The Effective Public Manager,
Third Edition

Steven Cohen, William Eimicke

The Effective Public Manager, Third Edition

Achieving Success in a Changing Government

JOSSEY-BASS
A Wiley Imprint
www.josseybass.com

Published by Jossey-Bass
A Wiley Imprint
989 Market Street, San Francisco, CA 94103-1741 www.josseybass.com

Jossey-Bass books and products are available through most bookstores. To contact Jossey-
Bass directly, call (888) 378–2537, fax to (800) 605–2665, or visit our website at
www.josseybass.com.

Substantial discounts on bulk quantities of Jossey-Bass books are available to corporations,
professional associations, and other organizations. For details and discount information,
contact the special sales department at Jossey-Bass.

We at Jossey-Bass strive to use the most environmentally sensitive paper stocks available to
us. Our publications are printed on acid-free recycled stock whenever possible, and our paper
always meets or exceeds minimum GPO and EPA requirements.

Jossey-Bass also publishes its books in a variety of electronic formats. Some content that
appears in print may not be available in electronic books.

Library of Congress Cataloging-in-Publication Data

Cohen, Steven, 1953-
 The effective public manager: achieving success in a changing government /
Steven Cohen, William Eimicke.—3rd ed. p. cm.—(The Jossey-Bass nonprofit and
public management series)
 Rev. ed. of: The new effective public manager. c1995.
 Includes bibliographical references and index.
 ISBN 0–7879–5938–3 (alk. paper)
 1. Public administration. I. Eimicke, William B. II. Cohen, Steven,1953-
New effective public manager. III. Title. IV. Series.
JF1351 .C574 2002
352.3—dc21 2002008569

FIRST EDITION
HB Printing 10 9 8 7 6 5 4 3 2 1

Contents

To Donna and Karen

Preface:
The Rationale for This Third Edition

We decided to write this third edition of *The Effective Public Manager* principally to communicate what we have learned about public management in the past six years and to update the examples used in the 1995 second edition. We have learned that the pace of change in the twenty-first century requires effective public managers to be creative and to constantly innovate. In the wake of the destruction of the World Trade Center in our home city of New York, we find ourselves with renewed admiration for the selfless public servants who sacrificed time, effort, and, in many cases, their lives to serve their fellow citizens. The American public's love-hate relationship with government continues, and the need for competent public organizations and effective public managers has never been more profound. The fundamental elements of management presented in the first two editions are the same, but the second edition devotes more attention to the need to rethink or reinvent government operations, and the third edition builds on the lessons of our 1998 book, *Tools for Innovators,* and presents a more detailed look at management innovation, which goes beyond the lessons presented in the second edition's chapter on Total Quality Management (TQM). In the first edition, the effective public manager is presented as an expert at working around constraints to produce results. Although such guerilla warfare tactics are still needed, our study of TQM and management innovation more generally leads us to try a bit harder to work to remove constraints. Sometimes, it is better to attack and eliminate an outmoded process than to waste resources working around it. The third edition also focuses

increased attention on the centrality of government in an era of global communication and transportation, economic interdependence, and the threat of global terrorism.

One question from the first two editions remains a driving force behind this third edition: Why does government have so much difficulty managing its programs? Let us examine the premise. Is government any worse than private nonprofit and for-profit organizations in managing its own operations? What measures do we use? How do we compare the efficiency of these forms of organization? We believe that the comparison is wrongheaded. Let us submit an alternative premise: that different types of functions are best organized with different forms of organizational governance. Some functions are best run by government, some by private organizations organized as nonprofits, and some by private profit-seeking organizations. However, although we reject the overall premise that government is worse at managing its operations than other sectors are, government certainly faces some challenges that private organizations do not confront. This book provides the reader with a clear understanding of those unique challenges.

The popular perception that government is incompetent is relatively recent. In fact, our constitution worked hard to limit government's power and, indirectly, its capacity. We need go back to the mid-twentieth century to see a very different popular perception of government. After the stock market crash of 1929 and during the Great Depression of the 1930s, private industry could do no right; in contrast, by the end of World War II, there was nothing that our government—the expression of the American collective community—could not achieve. Government was capable of the mass mobilization that defeated totalitarianism during World War II. It could accomplish anything. Today, we again look to government to protect us, in this time of vulnerability to terrorist attack. As we write these words, President George W. Bush has made "victory" over the forces of terrorism the highest priority of the U.S. government. Should the U.S. government achieve this goal, it could restore confidence in government to a level not known since

the end of World War II. Obviously neither the predominantly positive nor the predominantly negative images of government are accurate. There is nothing inherently evil about organizing human enterprise to make a profit; nor is there anything inherently inefficient about government organizations.

Government faces unique challenges. Trying to solve the toughest problems while under intense scrutiny is only the tip of the iceberg. More profound are government's well-intentioned but ultimately misguided efforts at self-regulation. The incredible array of rules governing hiring, incentives, promotion, firing, procurement, and work itself makes it difficult to create flexible, agile public organizations.

Finally, government has problems delivering programs because of the large size of public organizations and the dysfunctional Rube Goldberg contraptions created by imaginative managers to get around the system's constraints. One reason government organizations tend to be large is that government cannot be selective about its market niches. Unlike Federal Express, government cannot simply pick the areas it wishes to serve. Similarly, since government fraud robs the taxpayers of their money, we sometimes build regulatory safeguards that can cost more money to implement than they can save.

However, these patterns of large-scale bureaucracy and overregulation are not inevitable and can be avoided. Moreover, they must be overcome. Government is frequently characterized by large-scale, overly formal, overly hierarchical organizations. At the end of the twentieth century, we witnessed a downsizing trend throughout the private sector. This trend is accelerating in the twenty-first century. Huge vertically integrated companies have been broken up into smaller, more agile units. Much of the economic growth in the United States now takes place in small and midsize companies. In many respects, large companies are now networks of smaller organizations. Companies throughout the world have radically reduced their internal administrative overhead and analytic staff. Corporate headquarters have cut staffs from thousands to hundreds and from

hundreds to dozens. The information revolution and the growth of global communication have made it possible to knit together networks of organizations in many geographic locations working on a single production function.

Why is this happening? It is the result of fierce, global competitive pressure. How are these companies able to accomplish these staff reductions, decentralizations, and organizational reconfigurations? In part, such changes have been made on the backs of our white-collar workers. Several recent studies have documented the reduction in leisure time in the United States during the past quarter century. However, to answer this question fully, we believe we have to look at how technology has influenced organizational life.

If we look historically at companies such as Ford Motor Company—perhaps the extreme example of the strategy of vertical integration in production, we see companies that controlled every aspect of making a car. They owned iron and coal mines to make steel, and they owned steel mills, parts manufacturing plants, auto assembly plants—nearly everything it took to make, ship, and sell a car. Central control was needed to ensure adequate quality and quantity of the supplies that went into making a car. The strategy also assumed that profits would be maximized if they were all paid to the same company rather than to a variety of suppliers.

The theory worked for a while, but only when the vertically integrated companies had a head start on the competition and constituted a form of monopoly. However, once a free market in steel was established, car companies found it cheaper to buy steel from steel companies than to make it themselves. Steel companies had the advantage of seeing steel as their area of distinctive competence. They focused their organizational effort and brainpower on making better, cheaper steel. The same could not be said about a car company's steel division. In addition, since the in-house steel company had a single guaranteed customer, there was insufficient downward pressure on price and therefore less incentive for efficiency. After a while, the price of expensive steel and the cost of an overhead staff to coordinate steel and auto manufacturing is added

to the price of the car. If there is no competition, this does not matter. However, frequently there is competition and it does matter.

One reason competition can exist is that improved telecommunications and transportation technology allows a company to focus on its own area of distinctive competence, knowing that it can quickly elicit competitive bids for components (through Internet, telephone, and fax technologies). It can also quickly receive the components by air or by trucks traveling on interstate highways. The use of containers in shipping allows for supplies to be efficiently transported from ships to trains and from trains to trucks. If necessary, supplies can be delivered overnight by using companies such as Federal Express. Why own all of these suppliers if they can be accessed so easily? Moreover, organizations that do not invest in an extensive in-house supplier infrastructure can rapidly take advantage of new technologies and lower prices offered by competitive suppliers.

This simplistic description gives you an idea of what has happened to organizational management in the private sector. But what about the public sector? How can those of us concerned with public sector management ensure that government benefits from the advantages of small-scale organizations and modern telecommunications and transportation technology?

We believe that management innovations strategies such as TQM, benchmarking, team management, and privatization have already begun to facilitate changes in government operations and management. Although the term TQM is out of fashion, the principles of quality management have been widely adopted because they are about stimulating innovation at the grass roots of every agency—stimulating workers to constantly rethink how they work and stimulating managers to facilitate discussions and act on employee suggestions. It is, of course, not the only answer. In 2001, the Ford Foundation made a $50 million endowment gift to institutionalize the Innovation in Government project at the Kennedy School of Government to provide a permanent source of reward and notice for government innovation. An international network

of public management scholars has been established to exchange public management lessons across nations. There is room and need for all the creativity we can generate. The public sector needs fresh thinking and innovation, and we need an innovative public sector because public management matters.

Public management matters because public policy matters. Only government has the legitimacy and ability to address the problems facing our society; General Motors is not going to feed poor people and Wal-Mart is not going to arrest criminals. Public management matters because public policy is not enough. It is not enough to aspire to do the right thing and it is not enough to design a cost-effective solution in theory. We need to create the organizational capacity to deliver on our promises. The existing framework does not work; large-scale bureaucracy, with its centralized rules and overregulation of government managers, has failed. It is expensive, it is wasteful, and it prevents us from solving our most pressing problems. All over the United States, public management has become a political issue, and that makes this a critical moment. It is a time when we have the opportunity to clean up the accumulated mess of nearly a century of government growth. We have begun a long-overdue process of change, which we believe will in the end reinvent government.

The Goals of This Book

Public managers face a unique set of challenges in running governmental organizations. The complexities of modern, increasingly interdependent economies and societies increase the demands for governance. President George W. Bush's war against global terrorism is perhaps the most obvious example of the demand for enhanced governance. Crime, toxic waste, terrorism, world hunger, crumbling infrastructure, racism, AIDS, and economic growth are only a few of the critical issues thrust upon public managers. Although the problems faced by public managers continue to grow, most public managers are ill equipped to deliver quality leadership. Many of today's senior public managers are either untrained or poorly trained. In gov-

ernment, most promotions are based either on time-in-service or technical expertise. Scientists, lawyers, and engineers are promoted from staff to managerial positions without much consideration of the unique requirements of management. It is assumed that anyone can manage and that no learnable skills are involved.

The professionalization of public service and the growth of graduate study in public policy and management should begin to increase the number of trained managers in government. *The Effective Public Manager* is designed to provide practical help to those entering the ranks of public management and to those aspiring to become public managers. It is both a primer on public management and an essay that presents a vision of a new kind of public manager—an *innovative and effective* public manager, one who seeks to shape events rather than be shaped by them.

This book has several purposes. First, it describes the problems faced by public managers in managing an agency's internal operations and in communicating with the outside world. Second, the book provides strategies for addressing these management problems. Third, it provides personal advice to the public manager on how to build and maintain a professional reputation and how to advance in the bureaucratic hierarchy.

Management is the science of the simple and the art of common sense. Therefore, some of the points raised in *The Effective Public Manager* may seem obvious and some of the lessons might appear simplistic. But as simple as these lessons may be, most managers are unable to follow them. This book provides a core set of concepts that can guide the management of public organizations.

Overview of the Contents

The first chapter provides an analysis of the crisis in contemporary public management. It discusses why this crisis has emerged, what has been done to address the crisis, and what additional work must still be undertaken. It focuses particularly on the movement to reinvent and reinvigorate government.

Chapter Two provides an operational definition of effective public management. It summarizes the problems faced by public managers. Beginning with the negative image of the public manager, the chapter outlines a recipe for failure in the public sector and introduces a strategy for success.

Chapter Three addresses the most important issue faced by public managers: How can I get and keep the best people? It also discusses why hiring and firing are so complicated in the public sector and outlines a number of strategies for obtaining and retaining excellent staff members.

One of the recurring themes of *The Effective Public Manager* is that management is largely the art of influencing people. Developing a sophisticated strategy on paper is a waste of time if no one is willing to carry it out. Chapter Four discusses how to deal with and interact with colleagues at work. It provides advice on how to perform the mundane but essential task of keeping your boss and staff happy. It outlines the communication and listening skills that are essential to effective management and provides some practical tips on how to keep your organization functioning.

Assuming you have no choice and must retain most of your existing staff, what else can you do to improve an organization's day-to-day operations? Chapter Five examines how to rearrange organizational structures, task assignments, and standard operating procedures to increase an organization's effectiveness. Chapter Six takes the discussion of organizational effectiveness one step further by presenting our hands-on, real-world-tested approach to management innovation and the bringing of fundamental change to organizations. Our approach is based on over a decade of consulting work in government and the nonprofit sector and it reflects the hard lessons we have learned in trying to help organizations improve their performance. Chapter Seven focuses on an underdeveloped management skill in the public sector—that of the contract manager. With outsourcing increasing in the private sector and privatization increasing in the public sector, managers must become skilled at getting work done in organizations that they do not directly man-

age. If management now involves coordinating the efforts of networks of organizations, public managers must learn how to establish these networks, learn about their performance on specific contracted tasks, and learn how to influence their behavior.

Most managers are busy people who spend the majority of their time accumulating and digesting information. Organizing information and using it are increasingly recognized as critical management tasks. Chapter Eight outlines the problems public managers usually face when trying to improve the quality of information they receive. The chapter also provides a simple approach to managing an organization's information flow.

Chapter Nine poses the question How can I use the budget to control my organization? Financial management is the most important—and most overrated—influence mechanism available to public managers. Certainly no activity can occur unless it is paid for. However, paying for something does not guarantee that you will receive it. This chapter details the uses and limitations of the budget as a means of influencing organizational behavior.

Chapter Ten is devoted to the issue of formulating and implementing an organizational strategy. Every organization is expected to perform certain functions. An organization takes orders from above and is subject to expectations from outside groups. In the private sector, an organization's strategy is based on an estimate of market forces and organizational capability. In the public sector, political factors replace market forces, intensely complicating an organization's strategic decisions. In the private sector, an organization must decide if anyone will buy the proposed product and if the organization has the capability to produce, market, and distribute the product. In the public sector, an organization must receive permission and gain resources from elected officials before a product (or program) can be marketed. A public organization's strategy is highly constrained by political factors. This chapter provides advice for the public manager on how to interpret orders from above, read the signals sent by outside groups, and formulate a realistic operational strategy for the organization.

Public organizations operate in a fishbowl. The media, interest groups, overhead agencies, legislative bodies, and the public pay attention to where their tax dollars are going. Chapter Eleven summarizes the form and function of this often tortured scrutiny and gives some helpful hints for dealing with the outside world.

We conclude with an assessment of the costs and benefits of public sector careers and with a plea for more aggressive, risk-taking public management. We believe that public organizations can and must be made to perform more effectively. In Chapter Twelve we ask the question Why should anyone try to become an effective public manager? This last question is typically not phrased in this way, but is instead expressed as, Why should anyone bother to stick his or her neck out? The simple answer is that no one can succeed at public management without taking risks.

Many of us who have shuttled between government and academia bring to both arenas a set of images and perceptions about how government actually works. This understanding is built on important theoretical works in organization theory, such as the writings of Chester Barnard and Phillip Selznick, and on the work of political and policy scientists such as Herbert Kaufman, Theodore Lowi, Arnold Meltsner, E. E. Schattschneider, Harold Seidman, and Aaron Wildavsky. While working in government, we used the concepts put forth by these scholars to make sense of an otherwise unexplainable environment. This book attempts to provide both the beginning manager and the student of public management with a description of the problems of public management and the strategies we have seen used to successfully overcome those problems. *The Effective Public Manager* is designed to be practical and to pull together disparate areas of knowledge. It is not comprehensive and, despite the assertive tone of the advice offered, represents only a beginning. We hope that the answers to management problems presented here will help launch probing and innovative discussion among managers and policymakers in the public arena.

Acknowledgments

In the first edition, Steve Cohen acknowledged a number of people, all of whom we acknowledge in this edition, as this work has built on the first and second editions. These people are: Marc Tipermas, Steve's professor at SUNY Buffalo and his boss at the Environmental Protection Agency (EPA) and ICF Inc.; Lester Milbrath, professor emeritus at SUNY/Buffalo; Demetrios Caraley of Columbia University, Barnard College, and *Political Science Quarterly;* Harvey Picker, Alfred Stepan, John Ruggie, and Lisa Anderson, former deans of Columbia's School of International and Public Affairs; Fred Thompson, formerly at Columbia University, now professor at Willamette University; and former EPA managers and consultants Ronald Brand, Michael Cook, Mary Anne Froehlich, Thomas Ingersoll, James Janis, and Andrew Mank. Steve acknowledges the support and encouragement of former Columbia University executive vice provost, Maxwell School graduate, and Arizona State University president Michael Crow, and he thanks his colleagues Larry Brown, Nancy Degnan, former New York City mayor David Dinkins, Mel Dubnick, Lewis Gilbert, Don Hood, Sheldon Kamieniecki, Katie Mastriani, Louise Rosen, and Dan O'Flaherty for their excellent ideas, advice, and counsel. For this edition, we also wish to thank our talented, hardworking research assistant, Kelly Christensen. We also thank our research assistants Helen Eliassian, Vanita Gowda, and Misha Schubert for their excellent work on the book's reference section.

Bill Eimicke acknowledges Professor H. George Fredrickson of the University of Kansas, who helped start the reinvention movement twenty years ago with the New Public Administration, Professor Bruce Gates of Willamette University, former New York City mayor Ed Koch, and former New York governor Mario Cuomo. He also acknowledges the support and advice of his wife, Karen Murphy, and his daughter, Anne Marie.

Steve Cohen also acknowledges the love and support of his family: his wife, Donna Fishman, his wonderful daughters, Gabriella Rose and Ariel Mariah, his parents, Marvin and Shirley, his brother, Robby, and his sisters, Judith and Myra.

New York, New York
June 2002

Steven Cohen
William Eimicke

The Authors

Steven Cohen is director of the Executive Master of Public Administration Program and the Graduate Program in Earth Systems Science, Policy, and Management at the School of International and Public Affairs (SIPA) at Columbia University. He is also director of the Office of Educational Programs at the Columbia Earth Institute. From 1985 to 1998, he was director of Columbia's Graduate Program in Public Policy and Administration. From 1987 to 1998, he was associate dean for faculty at SIPA, and from 1998 to 2001, he was that school's vice dean. He is a 1970 graduate of James Madison High School in Brooklyn, New York ("Education is the true foundation of civil liberty"). Cohen received his B.A. (1974) in political science from Franklin College of Indiana and his M.A. (1977) and Ph.D. (1979) in political science from the State University of New York in Buffalo. Cohen served as a policy analyst in the U.S. Environmental Protection Agency (EPA)(1977–1978 and 1980–1981) and as a consultant to the EPA (1981–1991, 1992–1997). He is the author of *The Effective Public Manager* (1988) and is coauthor of *Environmental Regulation Through Strategic Planning* (1991), *Total Quality Management in Government* (1993), *The New Effective Public Manager* (1995), and *Tools for Innovators* (1998).

William Eimicke is director of the Picker Center for Executive Education at Columbia University's School of International and Public Affairs. He received his B.A. (1970) in political science, his M.P.A. (1971), and his Ph.D. (1973), also in political science, from

Syracuse University. Eimicke was director of housing for the state of New York (1985–1988), was deputy secretary to the governor of New York (1983–1985), was deputy commissioner of the New York City Department of Housing, Preservation, and Development, and was assistant director of the New York City Office of Management and Budget (1979–1984). In 1993, he served on Vice President Gore's National Performance Review, which sought to "reinvent" the federal government. He is the author of numerous articles on critical public policy and management issues.

The Effective Public Manager,
Third Edition

Chapter One

The Crisis in Public Management

The parks in New York City are in the best condition they have been in in a generation. This is so, despite cuts in operating expenses and staffing over the past quarter century. The city's imaginative commissioners, from Robert Moses to Thomas Hoving and from Betsy Gotbaum to Henry Stern, have all managed to do more with less and improve the parks. Parks are more important in New York City than in many other American cities because, although most of the land in New York City lies under single-family homes, most of the people in New York City live in apartments. For the children of apartment dwellers, the parks are backyards; they are where children go to run and play and toss a ball and be outdoors with their friends. Despite the improvements in the parks and the high level of public satisfaction (over 75 percent approval) with them, the city's parks and recreation department has been criticized for its management practices and suffers from a negative image in the press. In recent years, the department has been criticized for using welfare workers to clean parks, for charging nonprofit organizations that use the parks for programs sponsored by the nonprofits, for poor park upkeep, and for recruiting and promoting recent college graduates over civil service employees.

Reasonable people can criticize the parks and recreation department's management practices, but what is striking is the degree to which the public image of the department is dominated by these negative stories. There is little question that success is not as interesting a news story as failure or a scandal, but government's image suffers most from the public's lack of perspective. Government's

accomplishments are rarely discussed, but its controversies and failures are front-page stories. The proliferation of mass media in the late twentieth and early twenty-first century has added to government's negative image. Government is widely perceived as incompetent.

The current crisis of confidence in government in the United States began in the late twentieth century. Disdain for government is deep and profound and has developed into a collective American consensus. The common view is that government creates rather than solves public problems, and that government programs and policies detract from rather than add to the quality of life.

Although mistrust of government is an accepted part of America's political culture, government is still expected to provide services and enhance our quality of life. At times, the American attitude toward government reminds us of the superficial edge of toughness that characterizes residents of our home city of New York: beneath the tough exterior of the average New Yorker beats the heart of a caring person who is always willing to lend a hand. Americans say they hate government, but they venerate American political institutions and, particularly at the local level, consider them a necessary and positive force in their communities.

In times of crisis, such as the attacks on New York's World Trade Center and the Pentagon, we find renewed reliance, if not confidence, in government. We would term it a love-hate relationship. We Americans would prefer that government shrink and play a less significant role in our society, but in a complex world filled with threats and danger, we find ourselves looking to government for security and safety. During times such as these, we think of government less as a bunch of bungling bureaucrats and more as the tangible manifestation of the flag we are desperate to stand united behind.

The Crisis Defined

Still, there is a popular and, to some degree, substantive consensus that government is not capable of producing the public policies we might like to see implemented. In this view, the signs of failure—

crime, drug abuse, homelessness, high taxes, declining urban public schools, and corruption in high elected office—are everywhere. In contrast, we see the dramatic success stories of the private sector:

- Federal Express with its almost flawless computer-assisted delivery service
- Pizzas delivered in less than thirty minutes
- Amazon.com and its ever-expanding selection of everything
- Consumer items ranging from lightweight laptop computers with DVD drives to six-hundred-channel cable television with endless pay-per-view and home shopping options
- Increased emphasis on customer service from nearly every consumer business, with twenty-four-hour access and overnight home delivery of everything from mattresses to home entertainment systems

Consider the difference between standing in a long line at a local motor vehicles bureau, post office, or IRS office and driving up to the quick-service window of a drive-through fast-food restaurant, local bank branch, or Federal Express outlet. In the past decade, government has been moving to modernize its ability to provide rapid, high-quality customer service, but, for the most part, it lags behind the private sector.

Government is seen as wasteful and corrupt, business as lean and efficient. For example, the Reconnaissance Office of the CIA builds a $347 million headquarters office without telling Congress. Other examples are the famous $600 hammer and daily news stories about government waste and fraud, each contributing to an overall image of government incompetence. We won't comment on the fairness of this depiction (at least not until later in this book), except to mention the massive, coordinated response of federal disaster relief agencies to the flooding of the Mississippi delta in 1998, or the competence and heroism demonstrated by government officials in response to the destruction of the World Trade Center on

September 11, 2001—evidence that the common stereotype is not on target.

In contrast with the image of government incompetence, a new image has emerged—or perhaps we should say, it has reemerged: the wonders of the free market. The collapse of communist states throughout Europe in the 1990s and the surge of privatization in its wake have led to a new cult of the free market. Most acknowledge that privatizing communist economies has had a painful human cost, but the goal of developing a Western-style consumer economy is seen to be worth the price. The image of the American culture of consumption, built on Western-style free-market enterprise, is perceived as a model that works, in contrast with the failure of state-run enterprises.

The result of this has been the discrediting of the usefulness, and even the feasibility, of efforts to coordinate, regulate, and plan the private economy. In cities, the planning that we have maintained is now hidden in the site-specific designs of public-private partnerships. Efforts to regulate business practices continue, but they are done in an environment that favors deregulation.

Finally, we have seen a decline in the ethos of public service. In the 1990s, President Clinton worked hard to reignite the fervor for public service that he experienced as a youth during John F. Kennedy's presidency. He then impaired government's credibility when he had an illicit relationship with an intern and abused his pardon power on his way out of office. Despite the general disdain for government, there are countless examples of community spirit. Certainly, nonprofit community groups are well regarded by the average person. However, government has lost its image as a place where people go to do good and serve their fellow citizens, and government workers have suffered a significant decline in status over the past twenty years. It is increasingly difficult to convince public-minded students that they can effect change and improve people's lives by working in government. Even government's forceful response to the attacks on the World Trade Center and the Pentagon have not fundamentally changed popular perceptions of government.

The sum of these trends has been to cause a crisis in public management. We are not arguing that this crisis is necessarily a bad thing. Within the crisis there are tremendous opportunities to redefine and improve public management. However, to a considerable extent, the crisis is based on perceptions of government performance that are erroneous or are, at least, only partially accurate.

Nor do we argue that government operations are always as effective and efficient as they could be. However, all organizations—government, private for-profit, and private nonprofit—are flawed. Each experiences dysfunction and failure. Government is the most regulated and visible of these three forms of organization, but this does not mean that it is the least capable of the three. Our view is that each form is best suited to particular functions and activities. Our hope is that out of the crisis of public management we will eventually come to recognize the strengths and weaknesses of each form of organization. However, for the present, public management must deal with a profound crisis of confidence, a perception that government can't get the job done.

Reactions to the Crisis

Initial reactions to the crisis of public management came from those who first defined and articulated it: those in the conservative political movement. The tax-limiting initiatives in California and the Reagan "revolution" in Washington, D.C., were concrete reactions to the crisis of public management. The argument went something like this: if government can't deliver the goods, let's reduce the public sector and increase the private economy by reducing government's revenues. Furthermore, if government is the problem and not the solution, then we should certainly reduce the size of government—especially its domestic and social welfare programs.

Paradoxically, tax cuts at the federal level, increased defense spending, and cut-resistant government entitlement programs had the effect of increasing the size of the federal deficit. As the federal

share of state and local budgets was reduced in the 1980s, state and local taxes were increased in many places to make up for the revenue shortfall.

After a decade of attack, the second wave of reaction to the crisis in public management was an effort to reinvigorate the civil service. Two high-profile national commissions were established to set an agenda for reforming public personnel practices. The first, at the federal level, was a commission chaired by Paul Volcker, the former head of the Federal Reserve. The second commission focused on state and local public service and was chaired by former Mississippi governor William F. Winter.

It soon became apparent that the effort to revitalize the civil service was addressing only one element of a series of problems with government management. Thomas Peters and Robert Waterman's best-selling private management book, *In Search of Excellence* (1982), describes a quiet revolution in management technique that was taking place in a number of successful firms in the late 1970s and 1980s. Reduced hierarchies, a focus on quality, customers, and teamwork, and creative entrepreneurship were lauded in this landmark book. Public management scholars, journalists, and practitioners began to discuss the need to apply these ideas to public management. David Osborne and Ted Gaebler's *Reinventing Government* (1992) synthesized and popularized the ideas; the core reinvention concept was to rethink how government delivered, managed, and paid for public programs. Reinvention was an effort to "save" the public sector and the idea of promoting collective welfare by admitting that government sometimes did a poor job, and it proposed a series of creative methods government could use to improve its performance.

Osborne's emphasis on entrepreneurship was criticized by public administration scholars for its avoidance of issues of constitutional law and representational democracy. Three questions are typical:

1. What gives this unelected bureaucrat the right to take risks with the public's money?

2. What is the role of elected officials in authorizing these creative programs?

3. How can these programs be held accountable and be overseen by elected officials?

Despite the reservations of public administration scholars, public administration practitioners jumped on the reinvention bandwagon with great enthusiasm. Bill Clinton and Al Gore campaigned on the platform of reinvention in 1992. Mayors in the 1990s, such as Stephen Goldsmith from Indianapolis, Ed Rendell from Philadelphia, and Rudolph Giuliani from New York, became proponents of reinvention. The most important reinvention initiative took place at the federal level when President Clinton gave Vice President Gore the assignment of applying reinvention concepts to the federal government. The administration asked David Osborne to help lead the effort, which became known as the National Performance Review.

The National Performance Review

While clearly based on Osborne's reinvention philosophy, the vice president's National Performance Review was also rooted in the experiences of the Brownlow, Hoover, and Grace Commissions, the new public administration movement in the late 1970s, and even the privatization efforts of the 1980s. The National Performance Review was unique in its recruitment of borrowed federal bureaucrats to staff the task force, its use of consultants only on a pro bono basis, and its tight reporting deadline, just six months from the project's inception.

The review was initially conceived to focus on improved performance, but the commission leaders quickly succumbed to the political magic of cost cutting and led the final report with a commitment to cut $108 billion over five years and reduce the federal workforce by more than 252,000 positions. Whether or not such cuts made sense, the importance of the report of the National Performance

Review was in the reinvention philosophy that it expressed in four basic principles: (1) cut red tape, (2) put customers first, (3) empower employees to get results, and (4) get back to basics. Equally important, the report did not leave the issues at a philosophic level; there were also action recommendations.

To cut red tape, the report suggested creating a biannual budget, replacing full-time equivalent (FTE) personnel ceilings with cost ceilings, and permitting a 50 percent rollover of internal savings. It recommended the decentralization of personnel policies, including the phaseout of the federal personnel manual, department-based recruitment and examinations, a dramatically simplified classification system, and a much shorter and simpler termination process. Procurement procedures should be guiding principles rather than rules, with agencies permitted to test the marketplace. The report also called on agencies to cut internal regulations by 50 percent over three years.

To help put customers first, the vice president recommended ending government monopolies—such as the Government Printing Office—wherever possible and making agencies compete for business. To empower employees, the report recommended expansion of managers' span of control, more training and information technology support, family-friendly workplace options, the elimination of time sheets and time cards, and quality training for all federal employees. The report also recommended consolidation of the federal field office structure, expanded user fee financing, and electronic delivery of benefits.

The results of the National Performance Review were mixed. Although the vice president attributed a savings of $137 billion to the review, as a *New York Times* editorial pointed out, the claim was essentially not provable, as it was impossible to separate out the improvements brought about by the review from those related to the economic improvement of the nation as a whole. Furthermore, Gore attributed the largest reduction in government employment— over three hundred thousand employees during his tenure—to the review, but, in fact, the largest reduction occurred mostly within the armed services sector, because of the end of the cold war (Broder

and Henneberger, 2000). Undoubtedly, the Reinventing Government movement was responsible for some of this reduction, but the more important point is the new thinking in government that the movement represented.

Toward Addressing the Crisis

At the heart of reinvention is the need to radically revise the rules that govern government operations. Rules on budgeting, personnel, and procurement must be made more flexible if government is to achieve the agility and creativity needed to produce effective programs. We also need to develop and communicate a more realistic understanding of what public programs can achieve and a more accurate description of what they have achieved.

The issues of accountability to elected leaders and control by the institutions of representative democracy will not go away. If we are to reduce the rules governing hiring, we must develop a method for ensuring that political patronage does not reemerge. If we are to reduce contracting oversight and regulation, we must develop a method for ensuring that public procurement is competitive and as free of fraud as humanly possible.

In our view, there are three basic methods for ensuring effective but honest management.

1. Hold managers accountable for performance. If the parks are dirty, fire the parks commissioner.

2. Hold agency chiefs responsible for fair procurement and hiring rules. One element of performance is adherence to standards of merit hiring and competitively bid contracts. Again, if a bid is rigged or a manager is hiring his or her incompetent cousins, fire that manager.

3. Strengthen inspector generals and enforcement and empower whistle blowers so that corrupt officials are fired and jailed. But do not mistake a manager seeking to cut corners to deliver a service for someone who is stealing from the public's treasure.

The issue of accountability persists but is really a nonissue. Before a bureaucrat can develop and implement a public program, that program must be authorized by elected officials. The willingness of elected officials to permit such discretion may vary. We, of course, urge them to permit creative experimentation. This is not without precedent, although there are risks involved in permitting public entrepreneurship. One of the best examples of those risks is the story of Robert Moses, perhaps the quintessential public entrepreneur. At the peak of his power, he had massive influence on the development of New York City's infrastructure. For nearly fifty years, he built roads, parks, stadiums, bridges, beaches, and housing. He grew so powerful that he was beyond the control of New York's mayors and governors until New York state governor Nelson Rockefeller finally reduced his authority in the late 1960s. The lesson of Robert Moses is that unelected officials can become too powerful, and that is a danger in some places where reinvention is taking place. However, as long as elected leaders stay involved in the process and keep their grants of authority limited in scope and time, there is no reason to believe that creative government and representative government are conflicting concepts.

The final method for addressing the crisis in public management is to do a better job of training current and future public managers. That, of course, is one of the aims of this book: to help make public managers more strategic, creative, and flexible—more fundamentally effective. We believe that the creative values in reinvention can be coupled with a sense of ethical responsibility to the public and its representative institutions. We further believe that a professional public manager pursuing an explicit personal and organizational strategy can deliver effective public programs and help address the crisis in public management.

The work of public service is an honorable profession. But it is a profession requiring skillful use of analytic techniques, management practices, creative thinking, and modern technology. Social science is learning more about how to think about policy choices. It is helping us learn more about how people can interact and be

more effective in group settings. Computer and communications technology is making it easier for us to teach, learn, and exchange the information needed to be more effective decision makers and more productive workers. Managers in government, in the private nonprofit sector, and in parts of the private for-profit sector must learn to use this new knowledge to make their organizations more effective. The effective public manager of the twenty-first century will need to be creative, innovative, and entrepreneurial, as well as a lifelong learner. Stability, complacency, and routine will increasingly be replaced by change, new problems, and new solutions. Get used to it.

Chapter Two

Defining Effective Public Management

To define effective public management, we believe it is important to understand where the perception of ineffective public management comes from. In Chapter One, we discussed how the perception of government incompetence contributed to the crisis in public management. This chapter will discuss how the image of incompetence developed and how it can be countered.

In the 2000 U.S. presidential campaign, the desirability of a smaller government was accepted by both major party candidates. As Paul Light (2000) mentioned in a column published during that campaign, both George W. Bush and Al Gore claimed to be "the candidate of smaller government." Light noted Bush's claim that Gore's promises would add thousands of new bureaucrats to the federal workforce and Gore's counter-charge that his "reinventing government" campaign had pared the size of government by 300,000 jobs. "It hardly seems to matter that state government has grown under Bush in Texas, or that most of Gore's 300,000 jobs came from massive post-Cold War downsizing at the Defense and Energy departments" (p. A11). David Osborne (Osborne and Gaebler, 1992) sought to resuscitate the idea of an effective public sector through reinventing government. However, politicians throughout the country kept mistaking reinvention for budget cutback and program elimination. Even Al Gore, who should have known better, started to confuse reinvention with government cutbacks.

Why is the public sector in such disrepute? Are private sector people smarter? Are government employees lazy and corrupt? The

overwhelming contemporary image is that the government can't get any work done. It is difficult to argue with this perception, despite its inaccuracy. A huge number of government success stories could be cited if one wished to do so. Successful government programs have been established for rural electricity, food stamps, interstate highways, education, and many other endeavors. Although the examples of successful programs are almost endless, still, the image remains quite negative.

Whereas the public sector has difficulty implementing programs, private management is certainly no panacea. A failed public program gets noticed because the public sector is more closely scrutinized by the media than the private sector is; a failed *private* enterprise is just another of the more than thirty thousand businesses that fail in the United States every year. Public sector failures are more difficult to hide, particularly if the failure involves a topic that is in the public eye, such as health care. Still, one wonders why private firms can sometimes perform more efficiently than government.

The answer, though simple, is not satisfactory. The rules of government budgeting, personnel, planning, construction, and contracting are not designed to ensure rapid and efficient operations; they are designed to combat fraud and improper political influences. Whether a health care facility was built by a private firm or by the government, the project would use similar private design and construction firms to actually build the facility. In New York state, the Wicks law makes it difficult to hire general contractors, which means that even private firms working on New York construction projects end up wasting time and money. In most jurisdictions, public construction takes more time than private construction because of lengthy government procurement procedures.

If government procurement procedures are ignored, the media often assume that fraud has taken place. If incompetence, mismanagement, or bad luck is added to normal procurement procedures, massive delays are likely. Given the fishbowl atmosphere

surrounding government development projects, it is easy to see why the image of the public manager is tainted with failure.

The Bumbling Bureaucrat

Today's public servant suffers from a serious image problem, which is fed by stereotypes such as the picture of the inept bureaucrat reflected in the mass media and in the antigovernment rhetoric of a generation of faintly hypocritical elected officials. It is assumed that government operations inherently detract from the gross national product and are thus a drag on the nation's economy. Such simplistic notions do not account for the economic benefits of government programs such as the Internet (e-commerce), the space program (telecommunications satellites), the highway system (more efficient delivery of goods), and water and sewage systems (biological necessities). Without government and its effective public managers, we would not have, for example, the social security system, and a generation of young, upwardly mobile professionals might have to spend more time looking after their parents and less time creating wealth.

One reason for this negative image of the public sector is that bureaucrat bashing is a popular sport for the media and for aspiring politicos. Public policy decisions are often difficult and involve tough trade-offs, and the considerations devoted to such choices are not always acknowledged by the media. It is much easier to make officials look bad than it is to illustrate the complexities of their position, and it makes for much better headlines. Elected officials therefore devote a great deal of time to avoiding responsibility for certain decisions and pretending that imperfect programs result from bureaucratic incompetence rather than deliberate choices.

The second factor that contributes to the image of the bumbling bureaucrat is the practice of avoiding choices—"passing the buck"—and hiding decisions behind vague, convoluted language. In making decisions, a manager may expose him- or herself to

criticism from both internal authorities and the public. This fear of making decisions is a part of the culture of the public sector that the aggressive public manager must strive to overcome.

A third source of negative bureaucratic images has a more realistic basis. Public bureaucracies are excessively formal and overly reliant on written communication. This extreme formality, sometimes called red tape, is due both to the need for public accountability and to well-ingrained habit. Red tape in some routine bureaucratic processes can lead to ineffective and costly management practices. It can also lead to a very negative image in the mass media. A standard newspaper piece focuses on an older person or a disabled person who was denied health benefits because a form was lost or a bureaucrat ignored a key detail of the case.

Managing for Politicians

One of the biggest problems public managers face is their lack of control over goal setting. In the private sector, a board of directors is often controlled by, or closely related to, an organization's managers. But in the public sector, the board of directors consists of elected legislators and executives who are usually more concerned with their political health than with organizational performance. Anyone who has ever sat in on a congressional oversight hearing realizes that public managers do not control their elected board of directors. Fortunately for the public manager, the interests of elected leaders are sometimes served by allowing public agencies to perform effectively. Unfortunately for the public manager, political interests are difficult to project and frequently change with little warning.

Because political interests determine the goals of public organizations, public managers often face shifting priorities. The most effective public managers are those who learn to adjust programs rapidly to reflect changed priorities. Effective public managers learn to foresee changes in policy direction and build agile organizations capable of rapid redirection.

A Recipe for Failure

Most public managers are adequate performers, many are excellent, and far too many are inadequate, but all managers are subject to the same public image. It is not our objective to compare in detail the performance of America's public sector with that of its private sector. But given the strategic and managerial errors of some private firms, we suspect that our private sector is not generally better at management than our public sector. Certainly there are public managers who can match, if not exceed, the performance of any private manager.

Accepting the Negative Image

One reason for the negative perception of public management is the self-image of the public manager. Our government's managers are not isolated from society at large; they are subject to the same symbols and media images that bombard the rest of society. That negative image can take hold and become a strong self-perception in the mind of the typical public manager. It sometimes creates a psychology of failure that can become self-fulfilling.

The way that several Northeastern cities have housed their homeless families is a good example of negative public sector thinking. Cities such as New York are perennially in violation of court orders requiring them to provide housing for homeless families, and the experience of the Roper family is illustrative of how overwhelmed and negative-thinking bureaucrats often bring about this situation. Originally from New Jersey, the Roper children—five in all—were taken from their abusive and drug-addicted parents and ran a gauntlet of foster homes before their grandmother drove from South Carolina to take custody of them.

Despite the unavailability of any other options, New York officials refused them housing after their grandmother became ill and could not work. Their argument was that the family had a relative in the city—a sister, although she had three children and was living in a small studio apartment. Despite the children's contracting of pinkeye

and food poisoning, and the city's receipt of four letters from teachers and doctors pleading for housing for the Ropers, the city continued to deny the children respite from overnighting on the floor of the Bronx intake unit, claiming that the grandmother and the children were simply "ineligible," after several five-minute reviews.

In published comments, Leonard Koerner, a lawyer for the city, claimed justification, stating that many families "are not truly homeless" (Bernstein, 2001, p. 1). The commissioner, Martin Oesterreich, argued that the city had defended itself against false claims. Although city officials seemed overwhelmed with demand and resource constraints, the Legal Aid Society, a nonprofit legal group, continued to sue and obtain housing for families, including, finally, housing for the Ropers. The Roper story has a happy conclusion because of media attention. Because of reporting in the *New York Times*, readers flooded the family with donations. Eventually, a trust fund was set up for the Roper children, which would secure for them a better life. The Roper family story, however, is a good example of the psychology of failure that often grips overwhelmed public officials.

The self-defeated public manager is willing to define success as the absence of failure. Such managers lower their expectations, abandon any sense of vision, and ridicule those who retain ambitious goals. In many cases, self-defeated managers have good reasons for being negative. They may have been stabbed in the back by politicians, seen important pet projects overcome by inertia, or been subjected to any number of indignities.

In the private sector, such an unproductive manager might eventually be fired—or at least subjected to pressures to perform. In the public sector, it is not always possible to fire the manager, and it is often difficult to measure performance objectively. If success is difficult to measure, it may not be possible to hold a manager accountable for an apparent failure. In the business world, the balance sheet's bottom line is a relatively unforgiving indicator of success. In government, it is often difficult to determine whether an organization is succeeding. This ambiguity makes it difficult for a public manager to provide conclusive evidence of success.

A private manager can always take solace in a company's profits, claiming, "We may not make a perfect widget, but we still hold 22 percent of the market." The public sector analogue is to say, "Yes, the problem is not as bad today as it was ten years ago. The city only had 500 homicides this year, while ten years ago it had 550." Despite this improvement, no one is going to hold a parade for the public managers responsible for this 10 percent improvement in performance. Public managers often have no easy response to attacks regarding levels of government productivity; all too often, they accept the negative image that is presented to them. Such acceptance is the first ingredient of the recipe for failure.

Letting the Constraints Constrain You

Attitude is a critical factor influencing success. When managers accept a negative self-image, they are likely to fold at the first sign of an obstacle. Instead of figuring out how to get around a constraint, they cite the obstacle as an explanation for nonperformance. Every one of the problems that public managers face can be overcome. Solutions are sometimes complicated and are often circuitous, but they always exist. In Chapter Six of this book, we discuss how constraints can be eliminated by analyzing and improving work processes through Total Quality Management and a variety of other management innovation tools (Cohen and Eimicke, 1998). It is possible for public managers to deal imaginatively, legally, and ethically with the constraints placed on them.

In calling for a federal Quality Imperative, former vice president Al Gore advocated an assertive approach to quality in government when he said, "Our bedrock premise is that ineffective government is not the fault of the people in it. Our government is full of well-intentioned, hardworking[,] intelligent people—managers and staff. We intend to let our workers pursue excellence" (National Performance Review, 1993, p. 68). But, significantly, when he addressed the National Performance Review at all in the 2000 campaign, it was to distance himself from the concept of an activist government.

In a debate with George W. Bush, he announced that he would pursue a new Reinventing Government initiative to shrink government further, and said, "I'm the one who believes in limited government and I have believed in it long before it was fashionable to do so in the Democratic Party [through the first Reinventing Government program]. I don't believe there's a government solution to every problem" ("The 2000 Campaign: Second Presidential Debate Between Gov. Bush and Vice President Gore," 2000, p. A1). Gore's new position shows how difficult it can be to create a quality government with a positive workforce, given the prevailing negative view of government in this country. Recently, in one Midwestern city, the city manager canceled a popular street fair because liability insurance was unavailable. Rather than work with the legislature to secure public insurance or with the insurance industry to encourage private coverage, this city manager simply gave up. In contrast, when dealing with exactly the same insurance issue in New York City when he was housing commissioner for New York state, William Eimicke convinced Governor Cuomo and the state legislature to self-insure the Roosevelt Island tramway, thus keeping that highly visible and very popular transportation link with Manhattan operative in the face of astronomical increases in the cost of private insurance.

In the U.S. Department of Energy, a mid-level manager was told that he had authorization to hire fifteen people if he could get them on board in thirty days. When he discovered that it would take that long simply to get a position description approved and a job advertisement posted, he decided to make do with his existing staff. Rather than attempt to circumvent or eliminate an obstacle, this manager just gave up.

The passivity of some public managers in the face of obstacles is partly a function of their own inability and partly a function of the American political culture. Although government's role in our social and economic life has always been greater than American mythology would admit, the scope of government activity has dramatically expanded in the past fifty years.

Although the public sector is asked to resolve society's most vexing problems, Americans retain a love-hate relationship with government. They want government to do things *for* them but not *to* them. As Gerald Ford argued during his losing presidential campaign in 1976, "If the government is big enough to give you everything you want, it is big enough to take away everything you have" (Parker, 1960, p. 193). Even when government is successful in giving us the things we want, we really do not want to hear about it.

In our political culture, we are still not comfortable with the notion of an activist government. That is why politicians have been able to wage reelection campaigns by running against the governments they continue to lead. In such an environment, efficiency and productivity are not the dominant concerns of the elected leaders to whom public managers report. Symbolic victories are often more important than actual results. As a society, we continue to place a wide array of steps between the formulation of a public policy and the implementation of a public program. Unfortunately, these lengthy processes reduce not only fraud and political influence but also organizational efficiency.

There is substantial political pressure to slow down a program's implementation. Unless a program has high priority, it is subject to the leveling impact of routine decision making. Under routine conditions, obstacles such as time-consuming contracting procedures are frequently followed to the letter. Overt opposition to these slow procedures can often cost managers more than they gain. A contract or personnel office called on the carpet for inadequate performance has a thousand ways of subverting the organization that blew the whistle on them. Requests for proposals needed to hire contractors are sent back to the program office for revision twenty times instead of the usual eight. Job descriptions keep getting "misplaced" and phone calls are returned only when absolutely necessary. When public managers realize the difficulty of taking on the system, they start to accept constraints as a given rather than as a variable. When they allow the system's constraints to retard their

own performance, these public managers have discovered the second ingredient of the recipe for failure.

Allowing Caution to Become Inertia

The most effective public managers are careful people, whereas the least effective public managers are timid people. Careful managers understand that poorly thought-through actions can result in unanticipated consequences. However, it is very easy for caution to become paralysis. New projects are frequently abandoned when managers are confronted with tentative negative signals. At the federal level, we have seen projects aborted when overly cautious bureaucrats heard rumors that the Office of Management and Budget did not favor their proposal.

An instructive case involves the use of the Internet by the U.S. Postal Service (USPS). Despite the evolution of the Web over the last five years to include not only electronic mail but also electronic bill payment, the USPS was slow to make changes in its business model to include the Web. The Internet has caused a decline in the postal service's core business—first-class mail. First-class business matter, which consists of the bills and statements sent out by most businesses, has decreased dramatically in recent years, and almost the entire decrease has been the result of the Internet.

Despite these trends, and despite the fact that multiple competitors in the private sector have marketed electronic payment services that generate fees from this shift, the USPS was slow to react. Although it finally put in place a team to look at e-commerce activities in 1999, its bill payment products were slow in coming to market. The USPS was too cautious in choosing the right path to address the threat to its core business. While the USPS was deciding, the private sector was moving, depriving the USPS of a large potential market it still has yet to capture (Cushman, 2000).

A concrete example is on-line stamp and parcel postage purchasing, which had such a potential boon that it spawned two private sector start-ups, which began in 1999 with substantial venture

capital funding, as well as tremendous investor interest. These companies failed, however, blaming "an overly cautious Postal Service for making [success] virtually impossible." The USPS set a $500 monthly spending limit per customer, effectively shrinking the potential market. And it issued a seventy-nine-page rule book of technical requirements, which, for example, stipulated that stamps—printed onto the envelope from the computer—should be placed exactly one-quarter inch from the top and side. Despite the fact that these products would funnel revenue into the core businesses of the USPS, and the service had to do little but develop the flexibility to use this channel, inertia ruled the day (Weintraub, 2000).

Overhead and headquarters organizations frequently emphasize process over product. Local units of government and line organizations with direct client contact do not have the luxury of emphasizing analysis over action. Instead, line organizations tend to get bogged down in standard operating procedures. Caution does not degenerate into inactivity; rather, it leads to the repetition of known activities. In the case of the USPS and the Internet, the wait for the perfect opportunity took too much time, and the organization allowed caution to become inertia—the third ingredient in our recipe for failure.

Hiding Behind Ambiguity

An obviously disturbed man checked into a public hospital in a northeastern city recently, saying that he had heard God's voice and the Lord had instructed him to kill someone. After a day or so, the man calmed down, was released from the hospital, went out on the street, and killed several people. At a press conference, the city official in charge of hospitals announced that after careful study she had determined that the man had been "released prematurely." When the press asked if that meant that the man should not have been back on the streets, the city official said no; her only conclusion was that the man was "released prematurely." Naturally, the media made this public manager appear foolish for not agreeing to a logical conclusion based on her own statement.

Bureaucratic language is famous for being incomprehensible. Public managers have learned to hide their actions behind jumbled phrases, acronyms, evasions, and the passive voice. These techniques are used to prevent outsiders from understanding who is doing what to whom. Consider "preventative-retaliatory strikes" (invasions) and "revenue enhancements" (tax increases).

If confusing language were the only method used to create ambiguity, it might not be a serious issue. Unfortunately, some managers attempt to hide poor or nonexistent performance behind vague statements of goals, imprecise assignments of responsibility, or inexact performance indicators. Some managers learn to "game" the system and present the illusion of competence. They may create the impression that they are accomplishing important goals while achieving very little. Scheming managers of this type may do quite well personally. They may receive frequent, if undeserved, promotions. In some instances, a manager's image carries more weight than his or her performance. When image is rewarded in lieu of performance, the impact on an organization can be devastating. In the long run, then, these poor performers often outsmart themselves.

Forgetting That People Matter

The final ingredient in the recipe for failure is forgetting that organizations are made up of people and that people count. Management can be defined as the art of getting people to do things. Effective management is getting people to do the right things. Let us assume that for most people, the ideal state of existence is sipping margaritas on the beach while watching the waves roll in. The effective manager must convince people to leave that ideal state and do things they would not otherwise do. The manager must obtain resources to create incentives. Incentives are used to stimulate people to achieve organizational goals.

Organizations should be seen as organic entities—living, breathing beings. Organizations are not machines to be fueled and lubricated; they are organisms to be fed and nurtured. In order for an

organism to survive, it needs nourishment from its environment. Resources are made available to it because the organism is capable of performing some function that the environment requires.

In the crush of daily events, managers often forget these essential precepts. They forget that they need to interact and communicate with the people who work for them. Hiding behind their desks, they make decisions that frequently have an undesired and unanticipated effect on their organizations. Rather than deal with staff members as living components of a living organism, managers deal with them as abstractions. If this continues long enough, productivity is impaired and the organization ultimately loses its ability to attract resources.

One such decision that managers make—and attempt to implement without employee input—is to reorganize their units. A reorganization usually disrupts the dynamics of the office and can breed low morale and distrust of management's motives. As David Osborne and Ted Gaebler (1992) note, we need to reshape government institutions to reflect today's virtually limitless communication. We need to decentralize decision making, allowing more decisions to be made "down below" instead of concentrating them at the already stressed and malfunctioning portions of government.

A good example of empowering people is provided by the nonprofit agency Goodwill Industries of Tulsa. In 2000, the Oklahoma state government began providing grants according to outcome rather than output. Whereas previously the agency shifting the most people from welfare to work would get the most funds, most of the funds would now go to the agency that was most successful in achieving a *meaningful* welfare-to-work shift—that is, the agency having the highest percentage of people *keeping* their new jobs.

For Goodwill, this meant rethinking how they worked. Goodwill operated under a hierarchical model that was better suited to achieving outputs than incomes. Their management systems were designed to develop and implement standardized procedures that maximized labor efficiency rather than staff effectivness. Now, the front line would have to spend more time with a client to make

sure the client had a long-term chance of succeeding. Goodwill achieved this end by allowing the case workers a wide leeway in how much time they spent with a client and how they got the client into a new position.

First, Goodwill made sure that other tasks—such as marketing—were taken off the caseworkers' plates, allowing them to focus on what they did best. Then, Goodwill management removed many of the restrictions on how caseworkers pursued their goals. In the eyes of many frontline workers and managers, this change was just what was needed, allowing them to feel in control of how they did their jobs. The resulting improvements reflected a greater level of investment in daily maintenance operations and higher performance standards—achievements that would benefit any organization (Frumkin, 2001).

As a number of people have advocated, injecting competition into the delivery of public services can increase productivity. However, competition is not a cure-all, and at times government's work is so specialized that competition is not feasible (Kettl, 1993). Moreover, if the workforce is not supportive of change, competition may not succeed. It is critical that worker needs and concerns be considered as the move to competition begins. Indianapolis provides a good case of a carefully crafted move to competition. In the early 1990s, Mayor Steve Goldsmith shifted more than fifty government services into the marketplace by making city departments compete with private firms to deliver public services, saving over $20 million annually. He did this with the support of the public workforce, meeting regularly with workers in their workplaces and each week spending time on a department work team. Personnel cuts, when necessary, came from the ranks of the politically appointed middle managers. His success was accomplished primarily through participatory management.

We are not advocating that management become a roving encounter session with staff people, constantly trying to pry into their feelings. Managers do not need to develop personal relationships with all the people they manage. We are arguing that effective

public managers must understand the psychological, economic, and social needs that motivate their workforce.

Since most managers are not trained to manage, examples of inadequate management of personnel are easy to find. The most typical manifestation of inadequate management is simple rudeness—dealing with subordinates as though they really were not valuable human beings. Many managers have one personality for their staff and another personality for their boss. Others encourage staff members to take strong public positions on an issue and then refuse to provide support when a staff member is attacked. Sometimes, a manager will make no effort to understand a staff person's motivations and will reward a success with an entirely inappropriate incentive. Forgetting that people count is the worst mistake a manager can make. Managers who are not skilled in communicating and interacting with people tend not to succeed. Furthermore, managers tend to fail when they are forced to give orders. Organizations do not act because somebody pushes a button; they act because people decide to take action.

To illustrate this point, we examine the case of a small southern city's budget office. The city manager of this particular municipality hired a recently graduated M.B.A. to examine the operation of the budget bureau. As might be expected, this young man suggested extensive computerization and designed an elegant cash management and financial control system. As impressive as this system looked on paper, it proved to be a disaster in practice. Insufficient attention was paid to the preferences and talents of the people involved in running the system. A system that the staff understood and found comfortable was being abandoned. Staff members were not consulted about the development of the new system. They were ordered into a poorly designed, superficial training course, handed a procedures manual, and given thirty days to prepare for conversion. As might be expected, the city manager faced a small-scale revolt. The new system was shelved and the much-needed modernization was indefinitely delayed. This city manager learned the hard way that people are the heart of an organization and that people matter.

The Innovative, Effective Public Manager

We believe that the public sector can be effectively managed. The key to effective management is an active, aggressive, and innovative effort to overcome constraints and obstacles. In large measure, effective public management is simply the product of a positive, can-do attitude. It is easy to be frustrated by the roadblocks placed in the path of public organizations. It is easy to give up, take a conservative course, and wait to be told what to do. Effective public managers try to make things happen; they pursue programmatic goals and objectives by thinking and acting strategically. Effective managers attempt to understand why things are happening and how things can be changed. Effective managers are in constant touch with an informal network of informants who provide feedback on ideas and initiatives, and they are constantly learning, teaching, experimenting, and changing.

The best managers are those who understand their organization's environment. They are able to project the effect that their actions will have on that environment. They also have a keen understanding of how these outside forces constrain and influence their organization's activities. Effective managers are constantly identifying program areas to move into, resources that might become available, and potential sources of political support. They have, at least implicitly, a set of long-term objectives and they continually search for new ways to reach those objectives. Flexibility, resilience, and persistence are key attributes of the effective public manager. When obstacles cannot be overcome, new paths are pursued.

Embedded in the definition of effectiveness is the key concept of entrepreneurship. In order to pursue an agenda aggressively, a manager must design a course of action that can avert bureaucratic obstacles. Therefore, effective public management must be entrepreneurial public management. Given the array of constraints under which public managers operate, it is impossible for managers to be effective if they are unwilling to take risks. An effective entrepreneurial public manager organizes and manages a public under-

taking, assuming risk for the sake of organizational gain. Unlike the private entrepreneur, the public entrepreneur is not seeking personal or corporate financial profit; instead, he or she takes risks to ensure that government programs succeed and that the public reaps the benefits of that success. Unlike the private entrepreneur, the public entrepreneur's stakes are not private capital but, rather, public funds and his or her own professional reputation and advancement. Entrepreneurial public managers are characterized by their willingness to take on big policy problems and to rethink programs from the bottom up. This idea is so significant that we want to reiterate it: it is impossible to be an effective public manager if you do not take risks.

Why Risk Taking Is Possible

American public administration is at a critical juncture in its development. The activist federal government that began under Franklin D. Roosevelt is over seventy years old. John F. Kennedy's New Frontier is now more than four decades old. Today, a great deal of the creative force in American government is at the state and local levels (Osborne and Gaebler, 1992). This is essentially a return to the roots of American government. Before the New Deal of the 1930s, most policy initiatives were proposed by state and local governments. Whereas growth at the federal level has been relatively slow for the past several decades, state and local governments have grown considerably and have increased in scope and sophistication. In 1960, there were eight million civilian government employees in the United States. Of those, 2,421,000 were federal workers and approximately 6,387,000 were employed by state and local governments (U.S. Bureau of the Census, 1990a). By 1990, federal employment had risen modestly to 3,103,000. During this same period of time, the number of state and local government employees more than doubled—to 15,452,000 (U.S. Bureau of the Census, 1990b). By 1999, the number of federal

employees had dropped to 2,799,100, with state and local govern-ment employment continuing to grow to 17,432,000 employees. Whereas in 1960, 72.5 percent of all government officials were employed by state and local governments, by 1990, the state and local share of total government employment had grown to 83 per-cent. In 1999, this number had grown to 86 percent (U.S. Bureau of the Census, 2000). Counties have emerged as a significant new unit of government, filling a critical void between states and municipalities.

In recent years, we have seen a thorough professionalization of government service—that is, old-fashioned government clerks have been supplanted by scientists, lawyers, engineers, and general managers holding either an M.P.A. or an M.B.A. This change has been particularly dramatic at the state and local levels.

All levels of government now rely on private contractors to provide many services. Privatization, competition, and contracting have created an entire industry of quasi-governmental employees. Today, labor unions find that the public sector is one of the few growth areas for their organizing efforts. However, whereas unions at the state and local levels have enjoyed some modest success, at the federal level, they are relatively weak. Federal labor organizing was dealt a significant blow when Ronald Reagan fired striking air traffic controllers in 1982. Nor was labor organizing encouraged in the 1990s when Vice President Al Gore's National Performance Review called for a reduction of 252,000 federal positions, or 12 percent of the nonpostal workforce.

Although these trends seem unrelated, they provide evidence of the fluidity of contemporary public administration. Government does more than it used to, albeit not at the federal level and not always with public employees. Unions are a factor in some state and local governments and not in others. And government employees are increasingly better educated and better trained. For the effective public manager, opportunity lurks within this fluidity.

Government activities are no longer limited to simply raising and spending money. Many programs are funded through new and

imaginative mechanisms and are executed by combinations of public, quasi-public, and private organizations.

In Oregon, public and private officials are pursuing a novel arrangement to help rehabilitate former felons. While serving time, felons with good behavior can enroll in a new program through which they are sponsored by a local employer for training in a relevant trade or field, such as electronics repair. Once they have completed their training and served their time, they can then be hired by an employer. The state provides counseling services and helps ensure that inmates have the necessary support to continue in the community. The program has been a great success to-date (Butterfield, 2001).

In Texas, JCPenney and local officials developed a public-private partnership that creatively combined resources and addressed a pressing public policy problem. Recognizing that affordable child care was a constraint on keeping good workers, JCPenney met with officials and established a program to provide a mix of day care, after-school programs, and classes for children of JCPenney employees. The program was staffed by city teachers and social workers. It has been successful, and two other companies (Ford and IBM) are already designing similar programs of their own (Greenhouse, 2001). Public policy implementation increasingly relies on similar innovative partnerships.

The Need for Effective and Innovative Public Management

Despite the rhetoric of some politicians, the world is getting more complex and society's need for an activist government is increasing. The principal cause of this complexity is economic. We have decided as a society to exchange the simplicity of an agrarian lifestyle for the material, cultural, and intellectual rewards of modern industrial life. Each of us grows ever more dependent on others to meet our basic needs. Our labor gets further and further removed from the direct production of food, clothing, and shelter. Each year,

more of us manage information, provide services, or work in professions. In order to survive, this giant interconnected economic machinery must be constantly mediated, adjusted, and lubricated. If the economy falters, government must intervene. If a disease races through the population, government must develop a cure. If terrorists use airplanes as weapons, not only must the security issues of terrorism be confronted, but the economic impact of reduced air travel, due to fear of flying, must also be addressed by government. If harmful chemicals are entering our water supply, government must clean it up. If the homeless are sleeping on street corners, government must provide shelter. Government is involved in everything, from filling potholes to mating pandas.

A strong current in American political thought seeks to reduce the role of government because it fears that that government is a threat to liberty. Although such fear runs deep and has been reinforced by the emergence of fascist and communist regimes, antigovernment rhetoric is an anachronism. Economic interdependence is a far greater constraint on individual freedom than government power is. The political debate over more government versus less government is an irrelevant—or, at best, a symbolic—discussion. Despite conservative presidencies in the 1980s, total government spending as a percentage of gross national product rose by nearly 4 percent. Although the tenor of the federal government's programs changed during this period, the scope of governmental activity was not reduced during those years. The major trend during the 1980s was a steady increase in the cost of government transfer payments and a shift from domestic programs to defense programs. With the emergence of the compassionate conservatism of President George W. Bush in 2001, we again did not see reductions in the overall size of government. With President Bush's war against terrorism, we have seen a rapid increase in the size of the federal budget in response to security and economic challenges confronting the United States.

Growth in government should not be an ideological issue; it is merely a reflection of economic reality. Increased material con-

sumption adds transactions, volume, interdependency, and complexity to our social and economic relationships. Unless we radically change our social and economic order, government's role will continue to expand. If traditional values such as liberty, family, spirituality, and environmental preservation were to replace our society's main goal of economic growth, a simpler social and economic order could be created. If our social and economic relationships could be simplified, then the role of government could be reduced. However, in the United States, the preservation of our traditional values is dependent on our continued economic growth. Americans will sacrifice tradition to maintain a consumer society but do not wish to be forced to choose. The seductive power of material consumption is a fact of life worldwide. And preserving traditional values while pursuing economic growth increases a society's complexity and the need for social and economic governance.

Modern American society demands it all: plastic bags and a toxic-free environment, fresh fruit and safe pesticides, material wealth and spiritual fulfillment. A free market alone will not produce the type of society in which Americans wish to live; nor can government alone do the job. The free market is not designed to protect traditional values, and government is not very good at producing satisfactory levels of material wealth. A mixed public-private system is required. This obvious truth was implicitly accepted in the United States for most of the twentieth century, and nothing in the twenty-first century—so far—seems to challenge the need for public-private partnership. If anything, the need to make that partnership more sophisticated and better managed has become a central issue in public administration. Although the political dialogue attempts to mask it, there is a broad consensus behind activist government in the United States. Put another way, whenever our society faces a significant problem, we look to government for its solution. Government is considered a legitimate participant in virtually every field of endeavor. We may not want government to *dominate* a particular enterprise, but we frequently want it involved.

The demands placed on government are likely to expand at a faster rate than government's resources. As the gap between public demands and government capability widens, the need for imaginative public entrepreneurs increases. Beginning in the late 1970s and continuing today, the public has expressed strong opposition to tax increases and has generated political pressure to reduce taxes. Today, public officials often find it necessary to identify revenue sources when proposing new programs. Dedicated trust funds, user fees, leasebacks, and other imaginative revenue devices are being adopted with greater frequency. Today, there is an increased demand for public managers who are sophisticated about public finance and capable of "doing more with less."

Unfortunately, negative rhetoric has driven resources and talented people away from public service. Public officials have little prestige and are seriously underpaid. Jobs within the federal government are now more technical in nature and therefore require higher levels of educational attainment—a trend that translates into heavier recruiting from the fields of science and engineering. However, the private for-profit and nonprofit sectors' employment opportunities are often more attractive to the graduates of advanced science and engineering programs: "At the upper educational level of the technical fields, the national science and engineering job market [in 1990] absorbed 12,500 new Ph.D.s a year—6,000 in private industry and 5,000 in universities—leaving only 1,500 for the entire public sector" (Lane and Wolf, 1990, pp. 39–40). In 1990, 12 percent of the nation's 12,500 new Ph.D.s went into government, but by 1997, only 8 percent, or 1,220, of the nation's 15,250 new Ph.D.s entered government service (National Science Foundation, 2000). As the world gets more complex, government's appeal to the nation's best-educated citizens continues to decline.

The ideological debate over the size of government has drowned out the more important debate over the goals of government and how to reach those goals effectively. We accept as a given that modern societies and economies require activist gov-

ernments; however, governmental activism should not be confused with political liberalism or with any specific goal. A government can be quite active and yet have a goal of preserving the status quo. That is actually our point. We believe that an activist government is needed if we are to preserve our way of life. To minimize costs, this activist government must also become more effective. A new style of management is needed if we are to enhance government's effectiveness.

In the absence of a more agile, responsive public sector, several trends should emerge.

- The unanticipated effects of economic development will become greater and will have an increasingly negative effect on the quality of life.

- Our industries will be less able to compete with foreign firms, particularly those aided by more effective public sectors.

- Subtle threats to our security will grow and will reduce confidence in government and in the stability of the economic and social order.

- Additional resources will be devoted to public purposes, but the results of public programs will be less and less acceptable. Although resources may eventually be withdrawn, it is more likely that government's resource allocations will increase, as there are no other ways to address many social needs.

If you have read this far, you are probably interested in the concept of effective public management and may be interested in learning how to become such a manager. The first step is to analyze your own dissatisfaction with the way you've seen public organizations operate. Do not focus on the obvious disasters you have seen—the million-dollar or billion-dollar foul-ups. Think about all the little things you thought government organizations should have been able to achieve with ease but were not able to accomplish. That analysis and an unwillingness to accept poor results are the first

steps toward effective public management. Many public managers do not realize that there is something wrong. To these managers, public sector failures are system failures rather than individual failures. More often than not, these passive public managers refuse to acknowledge failures. Failures are explained away or are lost in an ocean of paper.

Let us reiterate that America's public management is probably no worse than its private management. Thomas Peters and Robert Waterman (1982) would not have had to "search for excellence" if the private sector were so effective. The weaknesses of our private management have never been more evident than they were over the past three decades of competition with Japanese auto manufacturers and electronics firms. At the same time, the popular success of Osborne and Gaebler's *Reinventing Government* (1992) and the attention received by Vice President Gore's National Performance Review make it clear that government management must be fundamentally reformed.

However, public management is different from private management, and public entrepreneurship is different from private entrepreneurship. Although many techniques of management are interchangeable, private companies and public agencies are governed differently. In addition, public organizations operate within a more rigid set of constraints than private organizations do. Private organizations are constrained primarily by the bottom line and secondarily by a system of law, whereas public organizations are constrained primarily by an extremely inflexible set of rules and procedures. The public entrepreneur must understand these differences and must learn to operate within public sector constraints. The next step toward effective public management is to develop a sophisticated knowledge of the constraints under which public agencies operate and the reasons those constraints exist.

The final steps toward effective management start in the mind of the manager and end up in concrete actions. First, the public manager must believe that public organizations are capable of pro-

ducing excellent results. That belief must be strong enough to overcome the inevitable frustrations that the manager will face. Then, the public official must adopt the management philosophy once articulated by Franklin Roosevelt: "It is common sense to take a method and try it. If it fails, admit it frankly and try another. But above all, try something" (Bartlett, 1992, p. 648). Small failures are acceptable if we learn from them and eventually bring about small successes. When a public manager believes that success is possible and aggressively pursues every possible course of action to achieve success, that manager has unlocked the secret to effectiveness. The difficult message here is that an effective public manager must take risks to ensure effective performance. The effective manager must learn to judge when caution is prudent and when conflict is necessary. Very little is ever achieved in conflict-free environments. To be effective, a manager must see conflict as an inevitable part of accomplishing goals. If someone in a public agency gets into a fight with someone from another organization, we should not assume that the conflict should have been avoided. It is foolish to pick fights for their own sake, but it is also foolish to assume that all conflicts should be avoided.

In his book *Innovation and Entrepreneurship*, Peter Drucker (1985) analyzes and demythologizes innovation and entrepreneurship: "Innovation is the specific tool of entrepreneurs, the means by which they exploit change as an opportunity for a different business or a different service. It is capable of being presented as a discipline, capable of being learned, capable of being practiced. Entrepreneurs need to search purposefully for the sources of innovation, the changes and their symptoms that indicate opportunities for successful innovation. And they need to know and to apply the principles of successful innovation" (p. 19).

Innovation is the key to learning to succeed, and it is possible to study the process of innovation. Innovation and entrepreneurship are not only possibilities, they are also necessities for effective management in the public sector. Drucker (1985) states that "to build

entrepreneurial management into the existing public service institutions may thus be the foremost task of this generation" (p. 187).

The remainder of this book addresses the problems public managers face in their daily work. This is not a "cookbook" or a manual; it is an approach to solving the problems faced by public managers. It provides examples of effective public management, but it is intended neither as a comprehensive treatment nor as the last word on the subject. In fact, we prefer to think of it as an attempt both to reorient the thinking of public managers and to demonstrate the possibility of innovative, effective public management.

Chapter Three

How to Find and Keep Good People

At its heart, an organization is simply a collection of people. Many companies are fond of saying that what makes them special is their people. This pronouncement often comes only a few months in advance of a massive downsizing. Finding employees, nurturing them, and motivating them form the essence of effective public management. In the public sector, the challenge is not losing good people once they are hired but, rather, getting them hired in the first place.

This chapter addresses the challenges of finding good people and then hiring them once you have found them. Next, we look at how to reward those staff members you want to keep and how to get rid of those you deem inadequate. Unfortunately, you may find it virtually impossible to fire those you do not want on your staff. If getting rid of unproductive people is not an option, you must develop strategies to work around these people.

Why Good People Are Hard to Hire

Government faces numerous vexing problems in hiring good people. Civil service rules often make hiring a long and tiresome process. In the past fifty years, there have been more than twenty attempts to reform the federal civil service rules in an effort to allow management more flexibility in dealing with personnel. The National Performance Review (1993) called for phasing out the ten-thousand–page *Federal Personnel Manual*, giving departments and agencies the power to do their own reviewing and examining for all positions and dramatically simplifying the classification system.

Unfortunately, personnel reforms, to date, have been largely unsuccessful, and hiring remains a difficult task (Hays and Whitney, 1997; McGrath, 1978). This frustrating history of failed civil service reform is at least in part attributable to the inherit conflict between the goals of a politically neutral public service and a bureaucracy that is responsive to the elected representatives of the people (Mosher, 1968; Hays and Whitney, 1997).

The Civil Service Reform Act of 1978 was enacted to address concerns about the civil service merit system, which is known to limit the discretion managers may exercise in hiring, rewarding, and firing employees. Yet the reform act did very little to actually eliminate those impediments, which make hiring and firing an arduous task for public sector administrators (Sylvia, 2000; Palumbo and Maynard-Moody, 1991). Commissions and reform legislation since 1978 have primarily focused on the theme of greater accountability of subordinates to superiors and of the bureaucracy to the elected executive and legislature. The 1989 Volcker Commission and 1993 Winter Commission reports are perhaps the most notable examples of this trend.

Hiring the right person for a government job is usually an extremely complex and difficult task. Finding the right person is just the beginning of the hiring process. In most cases, you cannot simply go out and hire the person. You must first determine whether you have the personnel allocation or "ceiling" to increase the agency head count. You must also obtain approval to hire a person in the salary he or she requires. Agencies are often limited regarding how many people they may hire above a certain salary threshold.

The person you wish to hire must meet the specific qualifications called for in the formal job description. Having done all this, you must then see that the job is posted and advertised for a free and open competition. If you have done your work perfectly, you may be able to hire the person you need. If not, you may have to make do with the staff you have or hire someone who meets the formal requirements but is not nearly as good as the person you wanted to hire.

Our own study of the New York City civil service system concluded that even those within the civil service system believe that the civil service system needs fundamental reform. Experts and participants in New York's system support the following reforms:

1. Reducing and redefining civil service titles from the current number of titles (three thousand) to one hundred
2. Eliminating title-specific written tests for hiring and promotion so that managers can select their staff members on the basis of experience and performance
3. Allowing city workers to share in their tangible successes; those departments that find ways to save money and reduce their staff should be able to benefit through merit- and performance-based bonuses
4. Creating a Senior Executive Service, modeled after the federal system, to develop a pool of professional, nonpolitical managers (Cohen and Eimicke, 1994a)

In South Carolina, a major civil service reform act was passed in 1993, stimulated by the reinvention movement. A subsequent study by the University of South Carolina concluded that the impact on many state agencies was "negligible" (Hays and Whitney, 1997). The authors of the study speculate that the resistance of middle managers who might bear the brunt of reform-generated cutbacks and have to shoulder the responsibility of interpreting and implementing the new rules helped minimize the impact of the reforms. They also theorize that worker resistance to change and paranoia regarding increased political control over the civil service contributed to the foot dragging.

As both New York and South Carolina demonstrate, it is difficult to manage organizations under the constraints of civil service. However, attracting good people to government is just as difficult. It is hard to bid for good people because public sector salaries tend to be fairly inflexible and extremely low when compared with private sector salaries, and government's negative reputation is an obstacle. During the economic boom of the 1990s, government salaries

fell even farther behind those of the private for-profit and nonprofit sectors (Walters, 1999).

Even graduates of public policy and administration programs are choosing private employers, right out of school and as a long-term career choice (Chetkovich, 2001; Light, 1999). It is simply not in vogue for the best and brightest of our young people to consider a career in government (National Commission on the Public Service, 1990).

The fact that government continues to attract some bright young people is a testament to the perseverance of those dedicated to public enterprise. It is also proof of the existence of aggressive public managers—those who seek out talent—and those talented people willing to swim against the tide and work in government. Rebecca Blank's study (1985) shows that a worker's choice between the private and public sectors is influenced by more than wage compensation. Among the individuals studied, those with the highest level of education and experience actually preferred public sector employment (especially at the state and local levels). Blank argues that the public sector provides other rewards for these workers. In short, interested and qualified people are available. It is up to the effective public manager to find them.

In 1999, a group of leading public sector practitioners and academics met to discuss the state of the federal civil service system and to outline a vision for the next century. Known as the Wye River Conference, participants reached a strong consensus on several major points. Among the key findings: the federal civil service is behind the curve with an aging workforce and nearly a decade of downsizing; federal employees should be viewed as a human capital investment instead of a budget cost that needs to be controlled; portable, individualized compensation and benefit packages are essential to effectively compete for quality employees; and performance incentives tied clearly to agency mission will enhance productivity and aid in retaining the best and the brightest (Ingraham, Selden, and Moynihan, 2000). The conference report also advocates greater emphasis on labor-management collaboration on mutual goals for performance.

Another closely related problem is getting rid of inadequate personnel. Firing workers protected by civil service rules is neither a pleasant nor a productive activity. Permanent government workers have fairly impressive job security protection and firing such workers can take an extraordinary amount of documentation and management time. Public managers face a tough choice when deciding whether to accept the cost of retaining an inadequate staff member or the cost of attempting to fire such an individual. The National Performance Review (1993) called on federal agencies to reduce by half the time required to terminate federal managers for cause and improve the system for dealing with poor performers.

Although civil service regulations may be cumbersome, they serve several important purposes. For example, civil service rules protect against some forms of political or patronage hiring. Political control of public bureaucracy is an important value in our political culture, but so, too, is a partial separation between politics and administration. Civil service rules attempt to separate politics from administration and also ensure that hiring is done through some type of merit-based process. In addition, these rules protect government employees from arbitrary or politically motivated dismissal. Managers must be able to discipline employees who are not performing, but, at the same time, employee "whistle blowers" must be protected when they seek to root out waste, fraud, and abuse. So the effectiveness of even a well-designed civil service system is constrained by conflicting goals (Cooper and others, 1998).

Although it is easy to be cynical about civil service regulations, the effective public manager should understand that these regulations were created to accomplish important public purposes. It is also important to note that some public managers face less civil service regulation than others. Some local governments are run by professional city managers, whose professional norms and values are expected to produce merit hiring. These professional practices operate in lieu of more cumbersome civil service rules. Some regional agencies and authorities fall outside of normal civil service rules. However, most public personnel management takes place in a highly regulated or unionized environment.

Unfortunately for the public manager, the job security offered by civil service protection can attract timid, risk-averse individuals to public employment (Bellante and Link, 1981). It is difficult to implement an aggressive and daring program strategy with passive, security-minded bureaucrats. Moreover, it is difficult to attract entrepreneurial-minded staff members to work in an uninspired work environment. This difficulty can be compounded by the problem of political patronage appointments. Here, the difficulty is not passivity but incompetence or inadequate socialization into organizational norms. A politically connected worker can demoralize nonpolitical workers if he or she is not subject to the same rules as they are. If the political appointee is powerfully connected, the situation may be a little like having a child of the company president assigned to your staff. Of course, this connection could enable an effective manager to increase his or her access to political information. Nevertheless, nonmerit appointments and promotions of any kind tend to discourage competent employees. It is difficult to attract good people to organizations whose staff members are routinely appointed on the basis of patronage or nepotism.

How to Find Good People

In order to find good people, you must know what kind of people you need. Dedicated, capable people are out there, but you must work hard to make them aware of your job vacancy. This involves going beyond the formal process of posting and advertising and tapping into your professional network to find out who is available, and then encouraging good people to apply.

Assessing Staffing Needs

The first step in this process is to assess your current staff members in terms of their skills, strengths, and weaknesses. To do this in a concrete, measurable way, focus on accomplishments. List your key people and determine what they have done in the past hundred days. Compare

these accomplishments with the goals you have set and the tasks you perceive your organization is responsible for achieving. What skills of current staff members were responsible for the accomplishments you have listed? What additional skills are needed to meet your goals? Are you looking for a different type of expertise, or do you simply need more of the same? Do not make the mistake of assessing staffing needs in terms of categories of skills that seem appropriate for an organization like yours. Instead, focus on the real work your organization performs.

When you conduct an assessment of staffing needs, you may have trouble identifying who was actually responsible for specific accomplishments and what particular skills contributed to success. An employee's responsibilities do not always coincide with his or her formal authority, so it is important to assess each individual's contribution (Contino and Giuliano, 1991). The process of judging performance is a central and ongoing function of management. If you do not have an intuitive feel for your staff's strengths and weaknesses, you are not paying enough attention to managing the work of your staff. If you create a matrix with accomplishments on one axis and staff contributions on the other axis, you should be able to fill every cell of the matrix. If you cannot do this, we would suggest that you first learn to manage the staff you have before attempting to hire any additional members. And let us be very blunt about what we mean by managing the work of your staff: talk to your employees. Find out how they spend their time and what tasks they are working on. Ask them to discuss with you the problems they are having with their assignments. Learn about their attitudes and abilities. Teach them how to perform better, or find other people to teach them what you cannot. That is your job; that is management. Honesty is often difficult and sometimes painful, but you owe your staff an accurate assessment of how they are performing and the opportunity to improve.

Developing a Recruitment Network

Assuming you have completed your inventory and assessed your true staffing needs, you should then communicate those needs. The

standard recruitment process in the federal system has long been viewed as slow, cumbersome, and filled with "hassles" (Abramson, 2001; Committee for Economic Development, 1978). The government is no longer considered by the public a desirable place to work, thanks to decades of bureaucrat bashing by the nation's political leadership. Government has always had to compete with the higher paying private sector for talent. However, the competition for the best and the brightest has intensified over the past decade, as non-profits have assumed a much larger role in delivering what were previously public services. These nonprofits are often viewed as more mission-driven and less political than government agencies, and the pay in this sector often exceeds public pay. In addition, the private sector is increasingly contracted to deliver public services.

Therefore, it is now easier to engage in public service work while employed in the private sector. Reports indicate that enrollment in government and public administration degree programs is declining and college graduates have an increasingly more negative view of government employment (Chetkovich, 2001; Lane and Wolf, 1990). In the aftermath of the attacks on the World Trade Center and the Pentagon in September 2001, there was a slight increase in government's appeal as a source of employment, because of the appeal of work in antiterrorist and relief programs.

Although some state and local governments are not as bad at recruitment as the federal government, few approach the private sector's level of aggressiveness in recruiting new employees. This is evident in the different job search strategies employed by those holding an M.B.A. from top schools, compared with those holding either an M.P.A. or an M.P.P. from those same schools. Business students are recruited by aggressive corporations at hundreds of on-campus interviews and can simply wait for prospective employers to find them. In contrast, students oriented toward the public sector typically find only a few dozen or so public agencies recruiting on campus. These students realize that they are expected to take the initiative and make their own job contacts within public agencies.

Effective public managers do not simply sit back and wait for excellent people to drop in. Rather, they find creative ways to make

the recruitment system more productive. They develop and nurture a network of contacts throughout government, academia, consulting groups, and industry, as well as within their own organizations. Successful public entrepreneurs develop the social skills to maintain such a wide-ranging professional network. This is often accomplished by actively engaging in professional associations, playing a productive role in interagency and intra-agency task forces, developing informal relationships with coworkers, doing favors and providing services whenever possible, and encouraging the productive members of their staff to leave the roost and accept promotions outside the organization. Bowes (1987) cites formal, informal, and conditional job links as components of the professional network. Each type of link uses a variety of mechanisms to put employers in touch with prospective employees. The mechanisms range from the conventional advertisement to recommendations from family and friends to temporary internships.

A distinguishing characteristic of entrepreneurial public managers is their attitude of enlightened self-interest. In the short run, it may be easier to deny a request for a favor or to discourage outward mobility for key employees. Yet the strong bonds needed to build a firm network may require granting the favor or encouraging mobility. Good employees need new challenges. An effective manager should recognize this and provide placement assistance. Similarly, such a manager should accommodate a colleague's request for assistance whenever possible. An entrepreneurial manager should see a request for a favor as an opportunity to help cement a relationship, and he or she should exploit that opportunity.

Getting the Word Out

Formal job postings and advertisements in trade periodicals are necessary but not sufficient mechanisms for announcing your staffing needs. These formal publications may be useful—and are often legal necessities, but you should not rely on them as your sole means of recruitment. Assuming you have a well-developed professional network, the job of communicating your staffing needs is

relatively simple. It is a matter of sending out e-mail requests and getting on the phone with people you trust and eliciting their suggestions. It is important that these conversations be confidential, and it is essential that you encourage these people to be frank. You should check out nominees' qualifications with as many members of your network as possible.

Although staffing decisions must remain the manager's prerogative, staffing searches should be as participatory as possible. Encourage your staff members to use their professional networks to identify applicants and to advertise job vacancies. When you use your staff in this way, it is important to avoid cronyism and to emphasize your wish to involve them in identifying rather than hiring new employees. Getting the word out is not simply a matter of broadcasting your needs. It is a two-way communication process through which you attempt to find personnel who fit your needs. It is not a passive process of advertising and waiting to see who walks in the door. It is an active process of intelligence gathering and information exchange and verification.

Encouraging Good People to Apply

Both direct and indirect approaches should be used to encourage qualified applicants. The professional network can be an effective means of indirectly communicating with promising applicants. If you and a prospective applicant share a common ally or friend, ask this person to encourage an application. Sometimes, a direct approach is needed. You may have to assure a prospective applicant that he or she has a reasonable chance of being offered the position, and you might also provide additional information about the position available.

Most conscientious people have a stake in the organization that presently employs them, so they may want the early stages of the application process to be informal and confidential. Reinforce the notion that an informal application can precede a formal application and that neither implies a commitment. It is also important to convince the prospective applicant that you are an excellent manager

and that your organization is worth joining. This becomes more important and is a more intense process when you are ready to extend a job offer, but it is also needed to encourage quality applicants.

Judging Applicants

If you have done a good job of advertising your vacancy, you will have created the delightful problem for yourself of deciding whom to hire. This is the kind of problem you should work hard to create. Applicants should be judged on such criteria as the following:

- Intelligence
- Experience, training, and expertise
- Demonstrated performance and organizational skills
- Social and group skills and overall personality
- Professional reputation
- Attitude, energy, and enthusiasm
- Written and spoken communication skills

An overarching criterion is the applicant's ability to fit the organization's specific needs. Managers often face a dilemma when they identify an excellent person but he or she does not quite fit the position that must be filled. This is where an overall analysis of the organization's staffing needs is most useful. By not hiring according to categories of need but, rather, according to needs related to real work, it is possible to mix and match staff members to assignments. You may be able to hire an excellent person who doesn't exactly fit your specific needs by altering the assignment of a current staff member.

The process of assessing applicants should vary according to the position you are filling and the organization you are managing. For example, if a position requires a great deal of interaction with other employees, you may wish to involve these people in the interview and review process. As a rule, you should never rely exclusively on your own judgment when assessing applicants. Get other people

involved in the review, and listen to what they have to say. Judging an applicant is far more an art than a science. Civil service obstacles to termination make government staffing decisions particularly critical. Anyone hired through civil service may well be with your organization for a very long time, whether or not he or she is a good fit.

How to Hire the Good People You Have Found

Once you have decided whom you want to hire, you must then convince that person to join your organization. Selling your organization and its mission should be easy. Navigating the civil service system hiring process is often quite difficult.

Learning the Rules of the Game

Every government organization has very specific rules governing hiring and firing. We refer to these as civil service rules, although that is not always the official title. It would make little sense to detail civil service rules here, because they change fairly frequently and differ across jurisdictions. Personnel procedures in some jurisdictions are fairly flexible. For example, the state of Georgia essentially eliminated civil service rules for hiring, promotion, demotion, and transfer for employees hired after July 1, 1996 (Walters, 1997). However, most public personnel systems have in common the following:

- Formal position descriptions detailing assignments and supervisory relationships
- Criteria for assessing applicants for each job or job title
- A formal process for advertising vacancies
- A well-defined process for reviewing and judging applicants
- A formal procedure for selecting the winning applicant

Hiring procedures vary by jurisdiction and even by agency within a given jurisdiction. Different degrees of flexibility are allowed in

applying rules to particular situations. As in all organizational endeavors, both formal written rules and informal unwritten rules exist. It is absolutely essential that you or a trusted associate learn civil service rules and develop a solid working relationship with the people who administer these rules.

Keep in mind that a personnel office derives its power from its control of the hiring process. Personnel offices tend to be rather inflexible. This is often a result of the rigid rules they enforce. One study points out that the profession of public personnel management has "adopted a methodology that emphasizes quantitative techniques [in hiring] to the *exclusion* of qualitative factors" (Hays and Reeves, 1984, p. 47, emphasis added). If you allow these experts to retain a monopoly of expertise on personnel issues, you place yourself at their mercy. In one regional office of a federal agency, the management and personnel office deliberately delayed implementing a nationwide order to streamline the hiring process. One of the reforms in the process permitted managers to allow applicant review panels to submit written appraisals of an applicant's credentials instead of providing that information at a meeting of the review panel. This shortened the hiring process by reducing the number of meetings that needed to be coordinated.

The right to convene these meetings was an important source of power for the personnel office. Friendly offices managed to have their meetings scheduled faster than hostile offices. In order to hold onto this power, the personnel office simply retained the old review process, even though it was allowed to modify the procedure. Although it would be foolish to try to fight a personnel office in its own area of expertise, you can certainly bargain more effectively with it if you know the rules of the game.

Using Temporary Appointments and Contractors

Bringing a person into the organization does not always involve filling a permanent or even full-time position. Sometimes, temporary appointments within civil service rules are feasible. Temporary

appointments can range from thirty days to several years. Longer temporary assignments are often called term appointments, connoting a definite term of service. Filling temporary positions does not usually involve the same degree of review as filling permanent positions. It is often possible to hire someone much more quickly through a temporary appointment. A frequent hiring strategy is initially to hire someone for a temporary position and then convert that person to permanent status. Conversion is accomplished by recruiting temporary employees into permanent positions.

In many respects, temporary employees are preferable to permanent ones. When managers attempt to infuse entrepreneurial spirit into an organization, it is often helpful to have staff members who are personally disposed to take risks. Temporary personnel tend to be less socialized into organizational norms and less inclined to follow standard procedures for their own sake than are permanent employees. Whereas temporary people may be feasible in management and senior staff positions, they are less feasible at the line and operating levels. Here, unionization is likely to be coupled with civil service protection, and the public entrepreneur is foolish to confront labor unions over staffing. In general, the public entrepreneur is wise to seek partnership rather than conflict with labor. Our study of civil service in New York City during the early 1990s found that under the then mayor, David Dinkins, the provisional employee clause was used to the extent that a full 9 percent of the workforce fell into that category (Cohen and Eimicke, 1994a).

When he was a mayoral candidate in 1993, Rudolph Giuliani was highly critical of provisional hiring practices in the Dinkins administration. Once elected, he launched one of the largest workfare programs in the United States. Beginning in 1995, the New York City Work Experience Program assigned public assistance recipients to work off their benefits in city jobs previously filled by civil service employees. As of 1998, 33,794 welfare recipients were carrying out maintenance and office job responsibilities, primarily in the city's parks and recreation and sanitation departments (Cohen, 1999).

When it is not feasible to hire even temporary employees, another approach is the use of contractors. Most jurisdictions follow the federal government's lead and prohibit using contractor labor to circumvent the civil service process. However, this has also encouraged a very strong movement to privatize public services at all levels of government—in the United States and around the world (Sclar, 2000). In several cities, unions have succeeded in restricting the amount of contracting that the local government can enact (Hays and Reeves, 1984). In some cities, such as San Francisco and Baltimore, this has taken the form of requiring that all municipal contractors pay their employees a "living wage"— defined by the contracting government entity (Brull, 2000).

Despite these barriers, however, contractors are frequently used as surrogate staff members. In local jurisdictions, the increased use of contractors is part of a general trend toward using private organizations to deliver public services (Savas, 1982, 2000). Many housing and local social services are now performed by private nonprofit organizations (Weisbrod, 1997; Salamon, 1995; Kammerman, 1983). With the relatively recent advent of severe financial constraints, local governments have come to regard private contractors as less costly than public employees and thus have turned to contracting outside of the government as a cost-cutting action (Savas, 2000; Goldsmith, 1997; Martin, 1993; Mansfield, 1978).

We are moving beyond even privatization and contracting out, to strategies that promote competition for public sector functions. Former Indianapolis mayor Steve Goldsmith opened up over sixty municipal services to compete with private firms to deliver city services, saving taxpayers over $20 million annually. Philadelphia, Milwaukee, and Chicago embarked on a similar course with equal success. In 1995, San Diego County, one of the largest local governments in the United States was on the verge of bankruptcy. Using a comprehensive program of privatizing its solid waste system and opening more than twenty county services to competitive bidding, the county was able to erase its deficit and actually enhance a number of county services. By 2000, the county had a

balanced budget and $300 million in reserves, and it spent $470 million more to expand and improve services such as child health care, libraries, and public safety (Eimicke, 2000).

Before staffing a public organization, it is useful to make the classic business decision to "make" or "buy." Should the organization create its own capability (make) or purchase it from a vendor (buy)? Public entrepreneurs are more constrained than their private sector counterparts. At the local level, a desire for patronage might force a "make" decision. At the federal level, a desire to limit the growth of official full-time government employees tends to encourage a "buy" decision.

The growth of federal "mission" contracting is an important phenomenon that deserves to be discussed in detail. Particularly in newer organizations such as the Department of Energy (DOE), the Department of Housing and Urban Development (HUD), and the EPA, unrealistically low staff ceilings have forced the government to use contractors as surrogate staff members. The DOE's Office of Civilian Radioactive Waste Management (OCRWM) illustrates this phenomenon. OCRWM is charged with siting and building the nation's first repository for the nuclear waste generated by U.S. civilian nuclear power plants. A trust fund based on a tax on nuclear-generated electricity will pay for this repository. The program is administered by a small staff in Washington, D.C., several field officers located throughout the country, and a much larger surrogate contractor staff. To perform its functions, OCRWM let a multiyear, multimillion-dollar contract to a team of consulting firms. The contract is a general-purpose mission contract to provide all manner of assistance to OCRWM in administering the program. A mission contract works like a checking account, in that the government deposits large chunks of funding into the account and then allows individual staff members to write checks (or issue task orders) against the account. In this case, the contractor created an organizational structure that mirrored OCRWM's structure. The only difference was that the contractor's staff was twice the size of DOE's and thus each DOE unit had a much larger shadow staff on

call. Contractor consultant employees were required to devote 100 percent of their time to this single contract. In addition, the contractor was required to set up shop in proximity to OCRWM.

Ultimately, the contractor secured offices in Washington's L'Enfant Plaza, in a building that adjoined the DOE's Forrestal Building headquarters. This is an extreme example of a mission contract, but it is also a logical extension of a long-developing trend. In most cases, contractor staff members work between 25 and 75 percent of the time for a single client and need not be located next door to their employer. They are not necessarily hired because they do work that the government lacks the expertise to perform; rather, in many cases, they are simply "extra hands" who are less senior than the government clients with whom they have contracted.

Mission contracting has both advantages and disadvantages. On the plus side, it allows an agency the flexibility to quickly hire the types of people it needs for a given task, and it allows the market to determine the price of certain types of expertise. Profits are regulated, and if the competition is intense enough, overhead is strictly controlled. It is also possible that contracted staff assistance can be provided at a lower cost than in-house assistance. On the negative side, the expertise that is developed is then owned by the private sector and not by the government. In certain situations, this may allow the private company to develop a monopoly or near monopoly on certain types of expertise. A problem with contracting is that unless government employees maintain strict management control over policy development, formal government accountability can be impaired, as private contractors virtually make policy. Most important, there is the potential for political corruption.

Some would argue that the use of private nonprofit agencies to provide housing, help for the homeless, adoption services, and job training in many states is a political nightmare for both the government and the private nonprofit sector. In some cases, elected officials use these agencies to generate political support for themselves and other political allies. In return, they pressure their agency heads to reward the agencies with contract renewals,

regardless of how well they have performed. Private nonprofits may initially pursue government contracts to serve their mission but soon find that the contract requirements and associated political pressures distort or even pervert the central goals of their organization (Weisbrod, 1997). Many success stories coming out of work-based welfare reform suggest that a multisector strategy can be effective in solving public policy problems. However, it requires careful planning and management from both the government contracting agency and the contractor managers and staff members.

Although contracting rules tend to prohibit government officials from formally requesting contractors to hire specific individuals, contractors tend to take such staffing suggestions seriously. In addition, contractor proposals for mission contracts usually include the résumés of the personnel being bid to work on the project. Although a measure of control over the hiring process is lost when contractor labor is used for surrogate staffing, a measure of control over product is gained. Under most rules of contracting, a private firm is not paid for a given service if it is not of acceptable quality. Even if a contractor must be paid for poor work according to the terms of the contract, the firm is well aware of the need to deliver quality work if the contract is to be renewed. Permanent government workers do not have an equivalent incentive to produce quality work because they are nearly guaranteed a job.

Contracting can be a useful tool for effective public management. It permits greater flexibility and allows a manager to exploit opportunities as they occur. However, productive government-contractor relations are far from automatic and are never simple. The government official must understand the profit and incentive system in place in the private firm. If you intervene in the management of another organization, you must be quite careful. In addition, you must train your staff to be effective contract managers. It is simply impossible for you to manage both your own organization and a shadow organization in a private firm. You must rely on your staff to manage contractors.

Borrowing People

Another way to staff an organization or task is to borrow people from other organizations. This can take a number of forms. For instance, you might assemble an agency or multiagency task force and elicit staff contributions through working groups. The level of staff commitment to work groups can vary widely. If the work group member's manager takes the task force seriously, a group member may be given the opportunity to make an important contribution to the group's work. In many cases, task forces perform symbolic rather than real work.

A second way of borrowing people is to ask to have them assigned or detailed on a temporary basis to your organization. The problem with borrowing people this way is that if the people you wish to borrow are particularly good, it is unlikely that they can leave their current posts. An exception to this rule may occur when a particular person is so valuable that management will do anything to keep that person happy—even loaning him or her out for a time.

A third way of borrowing someone is to ask another organization to perform a particular task. Many agencies have information technology specialists, policy analysts, lawyers, and financial wizards who are often willing to help out, but usually at a price. The price may be a piece of your budget or personnel ceiling, or it may be influence over some aspect of your program. When confronted with a difficult task and few resources, it is wise to be imaginative and seek help wherever you can find it. This search need not be limited to your own agency or even the government as a whole. Universities and interest groups might also be willing to help out. Although you seldom get something for nothing, you may find the price of outside help within your means.

Selling Your Organization and Its Mission

Whether you are staffing through permanent employees, temporary staff members, contractors, task forces, or borrowed labor, at some point staffing boils down to one human being convincing another

to contribute his or her labor to a particular mission. Typically, this involves selling the organization: "We have a great group of people who learn from each other and work and play together," or selling a mission: "We are undertaking the most important task facing our nation or the world today!" Although selling a public organization is no easier than selling a private one, public organizations often have more important missions than private organizations do. Therefore, it is likely that a great deal of public sector recruitment will focus on selling the organization's mission. Missions such as police protection, fire service, and environmental protection are easier to sell than flipping hamburgers, selling long-distance telephone plans, or marketing diet soda.

Private organizations attempt to sell their missions to prospective and current employees. For example, to this end, GE uses the statement, "GE brings good things to life." In the public and private nonprofit sectors, however, an organization's mission is usually the primary incentive for joining a given organization. Selling the organization's mission is often an easy task for the dedicated public manager—a matter of articulating his or her own deeply held beliefs. If your organization's mission impresses the person with whom you are speaking, you have an excellent chance of recruiting this individual. If it does not, you are probably better off without this person. As a manager, your job is not to recruit people who have no interest in what your organization is trying to accomplish; your job is to identify and recruit people who share your sense of mission.

Your job is to fine-tune your message and learn to articulate clearly what your organization is about. This is necessary for recruitment and for retaining and motivating staff members. One difficulty in articulating your organization's sense of mission is that it may be so ingrained in your actions and value system that you have difficulty identifying and conveying it. If you have this problem, you might find it useful to take some time and develop a brief written mission statement, which you can then use as the basis for your recruitment talk.

How to Reward and Keep the
Good People in Your Organization

The conventional wisdom that civil service and resource con-
straints prevent public managers from rewarding their employees is
simply not accurate. Knowledgeable and creative public managers
are able to access financial and other incentives to reward and
retain their top performers. The widely held belief that public
employees cannot be fired or even punished for poor performance
or nonperformance is equally untrue. However, to access incentives
and punishments, public managers must learn a complex set of
rules and procedures.

Using Incentives

Earlier, we discussed incentives and getting people to contribute
their labor to organizational work. To reiterate, organizations must
be viewed as organic entities. Incentives are the food that keeps the
organizational organism alive. Without the participation of its
members, an organization does not exist. In his classic work, *The
Functions of the Executive* (1968), Chester Barnard devotes consid-
erable attention to the issue of incentives. To Barnard, obtaining
individual contributions to group work involves both objective and
subjective elements. The objective element is the incentives you
can offer. The subjective element is the incentives a person is will-
ing to accept. Barnard identifies several classes of incentives,
including (1) material incentives such as money, (2) nonmaterial
inducements such as opportunities for recognition, prestige, and
power, (3) working conditions, (4) congeniality of the social envi-
ronment and a sense of shared purpose, and (5) participation in
organizational decision making. Subjective factors condition one's
willingness to accept particular incentives.

Under certain circumstances, some incentives work, whereas
under other circumstances, an individual may judge an incentive
to be inadequate to motivate action. An individual in jail may be
willing to accept one dollar per hour to wash dishes. However,

remove the element of coercion and that same individual may require ten dollars per hour to perform the same task. In other words, the element of coercion can persuade an individual to accept an incentive that, without coercion, he or she would not accept. A person's willingness to accept a particular incentive can also be affected by a manager's leadership or by the importance he or she assigns to the organization's mission.

It is the manager's job to obtain the resources needed to develop the organization's incentive system. It is also the manager's job to understand which incentives will be most effective in motivating individual members of the organization. Motivational level is a key determinant of employee performance (Lee, 2000; Kaye and Jordan-Evans, 2001; Steers, 1977). We are not suggesting that you learn the habits and values of every member of your organization; rather, you should use your organizational structure to create a cascade of positive energy.

If you manage an organization with several principal units, you must learn to motivate the managers of those units. They in turn must learn to motivate their key managers or staff members, and so on down the line. Motivation must be management's primary mission. Some managers believe that management is mainly knowing what needs to be done and giving orders to make sure that things happen. We believe that that has never really been true and that its likelihood is now even less, as more and more employees provide knowledge rather than manual labor.

Knowledge workers are very mobile and are often able to find work in all three sectors as employees or as independent contractors. Peter Drucker (1999) suggests that these knowledge workers be managed as if they were volunteers. Volunteers work for the satisfaction they get from helping the organization achieve a mission they care about, overcoming challenges, and seeing results. We have known for a long time that money is not the primary mechanism to motivate workers to perform (Herzberg, 1959). However, today's knowledge workers have many more employment options, so a manager who resorts to giving orders may soon become an unemployed manager.

The incentives public sector managers are able to offer employees can be quite constrained. It is usually difficult to provide additional pay, better working conditions, or other material inducements. However, this does not mean that providing incentives to your workers is impossible. You must simply be more creative. For, in government, material incentives may be problematic, but nonmaterial inducements are quite feasible. For example, instead of offering cash, you could emphasize the importance of public sector missions as the basis for both recruiting and motivating staff members.

Surveys indicate that most managers believe people stay or go because of money (Kaye and Jordan-Evans, 2001). Yet research indicates that pay is among the least important factors contributing to an employee's desire to stay with an organization. Employees report that what makes them stay with an organization are career growth, opportunities to learn and develop, exciting and challenging work, the chance to make a difference, great people to work with, being part of a productive team, a good boss, recognition, empowerment, flexible hours and an informal environment, and good benefits (Kaye and Jordan-Evans, 2001; Danziger, Kraemer, Dunkle, and King, 1993).

The city of Indianapolis has attracted international attention for its commitment to competing out public services. However, it may well be that the more significant and lasting contribution of Mayor Stephen Goldsmith's administration is the partnership forged between labor and management. Although some believe that Indianapolis won the prestigious Kennedy School "Innovations in American Government" Award for its competition program, it was the introduction of collaborative management by the city that earned the honor. In fact, the award was accepted jointly by Mayor Goldsmith and Steve Quick, president of the American Federation of State, County, and Municipal Employees (AFSCME) Local 725 (Rubin and Rubin, 2001). The accomplishments of the partnership included substantial increases in public employee productivity and dramatic reductions in the unit cost of public services. These public benefits were achieved in large measure through the provision of a

number of nonmonetary employee incentives, including increased job training, purchase of new equipment, time for union meetings "on the clock," direct e-mail communication with the mayor, employee involvement in key decision making, permission to attend relevant local conferences during business hours, and more flexible use of compensatory time. The union also secured a monetary incentive through which city workers received 25 percent of the savings generated by their productivity improvements (Rubin and Rubin, 2001).

The state of Iowa's Department of Management provides a good example of how agencies can make employment more attractive by seeking a balance between the demands of work and family. Responsibility for overseeing the state's budget and planning process means that the department faces fifteen-hour or longer workdays during the negotiation and approval process. Department director Cynthia Eisenhauer has introduced a number of incentives to help department employees manage their responsibilities at home and in the office. During the legislative session, some research projects are offered to volunteers and a thousand-dollar bonus is awarded for successful completion (Milz, 2001). Employees are also given broad permission to use flex time and comp time during the long business days, enabling them to escape some of the crisis mode that often accompanies a public budget negotiation season.

Encouraging Entrepreneurial Behavior

To reward and keep the good people you have, it is important to define what you consider "good people." For our purposes, good people are entrepreneurial innovators. What is an entrepreneurial innovator? We believe innovators are made, not born. Drucker (1985) maintains that there is no such thing as an "entrepreneurial personality." Rather, he states that "what is needed is willingness to learn, willingness to work hard and persistently, willingness to exercise self-discipline, [and] willingness to adapt and to apply the right policies and practices" (p. 173). Even mundane tasks can

be accomplished more effectively if some nonlinear, creative thinking is applied.

This is especially true in the public sector. Passive, conformist behavior is akin to gravity in large organizations. Without conscious, sustained effort, most large bureaucracies inevitably descend into a conformist mediocrity. To keep good people, a manager must provide an organizational environment that rewards innovation. The effective manager must also be willing to engage in activities that might increase employee creativity. Whether in an informal brainstorming session or at a formal retreat, the effective manager must create and participate in activities that stimulate organizational learning.

Creating such an environment is difficult in any large organization and is particularly so in government. An entrepreneurial environment encourages questioning, investment, experimentation, and action. It must tolerate failure that leads to learning. Rewards must be structured to encourage these entrepreneurial behaviors. Managers should reward not only positive results but also good questions, imaginative experiments, and even failures that teach important lessons. Entrepreneurs must take risks, and as long as the risks are not reckless, an effective public manager must encourage such risk taking. If rewarding failure seems too much for you, then you should at least avoid punishing the risk taker if the risky project fails—*unless* the risk taker is slow to admit that his or her project has failed or is unable to learn from the project's failure.

It is also important to structure incentives in order to discourage passivity and unquestioning behavior. This is especially difficult in light of the civil service restrictions in government, but it can be accomplished. All organizational units benefit from questioning and reexamination. Effective public managers must determine how much change is feasible and structure incentives accordingly. Managers must be conscious of the cues they provide employees by rewarding or punishing particular behaviors. If you talk like a risk taker but reward conservative, risk-averse staff members, your talk will be ignored.

Using Incentives to Promote Cooperation

Keeping good people and building an effective, entrepreneurial staff involves building a sense of group cohesion and teamwork. By widely distributing the fruits of an organization's victory, you can give everyone a stake in the organization's success. This means sharing credit, information, perquisites, and rewards with your staff. It also means building group identity and, when possible, distributing group rewards. Simple gestures such as praise, personal thank-you notes, and champagne "victory" toasts are important. Singling out groups, rather than group leaders, for recognition sends the signal that group effort is rewarded. As commissioner of New York City's Department of Parks and Recreation, Betsy Gotbaum invited employee teams to her headquarters office to honor their innovative suggestions. Everyone received a certificate of recognition, a token such as a department tee shirt, cap, or watch, and a picture with the commissioner. At the end of the year, all department employees were invited to a picnic in celebration of all the award winners to-date.

Sometimes, it is helpful to create a sense of competition with other agencies having similar responsibilities. Former U.S. Customs Service commissioner Raymond Kelly encouraged his employees to compete with the FBI, the U.S. Drug Enforcement Administration, the U.S. military, and state and local law enforcement officials to become the most effective force in the war on drugs. This approach can create an atmosphere of mutual interest and can increase the feeling of a shared stake in the organization's success.

Some incentives are inherently finite, and their distribution requires that only some people win and that others receive no obvious benefit. At the same time, a rising tide lifts all boats. If an organization succeeds, even members who may not get as much money or have as much power as their fellow staff members benefit from their association with a prestigious organization that is on the way up.

Keeping a Good Person from Leaving

It is not always wise to attempt to keep a good person from leaving your organization. Perhaps your organization offers inadequate pro-

motion potential for a high-quality staff person because of seniority or the presence of other excellent, more experienced employees. Sometimes, the effective public manager must take the long view and help a good person find a new job. Generally, it is better to lose valuable people at their peak than hold onto them as their productivity and morale decline.

Some jobs simply should not be held for a long period of time. In these jobs, burnout can be avoided by cycling people in and out after relatively brief tours of duty. In most cases, however, it is important to retain excellent employees.

The best way to prevent good people from leaving is to constantly communicate with the members of your staff in order to develop a sophisticated understanding of their personalities and needs. It is your job to be aware of your staff's level of job satisfaction. You must know whether they are challenged by their jobs and whether they believe they are receiving adequate rewards for their efforts. By paying attention to your staff members' needs you can readjust duties and incentives and thus prevent someone from leaving unnecessarily.

Although your goal should be to prevent unnecessary departures, you should never attempt to hold onto staff members simply to avoid the inconvenience of replacing a key person. It is important that you let a worker pursue paths that may help his or her development, even if those paths are sometimes not what you deem best for your organization. You should also avoid resorting to extreme concessions in order to retain key staff members. Such concessions often create unwanted precedents and send the wrong signal to staffers who are relatively satisfied with their work. If you have taken reasonable steps to motivate and retain your good people, do not be afraid to let them go if they remain dissatisfied.

It is important to avoid rapid staff turnover. You can accomplish this by learning from the cases of turnover you experience. Try to determine the reason for a turnover. Have you been looking for the wrong type of person for the particular job you are trying to fill? Should the job be redesigned because it is inherently unrewarding? Or did you lose a staff person simply because he or she wanted to move to another city?

In any event, you should see turnover as a potential opportunity as well as a potential problem. Turnover gives you the opportunity to infuse new energy into an organization. Furthermore, it is probably better to lose a good worker than to be forced to retain a bad one.

How to Get Rid of Inadequate Staff Members

Dealing with inadequate staff members can be a draining, time-consuming, unpleasant experience. Such workers can negate the positive messages an entrepreneurial manager seeks to communicate. Therefore, it is extremely important to deal with poor performance head-on.

Identifying Poor Performance

The first step in addressing the issue of inadequate staff performance is to define and identify it. Sometimes, poor performance is actually a result of poor communication between management and the staff. Management, working with the staff, must define an organization's objectives and then specify the work that must be performed to accomplish those objectives. This work must be clearly defined and within the capability of the staff. If management's expectations, objectives, and descriptions of necessary work are vague or inexact, it is difficult to identify inadequate staff performance. Often, managers expect employees to be able to guess what an organization is supposed to be doing, and to some extent, truly excellent workers must perform this task of deduction and organizational definition.

Inadequate performance should be divided into two categories. The first involves excellent employees who do not live up to high expectations; the second involves average employees who do not produce above-average work. Not everyone on a team can be a superstar, and most organizations cannot operate without a supporting cast of average workers. As a manager, you must be clear

about what you expect from your staff. Your expectations should not be general or organization-wide but must be set for each member of your organization.

Clarification is not simply a matter of setting formal performance standards and measuring their accomplishment. It requires extensive collaboration between management and the staff to elicit staff views on reasonable performance expectations. Clarifying expectations is a six-part learning and teaching process during which you do the following:

1. Determine what a staff member is capable of achieving
2. Decide whether the staff member's abilities are sufficient for your needs
3. Define the work the staff member must perform
4. Communicate that assignment to the staff member
5. Assess whether performance matches ability
6. Where necessary, identify why the staff member's performance was inadequate.

As these six steps indicate, the problem with inadequate performance may be inadequate management rather than inadequate labor. Perhaps you made an error of judgment in steps 1 and 2 and assigned a task to the wrong person. Perhaps you did not properly define the work, or you expected a staff person to exercise more judgment than he or she was capable of or willing to exercise. Perhaps you never fully communicated the assignment.

Encouraging Improved Performance

After carefully assessing a failed assignment, you may decide that you did everything you could to get the most out of your staff member. The reason for the failure is that this person simply does not fit in your organization. In a private company without a union, a manager might move to terminate such an employee, providing some reasonable

notice and separation benefits, depending on the length of service. In the public sector, where firing anyone is difficult, if not impossible, you must pursue corrective strategies other than dismissal.

The logical first intervention is to encourage improved performance. Many governments seek to create incentives for outstanding performance and consequences for underachieving through an annual performance evaluation process. It is definitely in the manager's interest to take as much time as possible in attempting to improve a staff person's performance. The alternatives are all resource-intensive and often more time-consuming. Unfortunately, public managers often view performance appraisals as time-consuming and with a high potential for conflict, even violence. So the process is either ignored or implemented in such a general and uniform manner as to render the evaluations useless as a management tool (Walters, 2001).

Knowing When to Give Up on a Staff Member

Sometimes, of course, it really is best to give up on a staff member. Certain signs indicate that a person is unlikely to ever be productive in your organization. Any staff person exhibiting more than a few of the following traits or practices is probably someone who should be encouraged or ultimately forced to move on.

- Wastes time in meetings with trivial or impossible issues
- Possesses poor listening skills—never seems to understand the last point made
- Refuses to work overtime
- Never arrives anywhere on time
- Is disliked by the rest of the organization
- Is pitied by the rest of the organization
- Spends much of the workday on personal business
- Agrees with everything you say

- Disagrees with everything you say
- Is at his or her best when analyzing why an assignment is infeasible, unnecessary, or otherwise not worth doing
- Rarely finishes an assignment on time
- Rarely finishes an assignment at all
- Is unable to explain or defend a product
- Undercuts members of his or her own staff

Incompetence manifests itself in a variety of shapes and forms, and it is not always easy to identify. The situation is seldom clear-cut. A person may be generally destructive but still perform an important function. An unproductive employee may be a very nice person in great need of the salary his or her current position provides.

It is never easy to give up on someone, and it is difficult to tell a person that he or she does not fit in your organization. However, it is absolutely essential that you deal with staff problems forthrightly. Jack Welch, the legendary CEO of General Electric, has long preached in favor of an annual performance appraisal system that forces out the bottom 10 percent of employees every year. A similar number are put on notice that unless there is a major change, they will be out next year. He argues that you do a person no favor by keeping that person in a job for which he or she is obviously not well suited.

Incompetence can be contagious. The time to give up on a staff member is when the organization's work becomes threatened and when "carrying" a poor performer significantly affects the organization's actual or perceived performance. You can detect this if external criticisms of the organization increase and if any or all of the fourteen behaviors previously listed occur more frequently.

Dealing with Inadequate Staff Members

Once you have given up on a staff member, you face the truly difficult task of getting that person to leave your organization. The first issue you must face is whether the problem is one of fit or one of

competence. Obviously, it is more difficult to deal with an absolutely incompetent person than with a competent person who happens to be holding the wrong job. Fortunately, in most professional situations, the issue tends to be one of fit. In these cases, you may be able to reorganize or transfer a person within your own organization. A performance evaluation system that clearly identifies the failure to meet even the minimum level of performance will facilitate such transfers (Walters, 2001; Kleeman, 1979). Unfortunately, these internal efforts at staff rehabilitation often fail because the staff person has developed a reputation for incompetence within your organization. Unless the organization is quite large, that image will follow this person to the next job. Often, it is best to simply ask the person to leave.

You should provide a strong message that the situation is not working out and that promotion is unlikely. It is best to carry this message personally and to deliver it in a variety of settings. Begin with formal evaluations, delivering your negative assessment personally in both formal and informal settings, and then follow it up in writing. Do not assume that your underachieving employee has gotten the message indirectly. We wish we could provide some useful advice on how to make this process easier. Judging staff members is difficult but necessary. It is never easy to tell someone that he or she is failing.

Managers are understandably reluctant to give employees a rating lower than satisfactory. This is particularly true in a civil service context, where protection of employee rights proliferates. Public employees generally have the right to appeal negative actions against them, with the burden of proof resting with the supervisor (Cooper and others, 1998). Surveys and anecdotal evidence indicate that managers are often unwilling to face workers whose work is substandard (Walters, 2001; Kleeman, 1979). In some measure, that failure is the manager's as well as the employee's, because the manager has not provided the support and guidance required by the employee.

Although there is no way to make this process pleasant, there are some simple steps you can take to help reduce the level of mis-

ery. First, be absolutely honest in your assessment. Do not attempt to sugarcoat or rationalize your assessment. Get to the specifics of the poor performance immediately and clearly state the gravity of the situation (DuBrin, 1980).

Second, confine your assessment to current job performance. You are not evaluating your staff member's professionalism or worth as a human being; you are simply saying that he or she is not suited for a particular job.

Third, if you honestly believe that the issue is one of job mismatch, then help the poor performer find a new job. If you are dealing with a competent professional, the chances are good that this person is just as frustrated with his or her performance as you are. If this is the case, then simply raising the issue of poor fit will help resolve the situation. A reasonably capable professional with a positive self-image will usually take steps to leave the organization immediately upon receiving a negative evaluation.

Sometimes, it is not an issue of fit, and you need to get rid of a truly incompetent individual. He or she refuses to leave the organization, and you cannot in good conscience help this person find a new position. In such a case, you are left little choice but to pursue the formal firing process. In some public organizations, this is so difficult and time-consuming that it is really not considered a viable option. In our view, pursuing a formal firing requires a careful balancing of costs and benefits. How bad is this staff member, and how much damage does he or she cause? Is it possible to work around this person? Can the organization afford to carry such a person and still accomplish its mission? Remember that trying to fire a staff member with civil service tenure is essentially an act of desperation. It should only be attempted when all else has failed.

It is very difficult to fire even a truly incompetent civil servant. This is simply one of the constraints of public management. However, it is important to note that an incompetent staff member is not an excuse for poor performance. It is the public manager's job to develop a management scheme for working around inadequate staff members and obtaining productive effort from competent staffers.

Managing Inadequate Employees You Cannot Fire

In most cases, public managers must take existing incompetent staff members as a given, and at the same time they must be careful to nurture excellence and avoid ruining good staff members. This involves the careful use of incentives.

Taking incompetent workers as a given does not mean relying on them to perform important organizational tasks. It is the responsibility of the effective public manager to prevent the bad habits and attitudes of the poor performers from spreading more widely in the organization. There are a number of ways to contain the influence of unhappy and unproductive workers. If you only have a few incompetent workers, you may be able to distribute them throughout the organization by reassigning them to different posts. Sometimes, people respond to the level of competence around them and work above their actual level of ability. If you have a large number of incompetent people working for you, it may be necessary to build a "turkey farm"—that is, detail people out of the organization, develop an unimportant special assignment, or use physical space to separate good staffers from bad.

Building a "Turkey Farm"

If radical surgery is required, it is sometimes wise to concentrate incompetence in a single location. "Turkey farms" are commonplace in large government organizations. Take the least essential function your organization performs and assign it to a team of poor performers. This has the advantage of removing your worst performers from the mainstream of your organization's life, thus preventing the spread of incompetence. Unfortunately, it can also result in a focal point for mischief and can create any number of unanticipated embarrassments. It is also possible that this year's unimportant function may become next year's hot issue. Nevertheless, a turkey farm provides a single, easy-to-spot organizational unit to avoid assigning the more important work to. If you have the

ability to keep this unit out of the public's eye and away from your organizational superiors, it may be a strategy worth pursuing.

Detailing Staff Members

Typically, a detail is an internal loan of staff members to another unit within a particular organization for a set amount of time (usually from 30 to 180 days). Sometimes, however, an individual can be lent to another organization or to another branch or level of government. Civil servants generally have fewer rights for challenging a time-limited reassignment than they would have in a permanent reassignment. A detail can remove a particularly troublesome staff person and break up patterns of dysfunctional organizational behavior. On the negative side, you are not likely to make very many friends by detailing your incompetent staffer elsewhere. Obviously, this is a strategy that works better in situations of bad fit.

Developing an Unimportant Special Assignment

A strategy that stands halfway between detailing and establishing permanent turkey farms is the formation of harmless task forces. This is essentially the creation of a temporary turkey farm. You might, for example, form a task force to investigate the subject of the future of office information technology. This is a task that seems important and might involve interviewing dozens of vendors, but it is unlikely to result in much damage to the organization if it is not performed competently.

Using Physical Space

As a last resort, you can use space to isolate your weak performers. Find space in another building or in a different wing of the building in which you work, and place your incompetent people there. If you do not wish to formally reorganize, simply use the allocation of office space to separate your good performers from your weak

ones. If you really want to send a strong negative signal, trade for less desirable space than you already have and move your incompetent staffers there.

Effective Management and Staffing

The negative and even desperate tactics to deal with poor performers that we previously described are not examples of good management practices. Management involves providing a support system for workers to deliver the best performance of which they are capable. You may develop highly imaginative, sophisticated, and innovative programs, but you will never put any of them into place if you do not motivate your staff. Segregating incompetent staff members may be necessary at times, but it is never a desirable course of action. Some managers reinforce their sense of self-worth by belittling members of their staff. This is a prescription for mismanagement.

The Necessity of Hiring Good People

Good people are needed to implement innovative programs, but staff performance and even competence are variable rather than constant phenomena. It is often possible to get more than you might expect out of a poor performer and less than you might expect from an excellent performer. Managers seeking to implement innovative programs must be imaginative in selecting and nurturing staff expertise. Obviously, this task is easier if you have the opportunity to hire new employees and if you hire good ones.

A common assumption is that workers are not willing to shoulder some of the responsibility for improving the workplace; however, an effective manager will encourage workers to transform their own work environment. Sometimes, a manager must allow the definition of the work environment to change. A program in the state of Washington has transformed performance evaluations into a cooperative effort of managers and employees (Walters,

2001). Three of the four parts of the evaluation form are worked on jointly by employees and managers. There are no ratings boxes, and the performance of the employee is described in a narrative fashion. The evaluation also includes a section on training and professional development opportunities and goals. Finally, the employee is given a formal opportunity to suggest to the manager how he or she might enable the employee to be more effective and efficient.

As W. Edwards Deming (1982) and others devoted to Total Quality Management have observed, the problem with productivity does not usually center on the worker but, rather, on management-designed processes and structures that workers use to complete their tasks. Workers must deal with conflicting demands for productivity, quality, customer service, and economy (Cohen and Brand, 1993). Instead of blaming workers for organizational shortcomings, we must depend on them to analyze and provide suggestions to improve work processes. Because workers actually do the work, only they have access to the information needed to improve the quality of our organization's outputs and outcomes (Bowman, 1991; Cohen and Eimicke, 1998; Deming, 1982; Beam, 2001; Scholtes, 1996).

Organizations are primarily a collection of people, and entrepreneurial innovation is dependent on organizational capability. Managers generally focus on hot issues and crises of the moment. It is important to remember that there is no managerial task more important than staff selection and staff development.

Revitalizing an Organization

Bringing new life to a tired organization is an art as well as a science. It involves many of the management techniques discussed in the following chapters of this book. However, waking up an organization centers on energizing its members.

A wide variety of methods are available to rekindle the organization's fire. You can bring in new, motivated staff people. You can promote junior-level people over less energetic senior-level people. You can also encourage competition between elements of

your organization. Reorganization, exhortation, and threats are other potential strategies. Each technique has certain costs and benefits, and each must be individually tailored to a given management environment.

A technique we have seen used to good effect at the federal level of government (in the EPA, NASA, and Customs) and at the local level of government (New York City's Department of Parks and Recreation and San Diego County's Health and Human Services Administration) is the creation of special projects. These short-term, high-priority efforts at program design and implementation can be used to shake up dysfunctional behavior patterns and can teach employees a new, more intense method of operation. Special projects create artificial but useful deadlines that force new work patterns to be developed to reach project goals. (The role of special projects in strategy formulation is discussed later in this book.)

As a manager, your key responsibility is to influence the behavior of your subordinates. You must always look for opportunities to assess and improve staff performance. Managers who ignore the job of staff development will substantially reduce their chances of success. Managers with entrepreneurial ambitions must pay particularly close attention to staff development. Brilliant strategies can fail miserably if executed by a weak and poorly motivated staff.

Chapter Four

Developing Effective Working Relationships

Effective management involves influencing people to behave in ways that help you implement your organizational strategy. Among the most important people for you to influence are the people you work for, the people you work alongside, and the people who work for you. This chapter provides some advice on how to perform that critical management task. It begins by suggesting methods for satisfying the demands of superiors, peers, and subordinates. The first step in this complicated process is determining whose demands you should try to meet and then learning to listen carefully to these people. It is critical that you meet their requirements as they see them rather than as you think their priorities should be. Among the skills you must master to establish effective working relationships are communication, time management, motivation, negotiation, conflict resolution, and empathy.

How to Satisfy the Demands of Superiors, Peers, and Subordinates

Organizational life involves a delicate web of interpersonal relationships. An effective manager must constantly assess and respond to the wants and needs of other members of the organization. However, the care and feeding of these relationships must not impede the timely production of important organizational outputs. This tension between task and relationship makes it difficult to satisfy all the demands you are asked to address.

Whose Demands Should You Try to Meet?

It is impossible to please everyone and meet every demand. On the other hand, it is easy to fall into the trap of reflexive rejection—automatically assuming that no new demands can be met and reacting negatively to every new initiative. The key to successful establishment of effective working relationships is determining which demands should be met and in what order of priority.

Instead of spending all your time thinking about whom you need to please, assess whether specific demands facilitate or impede important accomplishments. This is not to say that you should ignore the source of demands. In some situations, you will want to be responsive for reasons related to politics or enlightened self-interest. Most of your actions, however, must be guided by the dictates of your strategy. Without a relatively clear sense of purpose, your organization can become the repository for the demands of others. Similarly, without a strategy, you have no basis for resisting the demands of superiors. If you simply respond to the demands of your superiors without assessing their impact on your organization's work, you may not accomplish very much.

Staff demands should be filtered by means of similar criteria. It is critical to remember that you are completely dependent on your staff to accomplish work. Management-staff relationships are characterized by mutual dependence, a fact you should bear in mind when responding to staff demands.

Learning to Listen to Your Coworkers

Listening is an essential and undervalued skill. Since effective managers tend to be aggressive, they are sometimes better talkers than listeners. Most managers get promoted because they have been noticed, and people do not usually get noticed by being silent. Since your ability to express yourself may have helped you get your job, it is natural to assume that those same skills can help you keep your job. However, just as in politics, the talents needed to campaign are different from those needed to govern. Managers who are bad listeners tend to be bad managers.

The tendency toward one-way communication stems from the misperception that management involves ordering people around. Listening requires you to understand both intellectually and in the pit of your stomach that your staff is important. You must recognize that the people who work for you know some things that you do not know. Similarly, colleagues who do not work in your organization can provide you with critical information and advice. You will not be able to obtain these resources if you do not learn to listen. Assuming you are attempting to take risks to implement programs, additional information and advice can help increase your chances for success.

Listening involves paying attention to your role as a learner. It requires that you learn to interpret your colleagues' verbal and non-verbal messages. Learn to notice people's facial expressions and body language. Each individual has a unique way of signaling his or her acceptance, rejection, or comprehension of your message. Look hard for those signals and learn to identify them. If you are uncertain about them, do not be afraid to ask questions—such as, Does this make sense to you? or Is that acceptable to you?

Just as you wish you had more time to analyze a problem or rewrite a memo, so, too, will you wish you had more time to listen. These constraints are unavoidable, but they are not an excuse. Sometimes, action-oriented managers make the mistake of believing that speaking and doing are more important than listening. You may not be able to listen as well as you would like, but you can make listening one of your top priorities.

Why Informal and Interpersonal Relations Are Critical

Some organizational strategists, taking their cues from Machiavelli's prince, believe that fear is more reliable than love as a means of influencing people. It is true that if someone hates and fears you, his or her behavior may be quite predictable. If you have the clout to back up your threats, it may not be necessary for you to get along with the people you work with. But power in public bureaucracy is often a fleeting thing—as is powerlessness. Yesterday's powerless subordinate may be tomorrow's powerful boss.

In addition, it is unusual for a public manager to have authority over every aspect of a program. For example, you need the help of the personnel office if you want to hire someone. You need the help of the budget staff if you must obtain certain resources and need to move money from one cost center to another. Organizations operate informally as well as through a formal hierarchy. In order to get things done, you must sometimes exchange favors and information. An organization's formal communication is only a tiny portion of its total communication. Formal orders and messages are generally used to reinforce and codify decisions that have already been reached informally.

Your effectiveness as a manager will be a direct reflection of your ability to get along with people. You will find it easier to get your work done if people want to help you because they like you or even because they feel sorry for you. If you are feared or hated, you may get cooperation when people have no choice, but the minute you turn your back, your colleagues will find a thousand ways to undermine you. Organizational life involves a series of exchanges rather than power relationships. Like the rest of society, organizations are more complex in the twenty-first century. As organizations downsize, complexity does not decrease, because organizations increase their use of contractors and advanced technology.

The degree of interdependence in modern organizational life is striking. It is certainly possible to run roughshod over your colleagues, accomplish a great deal, and then move on to a new organization. But we believe that eventually this strategy will backfire. The old clichés are true: what goes around comes around. People you step on as you climb up the career ladder might very well see you again on your way down the ladder. Effective public managers take the long view. Aggressive management does not require you to disregard the feelings of coworkers. Managers who are committed to results usually become quite skilled at horse trading and at stroking key individuals within the organization.

Sometimes, you must deny requests or oppose a colleague, but there is no reason to be nasty about it. Roger Fisher and William

Ury (1983) argue that one should separate the people from the problem. Focus on understanding the values in conflict. It is natural in a conflict situation to assume that your opponent is a misguided fool. Even if this is the case, it does you no good to treat him or her as such. A little respect can have a very positive effect.

We have all experienced bureaucrats who receive great ego satisfaction from being able to say no. They seem to enjoy their small exercise of power. If your ego is so fragile that you need to push people around in order to feel good about yourself, you probably should not be allowed to manage the work of other human beings. You will be too prone to define management as the act of ordering people around, which, again, we argue is the most common misconception about the meaning of management.

How to Keep Your Boss Relatively Happy

Nearly all public managers report to someone. So every public manager is someone else's staff member. Just as your staff must adjust to your standards and management style, so, too, must you adjust to your boss's style.

Ascertaining Your Boss's Management Style

To adjust to your boss's style, you must, of course, figure out exactly what that style is. When you go to work for someone new, there is usually an anxious period of adjustment as the two of you settle into a working relationship. Part of the adjustment involves seeing whether the two of you can communicate and work with each other. You should work hard to adjust to your new boss's style, but it is possible, of course, that the relationship will not work and you will want to leave.

What do we mean by management style and standards? The answers to the following questions help to define a manager's style:

- How is the organization's work determined and assigned?
- How are assignments tracked and reviewed?

- How are successes rewarded and failures punished?
- What criteria are used to define success and failure?
- How are these criteria developed?
- How well does the manager listen and learn?
- How well does the manager communicate?
- How does the manager behave during crisis situations and general adversity?
- Does the manager share credit for success and absorb the blame for failure?
- How accessible is the manager at work?
- Does the manager develop informal social relationships with other managers and staff members?
- Does the manager treat subordinates with the same courtesy that he or she extends to superiors?

We all have our own preferences and tolerances regarding our supervisor's management style. Some of us prefer a great deal of direction, others fear being micromanaged. The same behavior from a manager can be perceived by different employees as too little or too much direction. Some of us need a personal relationship with our boss, as well as the ability to discuss both professional and nonprofessional concerns. Others prefer to separate these two spheres of life.

Whatever your preferences are, while you work for a particular manager, you must learn to understand and adjust your behavior to his or her style. If your boss prefers one-page memos and you prefer two-page memos, learn to communicate in one page. If you hate the telephone but can get more time from your boss over the phone than in person, learn to love the phone. If e-mails produce the fastest and most positive response, use that medium. If your boss is not very creative and expects staff members to suggest initiatives, learn to generate your own work. In short, learn your boss's style and figure out ways of accomplishing your organizational strategy within the constraints posed by that style.

Preserving Your Boss's Time

In most organizations, access to a manager is a valuable and scarce resource. Even if you have a close, informal working relationship with your supervisor, you should still treat his or her time as a precious commodity. The first rule for preserving your boss's time is to be prepared when you speak. Before you walk into a formal or an informal meeting, review in your head or on a notepad the points you want to raise. Arrange them in order of priority in case you do not have a chance to complete your agenda. Do not bring problems to your boss without some proposed solutions. If possible, resolve conflict ahead of time, and use your boss's scarce time simply to report the conflict's resolution. When possible, develop informal, rapid methods for delivering urgent messages. A quick discussion on the way to the elevator, a brief e-mail message, a thirty-second phone call, or a note left on her chair are only a few methods for delivering quick, simple messages.

At critical junctures in an organization's activities, you may need a longer period of uninterrupted time with your boss or with your boss and other colleagues. If you need extended time to speak with your boss alone and he or she does not mind the company, attempt to travel somewhere together. A long flight or train ride can be an excellent way to meet one-on-one with our managers. You are less likely to be disturbed by the phone, and it may be possible to have a fairly leisurely, wide-ranging discussion of policy or management issues. Every once in a while, you may need such a meeting to improve your understanding of your boss's current thinking.

The other type of session that can be useful is a half-day or longer retreat. Find a meeting space, preferably without a phone in the room, and convene a brainstorming or briefing session with a limited number of key staff members. If the meeting is properly organized, with a professional facilitator and a clear set of objectives, you can make excellent use of your boss's time. You can transmit data, receive policy direction, make decisions, or kick around ideas for developing creative answers to difficult management issues. The main point in any session with your boss is to develop a

concrete plan for using management time. If you waste your boss's time, your organization will be less productive and you will be a less successful manager. If you consistently waste your boss's time, eventually your own competence will be questioned.

Communicating with Your Boss

The first rule of communicating with your boss is to be prepared and to use his or her time sparingly. The second rule is to follow the format and style your boss prefers. Remember that your manager receives a tremendous number of messages every day. The ones that are going to get through are the ones that are most important and most easily understood.

Your messages should be labeled to fit within one of your organization's critical missions. If your message cannot be so categorized, it probably should not be communicated to your boss. No response to your message does not mean it is unimportant or unwelcome; it may simply be temporarily less important than other items. If you think something is particularly important, do not be afraid to send repeated messages until you receive some sort of feedback.

Working Out Disagreements with Your Boss

Sometimes, you cannot work out disagreements with your boss, and in that case, it is time for you to leave the organization. It is always possible to stay and make life miserable for others in the organization, but isn't life too short for such a terrible waste of energy? Unfortunately, most people in conflict situations stay where they are and engage in grumbling and sabotage.

If you disagree with your boss, there are times when you should simply repress your own views and fall in line. Sometimes, your commitment to the organization's overall goals will enable you to get over even a major policy disagreement. At other times, you will need to discuss the disagreement with your boss and perhaps forge a compromise.

The exception is deeply rooted ethical issues. Some issues must be fought over. However, most disagreements in public organizations do not involve major ethical issues. Typically, they are issues related to strategy and approach.

Attempt to work out your disagreements privately and quietly whenever possible. A public conflict will often require a symbolic response and an assertion of authority. In private, your boss need not be as concerned about appearances, and your chances of changing his or her views are far greater. Sometimes, an indirect approach may be even better than a direct private confrontation. You and your boss may share a trust relationship with a third party who can carry your message and possibly mediate a disagreement.

How to Keep Your Staff Relatively Happy

Part of the job of the effective manager is to maintain worker morale. This does not mean that you can make most of your employees happy all of the time. Rather, it means that for the most part, you and your staffers look forward to coming to work most days.

Learning What Motivates Your Staff

One of a manager's key roles is to learn about the specific incentives that motivate individual staff members. The main methods for learning about what motivates your staff are observation and listening. Self-consciously apply specific incentives and then observe their effects. Has a staff member reacted as you hoped he would? Has performance been maintained or improved? Remember that people change, and last year's incentive may no longer work. We all get bored if we do the same thing too many times. Your staff should be learning and developing on the job, and last year's plum assignment may very well be next year's routine task. The key is to be conscious of staff preferences, talents, and goals. Although it is not possible to always provide the perfect reward for the perfect

task, it is very sensible for you to attempt to maximize the impact of the incentives and assignments at your disposal.

Some people crave the spotlight. A reward for them is exposure to the media, staffing an event for a high-level elected official, or attending a national conference. Others appreciate sophisticated technology to accomplish their jobs more quickly and to play with when time is less pressured. Others really need more money and do not mind putting in long hours or taking work home to obtain extra income.

To effectively match tasks with talents and incentives with individuals, you must know who your people are and what motivates them. It takes time and effort to obtain this knowledge. You must develop a network within your organization to provide you with intelligence about staff attitudes and preferences. You should devote substantial personal attention to learning about the forces that motivate your key staff members. Information about your staff's preferences is far more important to successful management than understanding the status of financial or performance indicators. Motivating key staff members is the primary mission of management.

Communicating with Your Staff

Let us begin by discussing how *not* to communicate with your staff. Try to avoid

- Pronouncements from on high
- Frequent dramatic changes in direction
- Reliance on formal communication
- Establishing new policies without explanations
- Technical and confusing official language
- Long periods without communicating to employees

No single method of communication is appropriate to all situations. At times, formal written communication is necessary. If you have a staff of three thousand, you will need to use formal mecha-

nisms to reach them all. However, if you have a staff of five, internal formal communication can be offensive. Even if you have a large organization, your span of control should not exceed seven or eight direct reports. Those key people have informal influence over and communication with their own key staff people, and this effect cascades down throughout the organization.

Most of the important messages received by an organization's members are communicated through these informal networks. If the purpose of communication is to influence behavior, informal, oral communication has several advantages over written, formal communication. First, it ensures that the message is individually tailored to the person you wish to influence. Second, it projects intimacy and a sense of belonging to a privileged decision group if you deliver the message as part direction and part question. Third, an informal spoken message allows you to reconsider your request in light of new information or direct feedback. It is hard to withdraw a formal written memo without loss of prestige.

Most people appreciate a boss who relates to them as human beings first and as subordinates second. A respect for your staff members' dignity is critical. Organization members voluntarily give up some of their freedom to belong to an organization. It is not necessary or smart to frame your communications as if your staff has no free will. Attempt to minimize your use of command language and maximize your use of the language of persuasion and request. It may seem inconsequential, but it actually is important to try to keep track of the major events in the personal life of each of your staff members. Being sensitive to such events as weddings, births, illnesses, and deaths in their lives is not simply courtesy and manners, it is an important signal of respect for your colleagues.

Understanding the Role of Unions in Your Organization

The unionized portion of the nation's workforce is declining, but public sector unions continue to grow. Labor-management relationships vary considerably in government organizations throughout the

United States. In some larger cities, particularly in the Northeast, a large number of municipal workers are unionized, and the unions have tremendous influence on local politics and the behavior of government agencies.

At the federal government level, unions have very little power. This fact was made clear by the ease with which President Ronald Reagan eliminated the air traffic controllers' union in the early 1980s. When these controllers struck against the Federal Aviation Administration, Reagan fired them and disbanded their union. And federal unions grew even weaker during the 1990s. It is difficult to imagine a mayor of Boston or Baltimore getting away with a similar response to a strike of unionized municipal workers. In order to assess the role that unions should play in your organization, you must pay careful attention to the labor environment.

Many management experts dislike unions because they impose an unwanted element of formality on labor-management relations. Unions tend to emphasize the separate interests of labor and management rather than the collective interests of all the members of an organization. However, as long as hierarchy exists, labor and management will have some important and distinct interests. When a union exists and is part of an organization's tradition or when staff members decide that a union or professional organization is needed, it is not smart to oppose such organizations.

If your staff has made the choice to unionize, it is wise for you to respect that choice and learn to work with the union. This is not to say that you should abdicate your responsibility and turn over management decision making to the union. However, just as you must deal with your staff's individual preferences to influence individual behavior, so, too, must you deal with collective preferences to influence group behavior.

It is important to develop a good working relationship with unions, but this is sometimes difficult to do. Just as there are many terrible public managers, the quality of union leadership can also be uneven. If you are fortunate, you may find yourself working with a union leader who is willing to forgo symbolic opposition and develop a partnership. Sometimes, you may find yourself managing in an organization with a

history of poisoned labor-management relations. In these situations, you may have to take additional steps to build trust. At other times, you may simply have to fight a union. The conflict may be the reflection of a simple power struggle, or it may be the result of sincerely held disagreements over management policy. When you find yourself in a labor conflict, be careful to separate your ego from the conflict.

Here, again, we suggest adherence to the concept of principled negotiation as presented by Fisher and Ury in *Getting to Yes* (1983). They advocate identifying the policy issues that are at the heart of the conflict and suggest that negotiators work at compromising on those issues. They urge parties in conflict to attempt to separate the people from the problem. Sometimes, no matter how hard you try, you end up caught in the middle of a terrible fight. In such a situation, the best thing to do is either to duck or to practice the art of damage control. If you cannot stay out of the line of fire, it is wise to confront the issue as quickly and directly as possible. Absorb the bad news, accept the fact that you are going to make some people very unhappy, and attempt to move on as soon as possible. The worst thing to do in a labor conflict is to drag it out so that not only are the results unsatisfactory but everyone involved suffers a personal bruising as well.

Dealing with an Unhappy Staff

One of the principal tasks of management is to mediate internal conflict. If your staff is unhappy, your first job is to identify the source of the problem. The most common sources of staff unhappiness seem to be mismanagement, management competition, poor working conditions, inadequate promotion potential or staff cutbacks, personality conflicts, and external or environmental conditions. It is your job to monitor and maintain staff morale. If you identify a source of staff unhappiness that you can influence, by all means, attempt to do so. If low morale stems from causes beyond your control, involve your staff in a collective effort to develop a strategy for coping with the problem.

People need to feel that they are special. When early productivity experts experimented with light and other physical stimuli in

an effort to improve production line performance, they found that no matter what physical change they made, productivity improved. It turned out that the stimulus that affected production most was the workers' awareness of being observed; attention motivated people to work hard. Social scientists have termed this observation bias the "Hawthorne effect." Just as the Hawthorne effect has demonstrated that people are more productive when they are aware of being the focus of attention, simply exposing the cause of unhappiness can sometimes help people cope with a situation. It helps to know that other people share your frustration, recognize the problem, and can laugh about the situation or shrug it off. The worst thing a manager can do about a situation the staff finds frustrating is to deny the legitimacy of their frustration.

How Hands-On Should You Be with Your Staff?

Although you should avoid ordering people around, you cannot run an organization without setting direction. Directive leadership is even more important if you are taking entrepreneurial risks as a manager and departing from standard prescriptions and organizational patterns. The principles that entrepreneurial public leaders need to consider include taking personal responsibility for the policy process and its consequences (past, present, and future) and demanding thorough analysis and professional competence as an ethical imperative (Cohen, Eimicke, and Pérez Salazar, 2000; Levin and Sanger, 1994). The trick is to provide guidance and leadership without being condescending—to teach without lecturing. It will often be difficult to judge precisely how much direction your key subordinates require. If you set too little direction, they may not understand what you want them to do. If you set too much direction, they may resent your management style. If you generally treat people with respect, they will probably excuse your little excesses. Therefore, the best advice is to err on the side of too much information and too little direction, so that you set direction in a way that respects your staff members as professionals but does not set them up for failure.

Chapter Five

Structuring Systems, Tasks, and Responsibilities

With an excellent staff in place, an effective public manager must facilitate productive working relationships among the members of that staff. The degree and quality of staff interaction is influenced by an organization's structure. Structure helps determine who will work with whom and how talents will be used. Tasks, like organizations, can also be structured or arranged to maximize the talents of a staff.

This chapter focuses on organization and task structure by discussing how your organization's structure can help you manage. It will help you determine when reorganization is worth your effort and what it should accomplish. A manager also needs to appreciate the fine line between allowing a staff member's initiative and ideas to flourish and maintaining at least a semblance of control. A competent and effective manager knows how to break projects down into manageable tasks and how to ensure that tasks assigned are fair and reasonable. This chapter concludes by discussing how you can be sure that work is assigned to the right people and that tasks are effectively completed.

How the Organization's Structure Can Help Managers Manage

The structure of an organization can be used to influence the behavior of the organization's members. Reporting relationships can be rearranged and different missions can be emphasized by moving staffers into newly configured organizational units. Structure is important because most tasks in the modern world are complex and

performed by groups, and performance will suffer if an organization's work and structure are not in sync.

The Purpose of Organizational Structure

Formal structure is an obvious and somewhat overrated feature of organizational life. Max Weber (1946) noted that formal hierarchy is a defining characteristic of bureaucracy. In a formal hierarchy, everyone must report to someone. Knowing whom you work for and knowing who works for you are fairly important aids to effective management. In contrasting bureaucracy with other forms of organization, Weber observed that bureaucracy's great strength is its ability to break work up into small, efficiently performed tasks. Each task is performed by a distinct organizational unit. This division of labor allows organizational units to develop great expertise and facility with specific, narrowly defined tasks. Organizational structure therefore serves two essential purposes. It establishes how an organization defines and divides its work (division of labor) and provides mechanisms for coordinating and integrating the work of separate organizational units (Gibson, 1978).

Matching Structure to Organizational Needs

There is no such thing as a correct organizational structure. Administrative theorists made a concerted effort in the early twentieth century to develop scientific principles of administration (Rainey, 1991). These theorists specifically emphasized formal organizational structure. Perhaps the classic statement of their principles appears in a collection entitled *Papers on the Science of Administration* (Gulick and others, 1937). Herbert Simon (1957) spearheaded an intellectual attack on the science of public administration that effectively laid to rest the notion that administration could be guided by hard and fast scientific laws. Instead of deriving a "correct" organizational structure from pseudoscientific principles, we can judge a structure in terms of its appropriateness to or match with an

organization's unique needs. As Cyrus Gibson (1978) indicates, an organization's structure should be a function of three factors: goals and objectives, internal social structure, and external environment.

Obviously, an organization should be structured to emphasize the accomplishment of its principal policies and programs. If a high priority of an organization is to develop new technology, we would not be surprised to see a separate organizational unit for research and development. If an organization's principal focus is the enforcement of regulations, we would expect to see a group of lawyers working together in a large office of the general counsel. If an organization's environment is hostile, we would expect to see a structure that emphasizes defense against external threats. If an organization must deliver services over a wide geographic area, we might expect it to develop a decentralized structure to accommodate local needs.

Second, an organization's internal capabilities and attributes must be factored into decisions about structure. Sometimes a division of labor that seems totally illogical on paper works well in the real world because of a unique combination of talent that has developed within an organization. For example, organization A might perform a training function for organization B simply because the skill to perform the function has developed in organization A. At other times, an organizational structure may develop around a manager's individual strengths and weaknesses. For example, some managers may not pay close attention to detail and may require an organizational unit that is willing and able to follow up on initiatives and manage projects. Sometimes a manager's attributes or deficiencies can cause an organization to grow in illogical and dysfunctional patterns. When that particular manager is replaced, it may be necessary to reorganize the structure along more rational lines. Some organizational structures emerge due to the preferences of an organization's staff or manager. The key point is that organizational form should follow organizational function. Increasingly, those functions require smaller, less hierarchical organizations than the traditional government bureaucracy. As contracting, privatization, and competition become increasingly prevalent, and as government, to use

Osborne and Gaebler's phrase, spends more time "steering than rowing," the large, hierarchical government organization must adapt to this new situation.

External environment is the third element that affects organizational design. This environment is quite political, and it changes frequently. In fact, since public organizations are often assigned new missions by their political masters, we should expect reorganizations with some frequency. Unfortunately, a reorganization is often dictated by political rather than managerial considerations. Often, reorganizations are mandated by law, as in the formation of the U.S. Department of Energy or the creation of a new assistant administrator for hazardous waste in the EPA. At other times, reorganizations perform nonmanagement political and symbolic functions, as in the creation of the U.S. Department of Labor and the U.S. Department of Education. Both of these organizations were created in direct response to interest group pressure. Decisions on organizational structure often reflect policy priorities, and since these priorities are the organization's goals, such structural determinants are appropriate.

The Limits of Structure

Organizational structure can be viewed as a management tool designed to modify behavior patterns. If an organization is performing poorly, structure is one of a variety of mechanisms that can be used to stimulate improved effectiveness. However, structure has significant limits as a management tool. As with other management mechanisms, deploying different structural arrangements involves trade offs. Structure influences how tasks are differentiated and then coordinated. Harold Gortner (1981) notes that public organizations are frequently structured by policy or program area, management function—such as personnel, contracting, or budgeting, client type, and geography. Many organizations use more than one structural rationale, but one rationale tends to dominate.

The U.S. Department of Energy (DOE), for example, is organized by program, management function, and geography. It has pro-

gram offices in policy areas such as nuclear waste, nuclear power, fossil fuels, and defense. The DOE also has offices devoted to management functions such as policy analysis, legal services (general counsel), and personnel. And the DOE has a geographic substructure. Many of the department's program-based organizations establish field offices in various parts of the country. However, despite the use of three structural bases, the DOE is primarily organized by program. Most staff people are in program units, and these organizations frequently establish field units that report to counterpart offices at headquarters.

In contrast, the EPA is essentially a geographically based organization, with program offices in policy areas such as air pollution control, water pollution control, and hazardous waste cleanup. The EPA also has offices organized according to management function, including financial management, program evaluation, and information systems. However, the EPA's ten regional offices are headed by regional administrators who report directly to the national EPA administrator in Washington.

The assistant administrators in charge of the EPA's headquarters program and management offices are the organizational equals, not the superiors, of the regional administrators. Each regional office has program and functional organizational units that mirror the headquarters structure. Although these regional units are expected to follow policies made at headquarters, they report exclusively to their regional administrator rather than to an appropriate headquarters assistant administrator. Of the EPA's staff of approximately seventeen thousand, the great majority work in regional rather than headquarters offices. The EPA's decision to base its structure on geography allows it to modify national policies to fit regional environmental and political conditions.

The EPA traded nationally consistent policy and the efficient accumulation and communication of program experience for local flexibility and decentralized administration. The DOE sacrificed some ability to accommodate local political interests in return for national consistency. Presumably, the trade offs these

two organizations made were consistent with their organizational goals. The DOE was created in response to the energy crisis of the mid-1970s. It was designed to develop "crash programs" to meet national energy needs. Sensitivity to local political needs was not a priority for the DOE. The EPA, though, was designed to perform the politically sensitive mission of cajoling industry and local government into producing less pollution. Clearly, if progress was to be made, the EPA had to be capable of mitigating political attacks from local economic elites. In exchange for a structure attuned to local political needs, the EPA sacrificed a degree of the policy consistency that was a primary objective of national environmental legislation.

As these EPA and DOE macro-level examples indicate, decisions on organizational structure involve tough trade offs. Countless micro-level examples might also be provided to illustrate the same point: emphasizing one function or type of organizational unit necessarily deemphasizes another function or staff. The trick is to place your structural bets on choices that maximize the odds of successful program implementation.

What Reorganization Should Accomplish and When It Is Worth the Effort

Reorganization is an attractive management option because in the public sector it is relatively easy to accomplish, compared with other management techniques. Public managers have difficulty firing employees, abandoning unprofitable missions, and radically changing budget allocations. However, most public managers have the power to redefine the organization they control and can transfer staff members between newly defined organizational units.

The Uses of Reorganization

Earlier, we noted the importance of matching organizational structure with needs. The process of rearranging organizational units to

meet new needs is called reorganization. There are four basic uses of reorganization:

1. To break up dysfunctional patterns of organizational behavior
2. To create more logical combinations of functions in order to stimulate greater organizational efficiencies
3. To emphasize new or modified missions, goals, or objectives
4. To reward excellent performers

Dysfunctional Patterns of Organizational Behavior

As organizations mature, they sometimes take on characteristics that satisfy individual rather than organizational needs. Chester Barnard ([1938] 1968) notes that one of the key phenomena of organizational life is the development of informal organization. Irrespective of an organization's formal hierarchy and formal goals, informal patterns of communication and unsanctioned organizational goals develop. In a similar vein, Philip Selznick, in his classic work, *Leadership in Administration* ([1957] 1984), writes that as an organization develops, its members come to see it as more than a neutral piece of machinery; they consider it a valuable "source of personal satisfaction." One trivial but tangible sign of this sort of identification is office softball teams and their specially designed tee shirts. Anyone who visits Washington, D.C., at dusk during the summer will run into dozens of office softball games on the mall, between the Capitol and the Lincoln Memorial. Sometimes, organizational identification can help an agency accomplish important goals, as staffers will contribute extra effort out of affection for the organization and personal loyalty to friends with whom they work.

At other times, informal relationships can create dysfunctional patterns of organizational behavior as staff members establish relationships that thwart rather than facilitate the flow of information and the completion of tasks. According to Selznick ([1957] 1984), one of the functions of administrative leadership is to understand

and influence an organization's informal social patterns. One way of influencing informal communication and behavior is to modify the formal structure of the organization to facilitate the flow of information up the hierarchy. Although formal structure does not dictate organizational behavior, it certainly does influence such behavior. Let us assume, for example, that a staff member in program organization A is able to speed up contracting procedures because of an established relationship with a staff member in contracting office B. If you reassign duties so that office A no longer deals with contracting office B, this informal arrangement falls apart. Should you someday need to obtain a contracted service quickly, you may regret your destruction of the informal contracting arrangement your staff member had developed.

Creating Greater Organizational Efficiencies

The second use of reorganization is to create greater efficiencies and more logical combinations of functions. Although structure itself does not guarantee improved working conditions, reorganizing functions can sometimes improve work flow and communication. The city of Indianapolis, for example, undertook a massive municipal reorganization project, called Unigov, with the aim of consolidating a number of local organizations that performed similar functions.

In another initiative, a northeastern state transferred oil spill cleanup responsibilities from its transportation department to its environmental protection department. The governor's office believed that toxic waste, petroleum, and chemical spill cleanups should be located within one agency to facilitate development of expertise. The classical theories of administrative "science" claimed that efficiency is the primary goal of organizational structure and that a well-designed structure can promote efficiency, and most reorganizations are explained as enhancing that goal. Restructuring is a vastly overrated device for stimulating efficiency, but reorganizing functions can sometimes improve workflow and communications. Occasionally, you discover that, over time, a function has changed and organizational units that

once interacted extensively no longer work together. If these units report to the same supervisor, it might be time to place one of them in another area. Sometimes technological change can stimulate a reorganization. For example, before personal computers were invented, data management required large, centralized computer centers and organizations to staff them. Although mainframe computers are still used for payroll and certain research functions, the need for central computing support for each organizational unit has diminished. In some agencies, it makes more sense to break up computing units and disperse their staffs throughout the organization.

Emphasizing Goals and Missions

The third use of reorganization is to emphasize new or expanded missions and to accommodate the organizational growth stimulated by new work. Although the number of people a manager can successfully supervise is a matter of individual talent and preference, the number is never infinite. If an organization grows significantly, it must provide for additional reporting relationships. These new relationships are created by adding new organizational units. Increased size requires reorganization, and changes in policy can often be signaled and institutionalized through reorganization. A regulatory agency that is serious about enforcement might increase the prestige of its office of general counsel as well as the number of staffers assigned to it. An agency can communicate its seriousness about taking on a new mission by creating a new organization to implement that mission. In recent years, many state health organizations have created new units to address both AIDS and drug addiction. In fact, sometimes a mission can be obtained by anticipating a need and creating an organizational unit before legislation is even enacted (Cohen and Tipermas, 1983).

Rewarding Excellent Performance

Finally, reorganization can be used to create management positions and promotional slots for excellent performers. If an organization's

management level is not turning over quickly, it may not provide sufficient promotion potential to upwardly mobile staff members. In order to provide increased opportunity, it sometimes makes sense to subdivide organizational units, establish task forces, or create new management levels. Reorganizing to create new management positions can also create problems, however. Taking responsibility away from one manager and giving it to another may make the losing manager unhappy. If you do not divide responsibility, you must add a new level of hierarchy. If you promote someone from the position of branch chief to deputy division director, the existing branch chiefs may become dissatisfied. If you reorganize and raise all branch chiefs to the divisional level, you make everyone happy and create new management positions. However, you also add an additional level of hierarchy. At times, the need to reward and retain key staff members is great enough to justify such a reorganization. But one problem with this rationale for reorganization is that it can result in unneeded growth in the organization and in hierarchy. Unfortunately, many government promotion policies are based on the number of people an individual manages. This forces people who are not suited to management to become managers and it creates a tremendous incentive for managers to increase the size of their organization.

The Costs of Reorganization

Although reorganization can serve several useful purposes, it is not cost-free. If not strategically and responsibly conducted, reorganization can have a negative effect on morale. Reorganization can also disrupt informal patterns of communication, create insecurity, and cause a decline in productivity—particularly during the transition period, and it can result in less effective formal reporting relationships than those present before the reorganization.

Although formal hierarchy is a defining characteristic of the bureaucratic form of organization, most of an organization's communication does not follow the formal chain of command. Informal person-to-person contacts account for most organizational

communication. Such contacts are essential to the smooth functioning of an organization. They are the lubricant that makes it possible to implement the hierarchy's formal orders. Nevertheless, informal organization and informal communication networks are influenced by formal structure. A reorganized formal structure can disrupt both dysfunctional and productive informal behavior as well as communication patterns. In fact, it is difficult to imagine a reorganization that would not disrupt both positive and negative informal patterns. It is management's job to analyze the impact of a rearranged formal structure on informal behavior patterns. The decision to reorganize should be based in part on an assessment of the trade offs involved.

Studying the informal aspects of an organization can be difficult. The best way to assess the impact of a proposed reorganization is to "feel out" the reorganization's major participants. This includes holding lengthy discussions with all the managers involved as well as with a sizable sampling of professional and clerical staff members. You should pose alternative scenarios and survey colleagues about their thoughts on the reorganization's likely impact. You should also ask them to project the impact on the organization and on their own work. However, do not take responses literally. You are likely to confront a complex array of hidden agendas, but the composite of all comments should give you a feel for the trade offs involved in reorganizing.

Most reorganizations are sprung without warning on an organization's members. Occasionally, there are exceptions, where a major reorganization may include extensive employee participation. However, the vast majority are created in secret and imposed from above without much understanding of the human and social impact of the change. The suddenness of some reorganizations and the creation of new reporting relationships can create enormous uncertainty within an organization. During periods of transition, a tremendous amount of staff time is devoted to informal discussion of proposed changes. This is the typical justification used for developing the reorganization proposal in secret. However, since most people are unable to keep

secrets, the effort to develop a reorganization proposal in private usually breeds suspicion and insecurity. Once the proposal is released, most public organizations require internal review and possibly union approval before the new structure can be put into place. This transition period can be very nonproductive. For a staff member, a change of supervisor can be a disorienting and wrenching experience. Seeing trusted colleagues and lunch partners moved to another floor can create insecurity and lower morale. This in turn can lower productivity, the opposite of the desired effect.

The final cost of reorganization is probably the one most studied. Every organization's structure is based on some type of analysis or assessment of the functions that belong together or match. Most reorganizers ask the question Whom does A need to be in constant communication with? Lobbyists are located physically and organizationally near public relations specialists, management information specialists are located near budget analysts, and particular specialists or mixes of specialists are placed within the same organizational units. But when reorganizing, it is always possible to overlook efficiencies in the existing structure. Overall, the new design may separate functions that need to be together and link functions that could be separate. Although these problems are typically overcome through informal communication networks, an illogically structured organization can place too great a burden on informal mechanisms. Under these conditions, an organization's effectiveness can be impaired.

Deciding Whether to Reorganize

Rearranging the pieces of the organizational puzzle does not seem like much, but it may be all a manager can do to infuse vigor into a dormant organization. For the effective manager, reorganization can provide staff members with a strong signal that business will no longer proceed as it has in the past, and it can concentrate resources on programs that the manager has decided to take a risk on emphasizing.

We strongly believe that the effective public manager must shake up an organization to squeeze out increased performance, but we do not advocate change for its own sake. The decision to reorganize must be a strategic one. It must follow a rapid but thorough analysis of the costs and benefits of organizational options. This includes an analysis of the impact of rearranging formal functions and, as noted earlier, an assessment of the reorganization's effect on the informal organization.

Think of the cost of reorganization as the investment or risk taken to increase your organization's effectiveness. It is reasonable to spend something to get something, but it is unreasonable not to know what you are spending. Assess the real costs of reorganization in human terms and in terms of likely functional matchups, and attempt to weigh the costs against the benefits you hope to reap.

There is no cookbook to tell you how to conduct this type of assessment. The best counsel we can give is to seek advice. Speak to the agency's veterans and try to understand the organization's history and the effects of previous reorganizations. Talk to colleagues outside your organization and discuss with them your hopes and fears, and seek verification of your hunches and guesstimates. Consider a phased approach to reorganization, one that allows you to reconsider and make midcourse corrections. Listen to your staff, seek feedback, and do not be afraid to tinker with your initial design. Keep in mind that the sooner the process is completed, the sooner you stop paying the price of uncertainty and insecurity. Finally, do not assume that formal reorganization can solve your organization's operational difficulties. Management is not simply a matter of rearranging boxes on an organization chart. Ultimately, good management comes down to motivating people. Reorganization can create a more favorable climate for motivational initiatives and should be considered the start rather than the end of a management reform process.

What should reorganization accomplish and when is it worth the effort? The answer to this question is as varied as organizational type and mission. For the effective public manager, the risk is often

worth the benefit. Organizational malaise is a common disease in large organizations. There is often some benefit in simply shaking up the structure to see what falls out. The key here is to approach reorganization as a method of learning about your organization's informal social structure. If you see reorganization as the beginning of a long process of management reform, the risk will often pay off. If, however, you mistake reorganization for meaningful management change, it is likely that you will simply be disrupting behavior patterns. Like a child poking an anthill with a stick, you will reinforce your sense of mastery without causing any significant change. Before you turn around, a new anthill will appear in the same spot as the old one.

How to Maintain Control Without Suffocating Staff Members

It is critical to formulate a meaningful definition of management control. Control is *not* a matter of knowing and directing everything that happens in an organization. Control is *not* avoiding all mistakes. Control is the ability to direct organizational behavior to conform generally to organizational strategy, organizational objectives, and organizational values. Control is not preventing people from doing the wrong things; it is creating an environment that encourages them to do the right things. The organization's environment must be presented as a series of opportunities that the organization's procedures enable it to exploit. A manager has sufficient control of his or her organization if, on the whole, organizational behavior is carrying out the organization's strategy. It may be that the organization's strategy is faulty or its values inappropriate, but that is a separate issue.

Encouraging Staff Initiative

If you accept our definition of management control, it should be obvious that you cannot maintain control without encouraging

staff initiative. Such initiative is as appropriate in the public sector as in the private sector. The staff must constantly interpret a changing environment. Members must apply and adjust organizational routines to new situations. Without initiative, such adaptation is impossible. In the public sector, one critical part of that changing environment is the attitudes and perceptions of political players. This means that staff initiative must often take into account a greater number of external variables than might be the case in the private sector. However, this only makes innovation more complicated, not less necessary. To encourage innovation, a manager must learn to let go of specific responsibilities and delegate authority to subordinates.

Learning to Delegate

As managers move up in an organization and take on progressively broader responsibilities, it becomes increasingly necessary to delegate responsibilities to subordinates. We distinguish between delegating tasks and delegating responsibilities. Task delegation, or getting someone else to do your work under close supervision, is relatively easy. Giving someone complete responsibility for accomplishing an objective, however, can be more difficult. This is particularly the case if it is an area for which you were once responsible. It is likely that one of the reasons you were promoted and given broader responsibilities is that you were good at your former job. There is a very human tendency to attempt to micromanage in your former area of responsibility; your new job may be a bit unfamiliar, and initially you may even derive less satisfaction from it than from your former job. Delegation can be particularly tricky in the public sector because, in government, successful delegation requires both technical and political knowledge. Very few jobs in public management require only technical, internal management skills; most require a feel for the organization's political environment as well. The absence of a bottom line makes it difficult to determine whether you have successfully delegated an area of responsibility.

Successful delegation involves the following steps:

- Developing a clear understanding of the area of responsibility, including objectives and boundaries
- Establishing concrete performance objectives as a basis for measuring success
- Providing frequent performance review and feedback but not interfering in day-to-day tasks

Delegation is similar to teaching; it involves instruction and direction setting, but the student or delegatee must take responsibility and complete the assignment. Delegating responsibility is particularly important for the effective public manager. If you are to take initiative and innovate in any significant manner, it is essential that you have a cadre of associates whose performance you can rely on. It is difficult to look forward and exploit your environment if you are constantly looking over your subordinates' shoulders.

Nevertheless, delegation is never easy. It requires trust, teaching skill, and the ability to tolerate error, and it especially involves hard work. It is not simply casting off work and then forgetting about it until something goes wrong and you are looking for someone to blame. Delegation requires an active relationship between the delegator and the delegatee. The ability to delegate may be the most significant trait of the successful manager.

How to Break Down Projects into Manageable Tasks

Many assignments in public agencies are complex projects that require substantial expertise and involve a number of interconnected steps. This work is most effectively performed if it is broken down into simpler, more discrete tasks.

Planning Operational Programs

Many public organizations have adopted some form of program planning process, ranging from management by objectives to criti-

cal path analysis to traditional back-of-the-envelope budgeting. Every few years, a new fad, such as Planning, Programming and Budgeting System, Total Quality Management, or Zero-Based Budgeting, comes along. Although none of these techniques is ever the cure-all its advocates seem to imply, program planning and analysis is an important form of institutional thinking. If your agency has such a process and you have not been taking it particularly seriously, you may wish to reconsider. Although line managers have an understandable aversion to staff-generated paperwork, program planning can be valuable if it is done simply and quickly. Since you may be devoting considerable resources to pro forma compliance with these ritualistic processes, you should think about the adaptations you could make to a planning process that might make it genuinely useful. We particularly believe that agencywide quality initiatives can be particularly useful, especially if you are able to sidestep the inevitable paperwork such processes frequently generate.

A simple, effective program planning and monitoring exercise includes four major steps:

1. Determining your organization's short-term operational objectives
2. Describing and analyzing the activities that will be needed to accomplish these short-term objectives
3. Engaging in detailed activity or project planning
4. Tracking the project or activity

Determining Objectives

The first step in determining an organization's objectives is to develop or review current objectives. Is the organization doing what it says it is doing? Is it doing what it needs to do if it is to survive? A short statement of objectives should be developed and circulated for staff and management review. This statement of objectives should be as specific as possible, and it is important that the objectives be measurable and simple. We prefer short-term,

operational objectives because of the difficulty of determining success in the public sector. In the private sector, market penetration, market share, profit, and rate of return can all be used as discrete measures of organizational success. Although government does not have similar, well-recognized measures of success, each organization can develop its own set of management indicators.

A *management indicator* is a measure of an organization's ability to meet specific operational objectives. An *operational objective* is a concrete, measurable goal that is directly related to an organization's principal activities or operations. One example of a management indicator for a city sanitation department might be the percentage of streets rated clean. The department might set an operational objective of increasing the percentage of clean streets. Each year, you should set a number of such operational objectives and then manage your organization to accomplish those objectives. These operational objectives should be areas that are prioritized for improved performance rather than reaching specific numerical targets.

Frequently, managers will argue that the benefits brought by their organizations cannot be quantified or that setting operational objectives can distort an organization by irrationally focusing its efforts on accomplishing overly narrow aims; it can turn an organization into a group of uninspired bean counters. Again, we are not advocating numerical targets but are simply measuring current levels of performance and identifying areas that need to be improved. If the organization's operational objectives are seen as a set of specific operations targeted for improvement, it is not necessary to specify how much improvement is needed. In other words, it is not necessary to set numerical objectives. Since the objectives of public organizations frequently change, management indicators must be flexible and continually open to reexamination and modification.

Describing and Analyzing Organizational Activities

With a set of operational objectives in place, an organization can then begin activity, or what we prefer to call project planning. The term *activity* connotes a certain aimlessness, whereas the term *project*

implies a coordinated set of goal-directed actions. The first step of project planning is to identify the projects that an organization must undertake to achieve its short-term or operational objectives. The process of project identification begins with a rigorous analysis of current operations and levels of performance. Levels of performance are measured by analyzing the quality and efficiency of work processes and work outputs. Quality is determined by analyzing the satisfaction levels of the organization's customers—the people internal and external to the organization who will use the outputs of your organization's specific work process. The projects undertaken by an organization should be designed to improve the organization's current level of performance. Project priorities are determined by analyzing each of the projects according to their contribution to meeting overall operational improvement objectives. Those that do not contribute should be dropped, and new projects needed to meet operational objectives must be identified. A summary of objectives and projects designed to accomplish those objectives—perhaps in the form of what we call an operational program budget—should then be circulated for management and staff review. For ease of communication, objectives and projects might be categorized by organizational function or program. The operational program budget identifies an organization's

- Functions or programs
- Operational objectives (categorized by function)
- Projects (categorized by chief improvement objective)
- Staff leads and staff resources assigned to each project
- Nonstaff resources assigned to each project (such as contractor funding or equipment)
- Estimated start dates and end dates for each project

Detailed Project Planning

With projects identified and related to organizational objectives, it is then possible to begin detailed project planning. The staff leads identified for each project in the operational program budget

should develop a plan for carrying out the staff's assigned projects. These plans are designed to adhere to the deadlines and budgets identified in the program budget. They detail the schedules, milestones, deliverables, workload estimates, and resources for each project. The project plans should be described in words, presented graphically, and considered as commitments against which progress should be tracked.

Project Tracking

Deadlines and deliverables due within each project should be recorded, and progress should be tracked (at least) once each month. A periodic progress report listing milestones reached, missed, and modified should be developed. Project tracking and analysis should be conducted by the staff members who do the work involved in the project. This helps staff members increase their awareness of the project and provides a counterpressure to the temptation to ignore routine work and focus on crises. Government organizations have a tendency to careen from crisis to crisis, which is the antithesis of effective, entrepreneurial management.

Many of the managers who track work are compulsive and risk-averse. They track activities to cover their flank and defend themselves against criticism. Many entrepreneurs dismiss management systems as uncreative and as obstacles to creative action. We take the opposite view. We believe that program planning and tracking is a basic requirement for effective management. The most sensible risks are the calculated risks. It is impossible to calculate the risk of taking on a given program or project if you do not know what activities your organization is currently undertaking or what projects your organization is capable of undertaking. However, we do not believe that specific numerical targets or goals are useful in management. They either limit performance when a target is set too low or they limit quality as workers struggle to meet an unrealistic goal.

The Limits of Formal Program Planning

Although operational program planning can facilitate your organization's collective thought process, it should not be oversold. If your organization's environment is as dynamic as that of most public organizations, you will find that the world changes too fast for truly accurate planning. You should not expect to meet every milestone you set at the start of the year. In fact, you should try to avoid participating in a planning and tracking system that discourages modification of project milestones. It is silly to keep outmoded commitments and foolish to retain a system that encourages such behavior. However, it is inexcusable to be ignorant of your organization's operational objectives for improvement and the degree to which your organization is meeting those objectives.

One of the difficulties in launching an innovative public program is the complexity of obtaining the resources required to invest and develop your organization. Government programs tend to maintain the same resource base from year to year, and in this budget system an obvious source of public venture capital could be savings obtained by delivering current programs at a lower cost. How one determines where expenses will be reduced, however, is critical to effective management. It is essential that expenses crucial to delivering quality services not be mistaken for extraneous costs. The way to identify and understand your organization's various costs is through project tracking, and it is a necessary component of effective financial management. Project tracking tells you what you are buying with the funds you log in your financial management system (see Chapter Nine for more detail on financial management). It is easier to save resources if you have an accurate idea of what they are used for. Although formal project planning and tracking have these obvious virtues, in practice, such systems are often more trouble than they are worth. Often, they are not well tailored to the organization, and frequently they descend to empty ritual. Similar to reorganization, an organization's reporting or project control system is something relatively easy for a public manager to influence. The

people who are given the job of maintaining such systems have a tendency to forget about the organization's goals and focus instead on the effective reporting of organizational processes and outputs. After a while, some of these bean counters lose sight of the purpose of the reporting system. Rapid environmental change makes it very difficult even under optimal circumstances to ensure that these systems play an integral role in management. If reporting systems do not quickly adapt to change, they soon become irrelevant and unusable. Since such adaptation is quite difficult, project tracking systems are rarely effective in the public sector.

In an organizational environment that promotes management innovation, performance measurement is critical but will take a very different form from that of standard agencywide tracking systems. We suggest that you attempt, where feasible, to integrate performance measurement with efforts to improve quality through innovation. Performance measurement is central to quality improvement and other efforts to improve performance through innovation. Simply put, you cannot improve something if you do not know its current quality and quantity. If the measures in your agencywide system are too general to help you manage your operations, develop your own project-specific measures.

Formal project tracking can play a useful role in management by providing a general idea of what your organization is accomplishing, but it should not be used to manage every aspect of your organization's activity. Steven Cohen once worked for a manager who took project tracking to a ridiculous extreme. He had allocated the number of hours each individual on the staff was to devote to each of the organization's projects. If a staffer's time sheet indicated that he or she had spent too many or too few hours on a given task, this manager criticized and punished the staff person. So staff members decided that they would report the number of hours originally allocated to the project, regardless of the amount of time they actually devoted to it.

Each organization is uniquely capable of absorbing a given amount of reporting and tracking. A manager must understand

what type of planning and tracking system the institutional culture can sustain if such a system is to be successfully integrated into an organization's operations.

We find that the best-maintained planning, analysis, and tracking systems are those developed and maintained by workers for direct use in their own work. If information helps you do your job and improve your performance, you are more likely to provide accurate information to the system. If you have had a hand in deciding what aspect of your work you need to measure, you are more likely to understand why the measure is needed and you are more likely to pay attention to it.

How to Make Sure Task Assignments Are Fair and Reasonable

Assigning work to staff members is not simply a matter of listing their names on a planning document; it involves assessing their skills, needs, and capacity for work. There is no scientific method for conducting this type of assessment. Trial and error is probably the main method used to assess a person's fit for a particular task. If the task is critical, you may find yourself providing extensive monitoring and backup until you gain confidence in a staff member's ability.

Deciding What Is a Fair and Reasonable Assignment

When a new staff person arrives, it is important to begin a learning process to identify that person's talents and task preferences. Each of us is different, and work that one person considers drudgery another might consider delightful and fascinating. The best way to identify staff preferences is to be sensitive to performance and attitudes, particularly until a firm image of each person's capabilities is implanted in your mind. An appropriate and fair workload will be different for each individual. This will be determined in part by the individual's professional skills and in part by personal considerations. Some people work faster and more efficiently than others.

Some people are slow at delivering certain types of products but efficient in other areas. Staff members raising families or taking care of their invalid aunts may be unable to work in the office on weekends or evenings, but they may be willing to do paperwork that they can take home.

As a manager, you must determine a fair allocation of work, and you must take into account a wide array of personal and professional factors, but it is important to avoid free riders. Once again, the only way to ensure that assignments are fair is to get out from behind your desk and maintain ongoing communication with your staff. One point to keep in mind is that hierarchy inevitably requires some people to take on more responsibility than others. Those who demonstrate the ability to do more than their fair share are eventually promoted or rewarded for their efforts. Fairness is not a matter of evenly distributing work but of providing timely and appropriate rewards for excellent performers.

Allowing the Staff a Voice in Assignments

Communication with staff members should be a dialogue rather than a monologue. This does not mean that you should put assignments to a vote or allow your staff to refuse assignments. It means that you should be sensitive to staff preferences and take those preferences into account when you make assignments. You may have no choice but to assign someone an unwanted task. When you make such an assignment, it is important that you be aware of the cost to staff morale that you are incurring. Employees should also be involved in defining work. Presumably, you have a good idea of what the assignment is supposed to accomplish and what your organizational superiors expect to see, but your staff may know more than you do about the nuts and bolts of completing the assignment. When tasks are defined, a manager should play the role of listener as well as the role of director. Allowing staff members to help define the work can make assignments more practical and can create a sense of shared ownership. An individual's sense of control is heightened by involvement

in determining tasks. This increased sense of control can motivate people to work harder and more productively.

How to Ensure That Work Is Assigned to the Right People and That It Gets Done and Gets Done Well

Chapter Three discusses methods for assessing individual staff performance, and this section deals with analyzing and projecting organizational performance. Projecting organizational performance is not simply adding up the capabilities of individual staff members; it is also assessing the effectiveness of group processes and the productive capacity of organizational units.

Assessing Organizational Capability and Performance

The best predictor of future performance is past performance. Most managers search for similarities between new tasks and old tasks and use such links as the basis for new assignments. In some cases, the organizational structure helps determine assignments. Usually a task can be easily categorized by function or program—the two chief bases of organizational structure. However, past behavior and the current organizational structure may not be particularly good guides for assigning tasks. Some assignments may be unprecedented.

It is unlikely that you will be able to accurately project an organization's capability to perform unprecedented tasks. One indicator is the organization's agility. How has the organization performed during periods of extreme stress, demand, or rapidly changing environmental conditions? How has the organization performed in the past when given new tasks? What type of personality does the organizational unit's manager have? Does the unit's manager thrive on new challenges and get bored with routine tasks? Or is the manager better at refining old routines than at developing new ones? What type of staff capability does the organization have? Is there slack within the organization? Have staff members recently completed a major mission, and are they

casting about for a new one? Sometimes a new assignment is so important that it is too risky to give it to only one unit.

Sometimes a new mission is so important that it cannot be implemented by existing organizational units and must be assigned to a new unit. Franklin Roosevelt was famous for giving the same tasks to several organizational units and forcing them to compete against each other for the same mission. If he had no competing units, he sometimes created them. In fact, many of the New Deal's alphabet agencies were created because FDR was convinced that the older, more established organizations could not implement his new programs.

Once again, there is no science to deciding which units should be assigned which tasks. It is critical to understand your organization's capability and be flexible enough to switch assignments when failure is detected and deemed irretrievable. Detecting failure and deciding how to react to it involves the establishment and maintenance of a control and reporting system. (This subject is covered in the next section and discussed in greater detail in Chapter Eight.)

Giving and Tracking Assignments

Inadequate performance can be caused by both staff and management failures. One frequent management failure results from vague or imprecise assignments. This is particularly a problem in public organizations where goals often represent a compromise between conflicting interests. A legislative effort to finesse differences and mediate conflict inevitably lands in some bureaucrat's lap in the form of a vague instruction. Even where legislative goals are clear, a manager may not completely understand or agree with the goal and may therefore hedge a bit when giving the assignment. In any event, the first step in making an assignment is to define it in precise operational terms. By *operational*, we mean giving specific instructions that lead to discrete, feasible, and measurable tasks. These specific assignments must be clearly and consistently com-

municated. They must be explained in terms of their fit with the organization's philosophy and mission, and they must include a feedback loop—a preset method and schedule for reporting and evaluating performance.

Tracking assignments requires what Herbert Kaufman (1960) terms methods for detecting and discouraging deviation from preformed decisions (agency policy). This includes formal and informal reporting and evaluation methods—ranging from computerized management information systems to informal discussions around the coffee pot. (These techniques are discussed in Chapter Eight.) It is the manager's responsibility to create multiple channels for transmitting and receiving information on organizational performance. The manager should not passively wait for information to reach the front office but should aggressively seek out information about organizational performance.

For the purpose of assigning tasks, the most important piece of information a manager needs is whether the assignment has been accepted by the staff members assigned to it. A staffer's recalcitrance to an assigned task can take a variety of forms. The most obvious form is open opposition to the assignment. Passive resistance is a bit harder to detect, since it is usually characterized by the absence of activity. Most sophisticated bureaucrats have a wide array of methods for ignoring unwanted assignments. Token responses, slowed schedules, and paralysis at the first sign of external resistance are a few of the more popular techniques. Somehow the contract keeps being sent back to the lawyer to redraft an obscure provision—as a bureaucrat quietly kills a project. It is sometimes difficult to tell whether a project is failing because the person assigned to it is resisting or because it is simply a tough assignment. For this reason, measuring the quality of staff work is difficult. As you might expect, there is no simple method for ensuring that assignments are performed, and performed well, but Chapter Eight provides some help in improving the quality of the information you receive.

Chapter Six

Understanding and Applying Innovation Strategies in the Public Sector

This chapter identifies strategies for bringing innovation into public sector organizations, and it develops some ideas about how and when to deploy these strategies. In our view, a key element of being an effective public manager in today's dynamic environment is to be a creative and innovative public manager. In this chapter, we discuss management innovation conceptually, and then we discuss some specific techniques of management innovation now being experimented with in the public sector. These techniques include strategic planning, reengineering, Total Quality Management (TQM), benchmarking, team management, and privatization.

This is not an exhaustive list of innovation techniques but rather a set of the most common innovation techniques now used in the public sector. We will address each technique separately, although in the real world they tend to be used in combination and in no way should they be seen as mutually exclusive. In fact, a major assumption of this chapter is that despite the presence of consultants and others who advocate one technique as the "right" one to follow, effective management innovation requires the blending of a variety of innovation technologies and tailoring them to an organization's unique culture and environment.

The Concept of Public Sector Management Innovation

In *Tools for Innovators* (1998), we state that the "public sector management innovation is best defined as the development of new policy designs and new standard operating procedures by public

organizations to address public policy problems. It is important to emphasize that we are dealing with both the design and the management of policies and programs" (pp. 2–3).

The supposed failure of various organizational reform efforts is frequently a result of attempts to quickly and uniformly apply an organizational reform methodology throughout an organization. Rather than seeing these methods as instruments of incremental organizational reform, senior managers and their high-priced consultants see these ideas as all-encompassing organizational ideologies. They are oversold and misapplied and often fail for those reasons.

Successful innovation is often incremental and small-scale because the factors conditioning the success of innovative practices vary according to the organization's internal capacity, external environment, and goals or mission. Each organization is different and faces varied situations at particular points in time. The techniques required to promote organizational innovation must therefore be situationally determined. Furthermore, the stability of the organization's environment changes over time, requiring varied degrees of innovation. Finally, the internal social structure and capacity of an organization to support and carry out changed standard operating procedures will also vary. In other words, one size does not fit all.

In *Tools for Innovators* (1998), we developed an overall framework for management innovation techniques that delineated their characteristics as techniques of change and assessed their use in specific situations. In this chapter, we summarize the analysis of innovation tools described in detail in that work. If you would like more detail on the definition and application of management innovation tools, we urge you to consult *Tools for Innovators*.

Techniques of Management Innovation

To effectively apply innovation techniques, we need a shared definition of each technique. In this section, we describe and assess a select group of management innovation techniques, focusing on

strategic planning, reengineering, TQM, benchmarking, team management, and privatization. We define the technique, describe how it works, and discuss the typical benefits or impact, as well as costs, of using these techniques.

Strategic Planning

James Mercer (1991) observed that "at least three decades ago, Peter Drucker defined planning as actions taken right now to reach tomorrow's objectives. His definition still holds; planning means deciding what has to be done to prepare a given organization for the future" (p. 17). Hofer and Schendel (1978) define strategy as the basic pattern of current and planned resource deployments and environmental interactions that indicate how the organization will achieve its objectives. In our book *The New Effective Public Manager* (1995), we observe that "a strategy attempts to delineate the resources that will be used to pay for specific activities designed to accomplish specific objectives. Strategy formulation begins with the identification of objectives and the determination of methods for reaching objectives. These objectives and activities are then scaled to fit within resource constraints. Each element of a strategy (objectives, activities and resources) is constrained by political, social, economic and environmental variables. The objectives and activities of public organizations are constrained by the formal authority provided by statute" (p. 196).

How It Works. A strategic planning exercise typically involves an organization-wide initiative to reformulate goals and develop new methods of achieving those goals. At a minimum, managers from key organizational units are involved in the process. Sometimes, participation is broader, involving staffers from throughout the organization.

New information about the organization's environment is presented and assessed regarding its impact on the organization's goals and activities. Meetings are held to stimulate the creation of new

approaches to the organization's mission and work. An inventory of the organization's capabilities and needs is also conducted to determine the organization's capacity to implement the new strategy.

Benefits. Strategic planning gives the organization a chance to look at itself comprehensively, in light of the new information. When it is developed by a new management team, it provides that team with an opportunity to form a cohesive identity. When it is independently developed by a chief executive, it provides that executive with a medium to express and define his or her leadership. When a strategy is developed with broader participation, it can be used to create a sense of shared mission and values and can be used as a political tool to develop support for organizational change. In the public sector, an organizational strategy can prevent an agency from being taken in rapidly shifting directions by the political mantra of the moment.

Costs. A high-quality strategic planning process requires significant expenditures of management time and analytic resources. If the analysis is not done well, the organization may misread its environment, or it may misjudge its own capability. Although organizational change tends to be incremental, some strategic planning exercises assume that organizations are capable of massive, rapid change.

In the public sector, an organizational strategy can create political difficulties not only because it indicates what an organization is planning to do but also because it requires explicit trade-off decisions about what an organization will not do. This can stimulate political opposition to the organization and can also stimulate segments of the public and interest groups that were previously unaware of the organization's plans.

Reengineering

Reengineering is "the fundamental rethinking and radical redesign of business processes to bring about dramatic improvements in per-

formance," according to Michael Hammer and James Champy (1993, p. 32). Hammer and Champy's 1993 book popularized this innovation strategy. They emphasize key words—particularly "fundamental," "radical," "dramatic," and "processes," and they stress "starting over" and a "clean sheet of paper" as the reengineering way of thinking.

Hammer and Champy (1993) also focus on what reengineering is not:

- It is not downsizing.
- It is not restructuring.
- It is not a fad.
- It is not more of the same.

Reengineering has also become very popular. Two million copies of the original book (Hammer and Champy, 1993) are in circulation, and Hammer and Champy have each written a sequel. According to Hammer (Hammer and Stanton, 1995), reengineering consulting fees exceeded $7 billion in 1994 alone, driving $30 billion in related corporate investments.

How It Works. Perhaps to provide the maximum opportunity for consulting arrangements, none of the three books by the creators of the reengineering movement (Hammer and Champy, 1993; Hammer and Stanton, 1995; Champy, 1995) is very specific about how a reengineering project should be conducted, step-by-step. Hammer and Champy are clear that the larger the scale of the project, the higher the probability of success. They are also clear that reengineering is a top-down strategy, requiring strong and visible commitment from the CEO, as well as communication and enforcement of that commitment down the organizational hierarchy.

In general terms, reengineering begins with the appointment of a "process owner" by the CEO. The process leader then convenes a reengineering team, who will reengineer the process under

review, with the assistance of an internal reengineering "czar" and a hired, expert-reengineering consultant. A reengineering steering committee can also be established to provide a sounding board. Once the team has been assembled and all the aforementioned roles have been officially designated, the process can begin.

Although each reengineering effort is in many respects unique, there are common steps:

1. Mapping the current process
2. Identifying the steps that add value
3. Eliminating the steps that don't add value
4. Using a triage mentality—emphasizing speed, quick turn-arounds, prompt service, and a single point of contact for customers and suppliers
5. Reengineering first, and then bringing in automation and new information systems technology

As reengineering has been applied to government, some uniquely public concerns must be accommodated. Also, the realities of public organizational behavior have led to some modifications of the process. To begin with, government organizations must balance the constitutional requirement of due process in striving to meet consumer demands for prompt service. And while public organizations seek to include customers in the reengineering of public service delivery systems, they must remain attentive to the dangers of conflicts of interest and abuses of the public trust.

In his very instructive article, Russell Linden (1995) suggests seven principles to guide reengineering in the public sector:

1. Organize around outcomes, not functions
2. Substitute parallel for sequential processes
3. Bring downstream information upstream
4. Capture information once, at the source

5. Provide a single point of contact for customers and suppliers whenever possible

6. Ensure continuous flow of the main process

7. Reengineer first, and then automate

It is our observation that whereas reengineering in the private sector virtually always occurs within the same organizational framework, government reengineering often involves the transfer of the process from its current organization to a different (already existing) agency, or, more often, it is reestablished as a freestanding, new agency. Although many reorganizations are more symbolic than real, very often the creation of a new public sector organization is used as a way to reengineer a set of basic organizational processes.

Benefits. Hammer and Champy, together (1993) and separately (Hammer and Stanton, 1995; Champy, 1995), cite a long list of testimonial company case studies to document the efficacy of reengineering, including IBM, Ford, Kodak, Hallmark, Taco Bell, Capital Holding, and Bell Atlantic. Reengineering proponents identify increased productivity, growth, employee empowerment, higher morale, lower overhead, and improved customer service as benefits of the process. Its advocates also maintain that reengineering enables organizations to adapt to meet the needs of customers and the demands of competition and change. They argue that it recognizes the permanence of change and constructs a model of supportive competitiveness and growth with service. Moreover, it refocuses the organization on its vision and purpose.

Costs. Reengineering is a high-cost and high-risk strategy. Expensive outside consultant fees are only the beginning. The fear and subsequent dislocation caused by "blank sheet" analysis disrupts both the existing efficient processes and those in need of immediate improvement. The organization's functioning during the transition period is disrupted and slowed.

Despite the denials of its true believers, reengineering has become a cover for large-scale downsizings and the purging of analysts and middle managers. As a by-product, many of the organization's best people (those whom the organization does not want to lose) leave before the expected bloodletting starts. And although supporters also claim that it is "not restructuring," the costly and time-consuming process of shuffling the organizational boxes often accompanies the reengineering exercise, particularly in the public sector.

Reengineering's laudable emphasis on holism and seamlessness is also a limiting factor. Putting everything on the table can be daunting and can raise opposition from every corner of the organization. Moreover, while competition and change—technological and otherwise—march forward daily, a reengineering revolution takes about a year to accomplish. And is it feasible, in any organization, to have an annual revolution?

In the public sector, government operations are generally not disciplined by competitive markets. Ideally, public sector reengineering would be accomplished through consensus and universal participation. But the nonstop public and media pressure to cut the cost and size of government just about guarantees that public sector reengineering will become a closed, predestined downsizing exercise.

Radical redesign in the public sector is also severely constrained by partisan differences regarding government's mission, short-run considerations driven by the next election, legislative mandates, policy differences between the legislative and executive branches, civil service restrictions, and the opposition of public employee unions. And resources are seldom available in the public sector for reengineering consultants or the equipment and information technology needed to implement the recommended process changes. Finally, a great deal of cynicism has built up in public sector bureaucracies about the next innovation "silver bullet." Long-time middle managers have seen planning, Programming and Budgeting System (PPBS), Zero-Based Budgeting, Management by Objectives, TQM, and reinvention directives come and go with the next election or

change of commissioner. Protected by civil service, many of these middle- and higher public sector managers will wait out or even clandestinely sabotage the reengineering effort. That is why we believe that the transfer of the process to be reengineered, either to an already existing agency or to an entirely new agency, is the most likely way for reengineering to succeed in the public sector.

TQM

TQM can be reduced to three central elements (Cohen and Brand, 1993):

1. Collaboration with suppliers to ensure that the supplies used in work processes are well designed and fit for use

2. Continuous employee analysis of work processes to improve their functioning and reduce process variation

3. Close communication with customers to identify and understand what they want and how they define quality

How It Works. We have developed a government-oriented adaptation of TQM that we call project-oriented TQM. It includes the following elements:

Focus on production in the field. Management and workers should focus their attention on the process of producing goods and services. Understanding exactly what happens when work is performed is an essential element of TQM. Quality can only be improved once management and workers have completed a step-by-step description and analysis of the work process.

Worker participation. In order to increase the level of attention paid to production, management must depend on workers to analyze and suggest improvements to work processes. Since workers perform these tasks, only they have access

to all the information about how work gets done. If management does not obtain this information, it is very difficult to improve quality.

Communication with customers and suppliers. In order to improve quality, a worker must have supplies that are well designed and fit for use. Supplies can include computer equipment, forms, or directions from a supervisor. If quality is to be improved, suppliers must learn how to tailor their supplies to the needs of particular production processes. Similarly, in order to determine what customers want and how customers define quality, an organization must constantly be learning what its customers' preferences are.

Rapid changes in standard operating procedures and constant training. TQM requires that organizations constantly analyze and change work processes. Continuous improvement requires continuous modification of standard operating procedures and the communication of those new processes throughout the organization.

Small-scale projects at the beginning. To teach workers how to communicate with suppliers and customers and analyze their own work processes, it is best to start with small, easy-to-understand aspects of the organization's daily work. This builds a record of visible accomplishments quickly and avoids misinterpreting boundary disputes as TQM failures.

Eventual invisibility. After a few years, TQM is simply "the way we work around here."

Use of existing departmental procedures and structures as a foundation. Reinforce the importance of TQM through routine management processes. Avoid establishing separate quality organizations to implement quality improvement projects.

Benefits. TQM can enable an organization to tap into knowledge about work processes possessed only by workers. It can empower staff members to think and it can enhance morale. It can result in

higher-quality and lower-cost production as work steps are rationalized and supplies are improved. It can provide a means for bringing customer preferences into an organization, increasing the organization's ability to deliver what its customers want.

Costs. If the organization's overall strategy is faulty, TQM will have the effect of improving production of the wrong thing. Furthermore, if standard private sector TQM is applied unmodified in government, too much will be tried too soon and the effort will probably fail. Project-oriented TQM is public sector-oriented and recognizes the fact that government organizations are characterized by independent power bases. The leaders of these powerful independent units must be recruited to TQM; they cannot be forced to comply. If these middle managers do not support TQM, they will simply wait out the transitory elected and appointed officials championing the initiative and kill it at the first opportunity. Because it is so difficult to fire these managers, they cannot be swept aside by the top-level leadership as called for by Deming in his version of TQM.

Another cost of TQM in the public sector has to do with the difficulty of reconciling the claims of competing or contradictory customer demands. Unlike the private sector, the government cannot simply decide that it only intends to serve a market niche. Furthermore, the people who supply the resources for a service are sometimes not the direct users of the service. This means that you will have one set of customers paying and another set of customers receiving a particular service. For example, taxpayers pay for welfare programs, but welfare recipients (who may or may not be taxpayers) actually use welfare services.

Benchmarking

Benchmarking involves finding, adapting, and implementing best practices. Bruder and Gray (1994) define it as "a rigorous yet practical process for measuring your organization's performance and processes against those of best-in-class organizations, both public and private,

and then using this analysis to improve services, operations and cost position dramatically" (p. S-9). Fischer (1994) defines benchmarking in performance measurement terms: "Through a series of performance measures—standards known as 'benchmarks'—a person can identify the best in a class among those doing a particular task. Then, the best practices are analyzed and adapted for use by others wanting to improve their own way of doing things" (p. S-3).

How It Works. Benchmarking as a stand-alone management strategy is a relatively new and evolving set of techniques. Its roots go back to performance measurement, including the groundbreaking efforts of the International City/County Management Association to measure municipal activities in 1938, through Deming and his followers, the Hoover Commissions, and PPBS. In its current form, Bruder and Grey (1994) have set out the most detailed agenda in the following seven-step protocol:

1. Determine which function will benefit most from benchmarking
2. Identify key cost, quality, and efficiency measures for those functions
3. Conduct an expert opinion survey and literature review to find the best-in-class organization for each measure
4. Measure the best-in-class performance of organizations in the key areas identified
5. Compare your organization's performance against that of the best-in-class organizations and quantify the gap
6. Specify actions to close the performance gap to the best-in-class level, and, if possible, determine the steps necessary to "leap-frog" the current industry leader
7. Implement those actions and monitor your performance

Benefits. By continually seeking to identify the best-in-class organizations and duplicate or surpass their performance, an organization can embed in its culture and behavior a strong spirit of competitive-

ness, pride, confidence, energy, and striving for improvement. Benchmarking is also a relatively low-tech, low-cost, and quick response technique that almost any organization can adopt. Benchmarking also seems to be common sense and is easily understood by managers, workers, suppliers, customers, the general public, and the media.

Costs. Benchmarking can easily become bogged down in performance measurement and can lose sight of the real objective of performance improvement. This is particularly significant, as measuring the performance of organizations, particularly public organizations with multiple goals, is often a very difficult task. As Fischer (1994) suggests, no data are ever perfect, small differences should not be considered overly meaningful, and comparisons with competitors should be used to find red flags. Sometimes, significant factors may be too difficult or even impossible to quantify—for example, spirit, energy, and attitude.

Benchmarking can lead to limits on creativity by focusing on copying what already has been achieved instead of encouraging "out of the box" thinking and looking for quantum breakthroughs. Benchmarking can become a ceiling on achievement in a given field. It can also lead to blind attempts to imitate when more careful analysis would reveal cultural, temporal, geographic, or other characteristics that limit the replicability of the selected benchmark.

Finally, the cost of benchmarking is seldom noted in the literature or considered in the field. Research takes time, energy, and resources. The more extensive the benchmarking effort, the more likely it is to consume the organization's innovative capacity. Taken to an extreme and combined with a complex performance measurement system to establish baselines, benchmarking can begin to negatively affect the quality and quantity of services delivered.

Team Management

In a workplace context, a team is a group of people pooling their skills, talents, and knowledge in a mutually supportive effort to complete a project, reach a goal, or solve a problem. Or a team can

be defined as a group of people drawn from different disciplines, who work together on a permanent basis to carry out critical organizational tasks. Similarly, in their very successful book *The Wisdom of Teams: Creating the High-Performance Organization*, Jon Katzenbach and Douglas Smith (1993) define teams as "a small number of people with complementary skills who are committed to a common purpose, performance goals, and approach for which they hold themselves mutually accountable" (p. 45).

In modern organizations, project teams are rapidly becoming the primary mechanisms for innovation and change. The team focus can have a dramatic impact on the roles of managers and subordinates and on the functioning of an organization. The team focus can shift an organization from managing by control to managing by commitment. It can change the institution's emphasis from individual motivation and output to team motivation and output, and from traditional functions of organizing, staffing, and evaluating to coaching and facilitating.

How It Works. Teams typically consist of five to seven members, with one member selected by senior management to serve as the team leader. Teams are often created to complete a specific project or goal or to perform a significant ongoing function. The creation of a team is generally an indication from senior management that the work of the team is an organizational priority. Teams are usually organized as standing teams, project teams, or crisis teams.

Standing teams. Certain projects, types of projects, customers, or issues frequently recur within an organization. Standing teams can deal with issues that resurface seasonally or with issues for which a group of specialists is the most effective response. Unlike project teams, standing teams extend beyond the scope of any one project and can be characterized as a permanent part of the organization.

Project teams. Assembled for a specific assignment, this is the most common type of team and is typical in consulting

organizations. The appropriate mix of specialists from across the permanent organization are brought together to accomplish a project with clearly defined goals and deadlines. Once the project is accomplished, the team members return to their home base or join another team directed at a different set of objectives. A typical project for such a team might be installing a new computer system, relocating the office, or setting up a new program.

Crisis teams. The nature of a crisis team is obvious from its name. The typical governmental organization rocks from side to side as a herd of staffers run from crisis to crisis identified by headquarters, the White House, Congress, or the media. Crisis teams can be used to mitigate the constant disruption of the agency's regular work (which can later become a crisis when it doesn't get done), and they can be organized as project teams, assembling a new team of experts to deal with a specific crisis. A standing team—an ongoing swat team—can also be used. Generally, these projects would be very high-profile, and selection for participation on a crisis team should be accorded the proper organizational prestige.

Clear ground rules are essential for team success. Team members must understand the work they are to accomplish. There should also be a formal reporting structure and schedule for teams to input their activities into the organization's management structure. In addition, there should be regular, formal feedback from management to the team, with regard to their activities, including a method of evaluating team performance and the contribution of each team member to that overall performance.

Ground rules for each team should be established, in writing. Among the issues covered should be a process for assigning work, methods for reviewing work, the role of the team leader, an evaluation process for team and individual performance, and procedures for resolving conflicts between the team and other organizational units.

Some organizations execute an annual "contract" that details the specific deliverables that the team is expected to produce over the course of the year. It is particularly important that staff members be provided with increased levels of specificity and certainty in their communication with management, since the volume of communication will necessarily be reduced under the new management structure.

Clear goals, clear roles, constant and open communication, a plan of action, and well-established ground rules are essential. In addition, training in beneficial team behaviors and constructive feedback, balanced participation, informality, listening, civilized disagreement, knowledge of group behavior, self-assessment, style diversity, and well-defined decision-making processes all contribute to a successful team.

Benefits. A team approach to the accomplishment of work assignments has been common in many cultures for hundreds of years. Large multinational corporations have been using the team approach for a growing percentage of their work for the past twenty years. The team approach is prominent and is given credit for much of the success enjoyed at such leading corporations as Motorola, Ford, 3M, and General Electric.

Teams perform well because they bring together people with complementary skills and experiences that exceed the capacity of any single member. The broad base of teams enables them to respond well to a wide variety of challenges from customers, change, and technological innovation.

Second, the communication skills and network that successful teams develop create a capacity to respond quickly and flexibly to new problems and a changing environment. Individuals seldom have the resources in time, skills, and attitude to adapt to change or new obstacles as rapidly or as effectively as a team will.

Teams also facilitate the breaking down of barriers between genders, age groups, races, ethnic groups, and geographic biases. With such barriers reduced, an environment of greater trust and

mutual confidence develops, as well as a stronger commitment to organizational goals.

Finally, advocates argue that teams have more fun. This kind of fun is important because it comes out of meeting and working together to solve important organizational problems or striving to meet organizational goals. Teams work long, hard, and well in part because the members enjoy the process of collaboration and achievement. They often celebrate their successes and discuss their failures together, which reinforces the social and positive work aspects of the team experience. Katzenbach and Smith (1993) cite the phenomenon of being part of something greater than oneself.

Costs. A lack of conviction from management regarding team-work can communicate to the organization's members that work in teams is not serious business but, rather, more of a human resources, spirit-building exercise. Such a situation can reinforce the prejudice of some that individual performance is the only thing that counts and that work in teams just wastes time—in meetings and in conversations—when real work could be getting done. In such circumstances, time spent in teams will be wasted time.

Apart from participation in athletics, most of our formative experiences in school and social organizations reinforce individual work and evaluation. It is not surprising then, that many people feel at risk and uncomfortable when the team structure is introduced into their work setting.

The problem becomes extreme when performance evaluation and compensation systems are not modified to consider team accomplishments and therefore reward only individual achievement. Most members receive the clear signal that work in teams is not important. This reward problem is compounded when promotions are tied to progress up the supervisory ladder of the traditional bureaucracy. In such circumstances, expending time and energy in team settings is wasted time and effort and could possibly even damage one's prospects for a successful career in management.

Teams inevitably face obstacles which, if not overcome, can indeed waste the organization's resources, hamper morale, and ultimately lead to the organization's demise. To prepare individuals for effective team performance, initial training and ongoing access to help and advice are critical. Internal consultants, or those hired from outside the organization, are used, but in either case, an ongoing expense is involved.

It is even more expensive but just as important to revise the organization's performance evaluation and compensation system to reflect and reward performance in team settings. Career ladders must be created to ensure that talented employees do not come to view team assignments as a career dead end. There must also be clear guidelines regarding next assignments whenever a team completes its work and is disbanded.

Finally, moving to team management is tantamount to a reorganization, which involves the dislocation and expense of traditional reorganization efforts. Some will resist the change and others will seek to undermine it. Job descriptions, career ladders, and evaluation systems—and, often, office configurations—will need to be revised. And there is always the danger that the performance improvements anticipated by management will not meet expectations, and that the costs of another reorganization will follow.

Privatization

Using private or nongovernmental organizations in the implementation of public policy often replaces direct government provision of particular programs or services.

How It Works. Privatization takes four different forms. The first is contracting out functions that government agencies used to implement with their own staff. Management control is still retained by government, and the option of ending a contract and resuming direct government control is retained. The second form of privatization involves turning over a government-run enterprise, such as a phone

system, to the private sector by selling government assets and monopolies to private firms. The third form of privatization is a public-private partnership, where government and the private sector work jointly, with clearly defined roles, on a public purpose. New York City's Business Improvement Districts are examples of such partnerships. Under this model, the businesses located within a specific geographic area vote to create an organization to provide additional services such as security, cleanup, maintenance, and marketing, and in return, they agree to levy a tax assessment on themselves. The city collects these fees as part of the normal taxation process and returns the fees to the Business Improvement Districts organization. The fourth form of privatization is public policy designed to encourage private behavior. This often involves leveraging public resources to encourage private activity. Typical mechanisms include targeted tax credits or deductions and deregulation. Federal home mortgage insurance and subsidized flood insurance are examples of this leverage approach.

Benefits. Often accompanying the issue of privatization is a great deal of ideological baggage about the value and competence of government, relative to the value and competence of the private sector. Many of the most ardent supporters of smaller government believe that smaller government is a benefit in and of itself. We believe that the decision to privatize should be analyzed without the preconceived notion that it is the better way until proved otherwise. In our view, the chief benefit of privatization is that it opens up the possibility of competition in the performance of a public function. This is not to say that competition is a cure-all. There are some instances when competition is not possible or even desirable (see Don Kettl, 1993, on the competition prescription). However, in many cases, higher-quality, less expensive services and programs can be delivered when organizations compete for business and customer choice is maximized.

Another benefit of privatization is that it facilitates organizational differentiation and focus. It allows governmental policymakers the freedom to achieve the Osborne and Gaebler dictum to steer rather than row. It enables public managers to focus on policy

design and program evaluation and allows others to worry about the direct administration of governmental programs.

Costs. The principal costs of privatization stem from the loss of direct control over program administration. The production of goods and services needed to implement public policy is no longer in the hands of government. If a single private entity develops a monopoly of control over a service, or if it dominates that industry and holds a quasi-monopoly, government's ability to influence program implementation may be compromised. The skills and knowledge gained through administration belong to the private firm and not to the government. Government may come to lack the technical expertise or knowledge base it needs to effectively manage its private partners (Milward, 1994).

Conceptually, program implementation and policy formulation are interconnected. Policy design must account for organizational capacity. Effective program implementation requires a knowledge of administrative issues and the ability to influence administrative behavior. A reduced understanding of administrative issues and reduced leverage over implementation behaviors is a cost of privatization.

Integrating and Using Techniques of Public Management Innovation

In our view, all organizational innovation must begin with a strategy. Without organizational consensus regarding its mission and a road map for achieving its key objectives, better management has no meaning. A more efficient or economical method of producing a product or service few people desire is hardly worth the effort. So, for us, all management innovation initiatives must begin with *strategic planning*. With the organization's mission and key objectives articulated and agreed upon, the most effective method(s) to achieve them can then be selected.

Reengineering is a macro-internal strategy that is both comprehensive and expensive. It implies that the organization is still a viable vehicle to achieve its objectives but that it needs a radical restructuring of its methods. Reengineering has worked well in both the public and private sectors, but it is a high-risk option, requiring strong leadership at the top, extensive resources, and the time to succeed. To us, it is inconceivable that an organization would go forward with a reengineering project without first engaging in a serious, thoughtful strategic planning process.

In addition, some of the costs of reengineering could be mitigated by combining and/or setting the organizational stage with some of the other innovation techniques we have discussed. The fear of reengineering, which is particularly due to its top-down philosophy and association with downsizing, could be offset by ensuring the maximum feasible participation of the staff in the planning stage. A benchmarking exercise, involving a wide array of organizational units, could identify successful reengineering programs not requiring massive downsizing and, in the process, help create staff buy-in for support for the effort.

We also believe that mature TQM organizations—with their several years of staff involvement in analyzing their work, thinking in a continuous improvement mode, and seeing work as a continuum from supplier through the organization to customers—are better prepared for a reengineering effort. A level of trust and cooperation between management and workers that evolves from a successful TQM effort would help enormously in achieving support for the reengineering effort.

Recently, it has become very popular in the United States to criticize TQM. The supposed "failures" of TQM are often those of half-hearted whistle-and-bell consultant exercises that are not integrated into the regular work organization or are the inadvertent prelude to a massive downsizing initiative. We have seen and participated in successful TQM initiatives in organizations large and small, public and private, growing and stable. But as we have discussed, TQM in

the public sector has a greater chance of getting off to a successful start if it is project-based.

TQM provides an excellent foundation for other innovation strategies, as it can and should invite participation from all levels of the organization, as it encourages every member of the organization to think about his or her work in the context of continuous improvement, and as it establishes the framework of supplier-organization-customer. TQM can move an organization forward, but if an organization's basic systems are inadequate, the TQM improvements will tend to "bounce against" those ineffective systems. It is at this point and in this way that TQM helps identify fruitful targets for reengineering.

Benchmarking should be part of any effort to innovate within an organization. It is useful in strategic planning, TQM, reengineering, and even privatization. As each organization establishes its own innovation plan of action, it is usually instructive to learn how other organizations have approached changing similar processes (TQM) or systems (reengineering). It is also helpful in defining your mission or in setting objectives to know how similar organizations have completed that exercise. To bring team management into your shop, wouldn't you want to know how the organizations noted for their effective teams made their system work?

Benchmarking can also stimulate imaginative thinking. By presenting concrete models, benchmarking can help overcome the suspicion—particularly in government organizations—that the innovation strategy being planned is just another management "fad." But benchmarking without a management strategy to implement the desired innovation or improvement is a meaningless and wasteful exercise.

Team management can be a stand-alone innovation technique that can help facilitate cooperation and coordination among organizational members, cope with downsizing, and help flatten the organizational hierarchy. It reflects Drucker's observation that most organizations are increasingly populated by highly educated, highly skilled knowledge workers who are more interested in working

together to achieve shared objectives than in being told what to do. Team management is also an essential component of any successful TQM initiative. Without commitment and the ability to work in teams, TQM innovation is impossible.

Like other innovation techniques discussed in this chapter, an effective team management structure is rather meaningless without a clear mission and organizational consensus around key objectives. And, like TQM, team management can bounce against fundamental systems that do not work. In such circumstances, to achieve sustainable improvement, a team management innovation must be combined with either reengineering or some form of privatization.

Privatization makes sense only after the organization has gone through a strategy planning process to determine what it is about. The core functions essential to the organization's reason for being are the activities it can and should do itself. Functions that need to be performed but are not central to the organization's definition of self can be privatized. For example, the EPA's Superfund toxic waste cleanup program contracts with private organizations for the cleanup of waste sites. EPA staff members do not actually perform cleanup work, but they do decide where cleanup workers are to be assigned, as well as how clean a site needs to be. This allocation of work tells us what is central to the EPA's mission and what is not.

An effective organization must have a clearly defined focus. Once this focus is determined, the organization should then strive to shed functions that are not central to its mission. To do higher-quality, more cost-effective work, an organization must focus its resources on those functions that are central to its existence and it must shed or contract out any secondary functions. Too often, an organization's basis for privatization is not such a strategic planning exercise but is, rather, a matter of expediency—to raise immediate cash for budget balancing, to escape criticism for poor performance, or to fit into a blind commitment to the philosophy that the market cures all ills.

In sum, we see privatization as an alternative to internal management innovation, and it can be an effective tool if used thoughtfully and for the right reasons.

The Need for Innovation

We have written a third edition of this book because we remain convinced not only that the public sector can work well but also that an effective public sector is essential to a healthy, thriving society. In addition, we believe that much has been learned regarding management over the past decade. We still believe that an effective public manager must be an expert in working around constraints, but we also believe that we need to work harder at removing constraints. Sometimes, it is better to attack and eliminate an outmoded process than to waste resources working around it. Strategic planning, reengineering, TQM, benchmarking, and team management are viable innovation techniques, especially when used in combination. They can help public managers make public organizations more effective and efficient.

Chapter Seven

The Art and Craft of Contracting

In our book *Tools for Innovators* (Cohen and Eimicke, 1998), we note that the quality and cost of government services can substantially influence a nation's ability to compete in a global marketplace. To improve the management of government programs, public managers use such techniques as team management, privatization, reengineering, benchmarking, and quality management. Of these innovation techniques, the one used most frequently is contracting out to private for-profit and nonprofit organizations to help deliver public goods and services. Although this trend may reflect an ideological preference for smaller government, public managers have correctly concluded that they will more successfully implement public policy if they learn to work with private organizations.

There is a good deal of scholarship devoted to analyzing the decision to use contractors and to providing advice to decision makers about how and when to contract out (Avery, 2000). A number of scholars express doubts about contracting out (Harrison and Stanbury, 1990; Hirsch, 1995; Sclar, 1994, 2000). Some analysts have expressed concern about the long-term impact that contracting out has on American democracy. Perhaps the most compelling of these analyses is Brinton Milward's path-breaking work on what he calls "the hollow state" (Milward, 1994, 1996; Milward and Provan, 2000). The notion is that it is difficult to manage a program and assure accountability if government no longer has direct control of the organizational capacity to deliver programs.

Bardach and Lesser (1996) raise the issue of accountability to particular parties versus accountability for results. They note that

before developing accountability mechanisms one must decide who management is accountable to and what government is accountable for. Concerns about the hollowing out of government are important—and worrisome, but increases in contracting activity are widely reported (McDavid and Clemens, 1995; Green, 1996; Light, 1999). A number of observers have discussed the need for more sophistication in government contract management (Johnston and Romzek, 1999; Romzek and Johnston, 1999; Gordon, 1998; O'Looney, 1998). Whether one favors or opposes contracting out, its growth is indisputable. Those of us in the business of advising and training public managers must learn to understand this management tool and teach public managers how to use it more effectively.

We anticipate that governments will continue to contract out and the role of contracting will continue to grow. In our view, this mirrors the outsourcing trend in the private sector. As we have noted (Cohen and Eimicke, 2000b), the trend toward multisectoral public service delivery creates several critical and difficult operational problems that must be addressed, including:

- Finding out what contractors are doing
- Developing and implementing systems of contractor incentives
- Getting a fair price for services
- Developing the skills needed to negotiate contracts and manage contractors

The importance of performance measurement to managing contractors has received a great deal of attention, as scholars have sought to identify the conditions that lead to successful outsourcing (Wulczyn, Orlebeke, and Melamid, 2000; Campbell and McCarthy, 2000; Cohen and Eimicke, 2000b; Heinrich, 1999; Panet and Trebilock, 1998). In an earlier piece (Cohen and Eimicke, 2000b), we discussed the reason performance measurement is so critical to contract management:

Management of interorganizational networks and contracts means that leaders cannot depend on traditional hierarchical controls to influence the behavior of subordinates who are responsible for performing particular tasks. This means that management cannot use organizational culture, personnel promotion, demotion, termination, or authoritative command structures to influence behavior. . . . In contrast, contractual relationships with private and nonprofit firms provide the surest way to punish poor performance: contract termination. While there are limits to the use of this technique—it is difficult to terminate contracts in mid-term—they do provide incentives that are clearly understood by the people who work in the organizations holding the contract [pp. 101–102].

We have also written about the use of performance measurement techniques for learning about contractor inputs, work processes, outputs, and outcomes (Cohen and Eimicke, 2000a, 2000b):

The need for vertically integrated, hierarchically controlled organizations has been reduced as technology has made it easier to communicate ideas and information and transport goods and components of goods around the world. Satellite communication, cellular telephones, hand-held computers, containerized shipping, and multinational organizational networks make it possible to create goods and services in a variety of locations. These goods and services can be assembled throughout the globe, from components made all over the world. They can be tailored for use in a particular location or market. The creation of a world-wide system of production means that organizations must constantly ask and then reexamine the "make or buy decision": Should we do this task in-house or hire a consultant or another firm to do this work for us [pp. 99–100]?

Public managers are capable of managing contracts and contractors, but this management task requires new skills and training for those managers (Cohen and Eimicke, 2001). Contracting not only solves problems but creates them as well. Public managers must

learn how to identify and solve the problems that contracting creates, such as the following:

- Flawed Request for Proposal (RFP) or contract language
- Overly bureaucratic contracting procedures resulting in delays and high transaction costs
- Too few bidders or contractor monopolies
- Poor communication between government and contractor management
- Poor communication between government and contractor staff
- Inadequate direction from government to contractors
- Contractors that give an agency's work low priority
- Insufficient contractor staffing, training, equipment, and facilities
- Poor contractor management
- Political opposition to contracting
- Political interference in contractor selection and management
- Underestimating or overestimating resource needs for contractor-performed tasks
- Insufficient or excessive profits
- Inappropriate or outmoded performance measures and insufficient systems for communicating performance data
- Incomplete methods for auditing performance reporting
- Inadequate methods for incorporating performance data into government and contractor decision making
- Misdirected or inadequate contract incentive provisions
- Conflict of interest issues
- Union opposition to contracting
- Media and political attention to contractor failures

Skills Needed to Manage Contracts and Contractors

The list of obstacles to contracting could be duplicated for any management task. It is the job of those of us who teach managers or who manage managers to identify and impart the skills required to successfully overcome these obstacles and manage the process of contracting.

Letting a contract. The process of letting contracts involves skill in

- Drafting contracts and structuring tasks and incentives
- Measuring performance
- Advertising for contractors
- Assessing contractor capabilities
- Understanding the laws, regulations, and standard operating procedures governing procurement
- Understanding the business that is the object of the contract

Drafting contracts. Program managers who hope to implement some part of the program they manage with outside help must understand the shape and form of contract language or have a staff member who can do this. A deep knowledge of contract law would be helpful but is not needed for this task. A staff member with a great deal of experience in drafting contract language or in working on procurement will suffice. Inevitably, the procurement office will review or draft the contract's language and that office will have access to legal assistance. The program's manager will need to have someone on staff capable of communicating with these internal agency procurement experts and experienced at balancing technical procurement concerns with the program's needs.

Measuring performance. The contract must include reporting requirements that obligate the vendor to participate in the government's performance measurement system. This means that the staffer who is expert at performance measurement must be involved in the process of drafting contract requirements. Again, someone

with experience in drafting contract language must be involved to ensure that the organization that wins the contract is formally obligated to participate in the agency's performance measurement and management systems.

Advertising for contractors. Most governments have formal requirements for advertising requests for proposals (RFPs) or requests for qualifications (RFQs). Federal contracts must be listed in Commerce Business Daily, and many states require newspaper posting. These are necessary steps, but they are not always sufficient to elicit a large enough number of high-quality bids. In some of the newer areas of privatization, government may learn that there are no qualified vendors interested in bidding on the contract. Government's dominance of the service may have reduced the probability of a private vendor entering the field. The price structure for the contract may be too low because of off-budget infrastructure or capital costs that do not come out of the contracting agency's budget but must be incurred by a contractor. It may be that the true costs of contracting are lower than those of direct government service delivery, but the government agency letting the contract does not pay the full cost of delivering the service. These issues must be fully analyzed before the decision to contract is made. Subsequent to an affirmative decision to contract, the government must work to ensure that private organizations are encouraged to submit bids and that the cost and fee structure is realistic. Sometimes, it may be necessary to contract with a firm to develop the capacity to provide the good or service that the government wants to purchase.

The skills involved in finding qualified contractors include business and cost analysis, but analysis alone is not sufficient; also required is a kind of business sense. This is where contracting becomes art rather than science. In the private sector, the skill is held by purchasing agents, who know where to find ample quantities of supplies at the best possible prices.

Assessing contractor capabilities. Once bids are received, government employees must be skilled at reading proposals and judging capabilities. This means that staff members must have the ability to

read into the statement of qualifications to determine what is real and what is not. They must also be able to check on the accomplishments that organizations cite in their bids. A firm or an individual may claim credit for the work of other organizations, and sometimes these other organizations may be part of a team that the bidder worked with on a previous assignment. Strictly speaking, the bidder may be entitled to claim the work of a subcontractor, but if this subcontractor is not part of the new bid, such a claim is misleading. This type of reference check requires that your staff have an informal network in the business in question. In new areas of work, it may require structuring a pilot test or a competition among several "best and final" bidders.

Many contract review processes have a point system to assess the quality of the bid. That system can make it difficult to award the contract to the most qualified bidder if the weighting system is poorly designed and places value on factors that turn out to be irrelevant. Moreover, the actual scoring of a proposal is far more art than science, and it depends on the subjective assessments of the review panel. In the end, initial contractor selection always involves an element of risk. The key is to learn from mistakes and to build a core of staff members with experience in analyzing bids. When you have found a good vendor, try to assess the qualifications that contribute to the firm's success in doing your work and design re-bids to elicit those qualifications.

Understanding the laws, regulations, and standard operating procedures governing procurement. Government purchasing requires you to understand an arcane and complicated set of laws, rules, and standard operating procedures. An understanding of these procedures is needed to deal with the agency's internal lawyers and experts that govern contracting. If you do not have an expert who is loyal to your program and purpose, you are at the mercy of your agency's internal process experts. Many of these folks have trouble remembering the purpose of the agency, let alone the importance of your contract in implementing an important piece of public policy. You need to remind them of the agency's mission—and in the language of contracting.

Understanding the business that is the object of the contract. Finally, to let a contract, you need to have someone on your staff who either has worked in or has a deep knowledge of the business you are contracting with. This is one reason developers typically hire a general contractor for construction projects. All the general contractor does is manage the work of other contractors. The most competent general contractor has staffers who have worked in all aspects of construction and know "where the bodies are buried"—they know the tricks of the trade. They are more difficult to fool and are good to have on your side and working with you rather than against you. When contracting for a service or a product, your best defense is a staff person who knows the business, how it makes money, and where things typically go wrong. This will enable you to structure your RFP and the contract itself in a way that increases the probability of success.

Managing a contractor. As difficult as obtaining a contractor is, it is even more difficult to manage the work of a contractor once that contractor has been awarded a contract. The process of managing a contractor involves skills at the following tasks:

- Understanding the purpose of the contract and the work it is designed to elicit
- Communicating agency needs, culture, constraints, and mission to the vendor
- Communicating the firm's capability, culture, constraints, and incentive system to colleagues within the government
- Deploying incentives and disincentives to the contracting firm
- Understanding and monitoring contractor accomplishments

Understanding the contract's purpose. A person on staff must be assigned the task of communicating with and managing the work of the contractor. In a complex contract, this might need to be a team of people. In order to do this job, the staff member must be clear about what the contract is designed to accomplish. At times, the final RFP might resemble a compromise within the agency. By

the time the contract is let, operational ambiguity must be eliminated, if at all possible. If the government agency is not certain of the purpose of the contract, what chance does the contractor have of understanding what is supposed to be done?

Communicating with the vendor. When two organizations interact in the performance of critical tasks, it is important that they develop an understanding of each other's capacity and culture as well as an empathy for their colleagues in the partner organization. The skill required is the ability to communicate opportunities and obstacles while keeping the work process moving. This requires a skill at developing informal networks and in developing and maintaining trust, and it requires constant effort to stay on top of the shared activity of the two organizations.

Deploying incentives and disincentives. In addition to communication, contract management requires a person skilled at understanding motivation. What is it that elicits effort from the contractor? What types of punishment can help prevent large-scale mistakes? Cash incentives may work in some instances, but government should not assume that money is the only incentive that works. Nonprofit organizations may be motivated by shared mission, and technical experts might be motivated by access to interesting tasks or new equipment.

Ensuring ethical practices. Government contracting is big business. Whereas George Washington Plunkitt thought, in the early twentieth century, to distinguish honest from dishonest graft in New York City's Tammany Hall political machine (Riordon, 1963), government officials are now held to higher standards, and even the appearance of impropriety must be avoided. In Plunkitt's day, acting on insider knowledge and buying the land needed for a new public park or reservoir was simply "seeing your opportunities and taking them" (Riordan, 1963, p. 3); today, it is fraud that can land you in jail. The rules of ethical behavior may be painful to follow, but they are really not very complicated. Avoid rewarding friends and family with government's largesse. If a friend or family member is bidding on a contract, recuse yourself and ask other officials to judge the bidding.

Understanding and monitoring contractor accomplishments. Finally, staff members must learn to track and fully understand the output and outcomes of contractor work. This requires visits to the contractor's offices and to any field location were work is being done and where customers may be present. It involves a profound understanding of the nature of the contractor's work and an ability to separate real work from symbolic acts. The agency's staff not only should receive and analyze performance reports and other forms of regular feedback but also should ensure that independent reports and audits of performance are conducted with some frequency. Government staffers not only should rely on the perceptions and judgments of others but also should learn to assess performance and extrapolate the contractor's overall performance from key indicators. But understanding the science of performance measurement, although a key part of this skill set, is not all that is required. Government staffers and managers must also develop gut instincts that are based on experience and lore to assess and improve contractor performance. This requires respect for senior staff members who have managed contractors before, as well as an attitude that questions conventional wisdom and easy answers.

Obtaining and Deploying the Skills Needed to Manage Contracts and Contractors

Letting contracts and managing contractors is not simple and is far from automatic. So if it is so hard to do, why bother? The answer is that modern service production requires high levels of specialized skill and complex, up-to-the-minute information. Large organizations set up as traditional vertical hierarchies are not as good at performing these functions as smaller, more agile, less hierarchical networks of organizations. This is a finding that cannot be verified by organizational theory but is demonstrated by data on increased levels of contracting out by government and outsourcing in the private sector.

We have outlined a large number of skills needed to let contracts and manage contractors. How are these skills to be obtained?

What kind of people must be hired? How are they to be trained and deployed? In general, our approach is to proceed simultaneously on two paths. The first is to develop creative methods for letting contracts and tracking and rewarding contractor performance. The second is to self- consciously have more experienced staff guide and mentor less experienced staffers, and to develop mechanisms for learning while doing and codifying the lessons drawn from experience.

Creative contracting. With increased contracting and outsourcing, we have noted the growth of creative contracting practices. One example is using the Web to elicit contract bids and receive proposals. Another is to use the Web to routinize and speed up performance reporting, measurement, and analysis. The Web is also being used by smaller cities to elicit contract bids from national firms. Another creative idea is the use of performance incentives. For example, for each day that the subway track repair is completed ahead of schedule, the vendor receives a $10,000 bonus, and for each day that it is late, a penalty of $10,000 is taken off the vendor's fee. Another example is shared overhead: hiring teams of contractors, including multiple subcontractors, is a very old practice, but some team arrangements now include shared facilities and equipment as a means of reducing overhead costs.

Another new contracting practice comes out of the quality improvement movement. Prime contractors, subcontractors, and government clients meet to attempt to solve operational and management problems. They review a collective production process, discuss management and logistics issues, and try to reduce communication gaps. For example, if client direction is late or vague, or if a subcontractor needs a supply from another subcontractor and it is late, these discussions can help solve any ensuing problems.

Benchmarking contracting mechanisms with other jurisdictions should be a good way of discovering innovative contracting practices. As contracting increases, we should expect to see new practices develop as well as new methods of working with vendors and improving their performance.

Mentoring and learning by doing. Despite the increased level of contracting activity, contracting is not a new practice in American government. Don Kettl (1988) mentions George Washington's complaints about the shoddy work of contractors during the American Revolution. Governments, by necessity, buy a great deal more than they make. The work of letting and managing a contract is considered less important by senior government managers than it should be. Agencies should devote more attention to debriefing their best contract managers and getting them to impart their wisdom to junior staff members.

There are a number of formal contract mechanisms that can be employed, depending on the good or service being contracted (O'Looney, 1998). There are different methods that can be used to set a contract's pricing structure, ranging from "time and materials" to "costs plus fixed profit" to "fixed service fees," or what John O'Looney has termed "per unit payments." There are also a wide variety of reasons that contracts are entered into. These in turn result in a range of relationships between the government and the contractor. We strongly agree with O'Looney's assertion that "building trust or positive interdependence in contract relationships must begin with trust-enhancing measures on both sides. However, the government's contract manager must take the lead in making this effort a meaningful one, as it is usually inactivity on the part of government that allows a contractor to wander into a state of non- or poor performance" (p. 195).

O'Looney then identifies methods that can be used to build the trust relationship between government and contractor, and we have also discussed these relationship-building steps (Cohen and Eimicke, 2001a). The key question here is, how do staff members learn how to do this? How do they learn to select contract mechanisms and pricing structures? How do they learn to establish the correct and most effective relationship with a vendor? How do organizations institutionalize this learning process?

In our view, the first step in this process is to identify the need to manage contractors as if their work were an integral element of

the agency's organizational effort. This means that the program office involved in the task must learn the details of the contracting process and not simply leave it to a central contracting office. These details condition and set the boundaries for the type of working relationships that can be established with contractors.

The second step of the mentoring and learning by doing process is to establish a team of experienced experts as mentors and train them to teach contract management. The third step is to establish a set of organizational routines that involve these senior staff members in training junior staff members. The fourth step is to involve senior staffers as consultants in the early stages of a contract solicitation and management process. The fifth and final step is to imitate the sneaker company and "just do it" (steps 1–4). All of this presupposes that you have senior staff members with experience in managing contracts and contractors. What should you do if you do not have such staff people? You have two choices: (1) hire at least one person with this background or (2) hire a consultant to help your staff learn how to manage contractors.

Once you have brought this practice into your organization, it is important that you retain the lessons you are learning and develop methods for sharing information throughout the organization. It is particularly important to learn from mistakes and try to avoid their repetition. Contract management tasks must be factored into the organization's resource planning. These tasks should be part of individual performance appraisal and organizational performance measurement and management. The goal is to make the function of contracting out a seamless element of an organization's typical work and management.

Conclusion: Implementing the Art and Craft of Contracting

Much of the academic literature on contracting is devoted to its long-term impact on government operations and on society. The purpose of this chapter is to contribute to the process of exploring

the operational management challenges caused by increased contracting. The issue we are concerned with is the effective use of outsourcing as a management tool. In what ways do organizations need to adapt to become effective contract managers? What skills are needed? How are those skills developed and maintained? These issues may be prosaic from the standpoint of academic inquiry, but they sit at the center of the concerns of practitioners. What must I do to get better at using contractors? How do I build the capacity to outsource effectively?

The use of contracts, though not new, is becoming a central task of public management. Just as we focus M.P.A. students on financial management, information management, policy analysis, political management, and human resource management, we must now add contract and contractor management to that core list of analytic and managerial skills. We need to ensure that our case literature focuses more attention on contract management. We need to remove contract management from its subterranean home—as a topic fit only for the worst sort of drones, and move it to the heart of the field of public management. Its effective practice is an art and a craft that builds on lessons taught in all of the other management fields. It builds on the techniques of team management, performance measurement, financial management, strategic planning, and conflict resolution, and it integrates them within the task of finding quality contractors and inspiring their best possible work.

Chapter Eight

Gathering, Organizing, and Using Information

Time is a manager's most precious commodity. As Herbert Kaufman (1981) observes, public managers spend most of their time accumulating and assimilating information. A critical function of management is to ensure that information is properly organized and filtered. A manager's own use of time, as well as the time demands on subordinates and superiors, is dramatically influenced by the organization of information. This chapter discusses how to project and influence the flow of information into your organization, and how to structure information flow within your department. We will also discuss methods for improving the description, synthesis, and analysis of information, and conclude with an analysis of information dissemination.

How to Avoid Having Too Much of the Wrong Information and Not Enough of the Right Information

Information is a bit like water: too little and you die of thirst; too much and you can drown. In *Information for Collective Action* (1973), Stephen Skjei analyzes the use of information in decision making. He associates information with control. With perfect information, a decision maker can accurately assess a situation and know with absolute certainty the effect of a given action within that situation. Without information, Skjei notes, "a problem cannot be defined, there is no ability to choose and thus no question of control capability" (p. 2). Hadden (1986) adds that information is something to be "managed" so that it can be brought to bear on

various organizational decisions: "Data needs to be managed because there is so much of it that (1) it may overwhelm the user, (2) it may be hard to find when needed, or (3) its very existence may be forgotten" (p. 572). Naturally, decision makers are never confronted with either total or zero information. In fact, decision makers constantly face the choice of whether to develop additional information, whether to make a decision based on existing information, or whether to ignore information. Skjei divides decision-making information into three categories: (1) information that defines the problem, (2) information about the decisional environment—the conditions that set the parameters for decision making, and (3) information that describes and projects the impact of alternative solutions to the problem.

The Role of Information in Governmental Decision Making

In addition to the information needed to set programmatic direction and build policy, managers require information related to the implementation of programs, such as data on activities and resource expenditures, program outputs, and the impact of program outputs. Public organizations face problems that are more difficult than those faced by private organizations. Hence, public organizations tend to operate in a more complex decisional environment. Addressing the problem of global climate change is more difficult than making a beverage that is "less filling but tastes great."

Public programs and policies tend to attract more attention and stimulate greater political conflict than private actions do. Issues do not generally enter the public sphere unless they are too complex or too difficult to be addressed by the private market. Therefore, the need for information tends to be greater in the public sector than in the private sector.

Accordingly, the probability of achieving managerial control tends to be lower in the public sector than in the private sector. The greater complexity and information requirements for public management account for some of the caution and slow pace of public pro-

grams. Successful information management is therefore absolutely essential for the public entrepreneur. The public sector's greater information needs tend to increase the cost of having too much of the wrong information and not enough of the right information. Sufficient information can reduce risks and increase the probability of successful entrepreneurship.

Factors That Influence the Information Received

In his classic work, *Inside Bureaucracy* (1967), Anthony Downs assesses internal communication within public organizations. Downs discusses the factors that distort information before it reaches the public manager, and he finds that one of the primary forces distorting messages received by senior managers is hierarchy itself. Each time a message passes up through an organizational level, it may be modified. By the time it reaches the top, it may bear little resemblance to the message originally sent.

Distortion is also caused by the different perspectives of individuals within distinct organizational units. As Harold Seidman (1980) observes, "Where you stand depends on where you sit" (p. 21). Downs (1967) observes that experienced managers prevent such bias by filtering information according to its source. Downs also identifies a number of "antidistortion factors in the communication system" (p. 118). These include (1) multiple internal information sources and/or overlapping responsibilities, (2) external sources of information, (3) direct communication through hierarchical levels or through the elimination of such levels, and (4) creation of distortion-proof messages.

The presence of these factors will influence the type of information you receive. Standard operating procedures and organizational culture and tradition will also influence the information you receive. Some types of information will routinely be sent to you and some types of information will not. Some information will be sanitized and some will be provided in relatively raw form. Your level in the hierarchy will also influence the type of information to which you

are given access. Finally, your own ability to pursue and obtain information will affect the information you receive. Pursuing information requires developing both external and internal sources.

Assessing Information Needs

Although it is important to understand the information environment within which you operate, that information should not be seen as a constant. Later in this chapter, we discuss methods for influencing your access to information. At this point, it is sufficient to reiterate the necessity of good information for the public entrepreneur. An innovative public manager must have an information strategy, and that strategy begins with an assessment of one's information needs, which do not exist in a vacuum. It is difficult to know what type of information you require if you do not have a clear idea of what your organization is supposed to do and how it is supposed to do it. Assuming you have participated in some type of program planning exercise, you should have a sense of your organization's operational objectives. Thinking back to the type of information needed for decision making and administration, we may be able to construct a simple needs matrix.

Exhibit 8.1 provides a guide to developing such a matrix. The first question you must address concerns the importance of the information "type" in accomplishing specific operational objectives. If the assignment is a staff-level diagnostic or policy formation task, information types 1 through 4 will be critical. If the objective is a routine task such as negotiating a contract, information types 5 through 8 will be most important. At the highest levels of administration, it is likely that you will need information in each of the eight categories. You must then ask how much information you need and what questions must be answered to accomplish a specific objective. For some managers, information is like a security blanket. These managers do not think strategically about the type of information they need but assume that the more information they can collect, the better. This is often manifested in a

Exhibit 8.1. Information Needs Matrix

Information Type	First-Priority Objective	Second-Priority Objective
1. Problem data		
2. Environmental data		
3. Solution options		
4. Projected solution impacts		
5. Internal actions		
6. Resource expenditures		
7. Outputs produced		
8. Actual solution impacts		

fascination for computerized management information systems (MIS). There seems to be something seductive about a computer terminal, fancy graphics on a color monitor, and a laser-printed, spiral-bound report with four-color pie charts.

Given the volume of information that public managers must deal with, it is not surprising that many are attracted to a technology that promises to simplify and organize the flow of information. Unfortunately, information management is not an automatic process. Like most aspects of management, it also involves prioritization and painful trade-off decisions. Later in this chapter, we discuss the use of information systems as a method of organizing information. We mention MIS here because a poorly planned system can be a major cause of misinformed management.

To reiterate, there are a number of reasons why you have too much of the wrong information and not enough of the right information:

- The information you receive may be distorted as it passes through hierarchical levels.
- The information you receive is biased by the organizational and political interests of the sender.

- You may not be aggressive enough in seeking out external information sources, nurturing a network of information sources, or planning an information strategy.

How to Project Information Needs

Exhibit 8.1 provides a framework for thinking about information needs. It requires that you consider the types of information available for decision making and implementation and that you assess the pieces of information that might be relevant to reaching specific operational objectives. Although the matrix can help structure our thinking, it does not really provide much guidance on how to describe, project, and prioritize information. Projecting information needs is not a precise science. The ability to make such projections is best informed by pertinent experience, from which you can recall analogous situations. If you do not have a great deal of experience, it is important to learn from someone who does. An organization's veterans are a management resource too frequently ignored. You should actively seek out and tap into this living institutional memory. You will need two basic types of information: (1) information necessary for completing the task and (2) information necessary for obtaining, explaining, and defending the task. In short, you will need information for internal use and information for external use. This section discusses internal information, which you will need to get the job done.

Projecting Information Needs to Get the Job Done

As Exhibit 8.1 indicates, you begin by specifying operational objectives and thinking about the types of information that might be germane to achieving those objectives. To project the information you need, it is necessary to identify what Ron Brand, former director of the EPA's Office of Underground Storage Tanks, calls the "real work." What tasks must be completed to achieve this operational objective? Who will actually perform these tasks? When is

each task scheduled to be completed and how can we find out if it
has been completed? If you can answer these questions, your own
role in the process becomes clearer, and it becomes possible to iden-
tify the kind of information you will need to get your work done.

Your basic approach should be to think small. What is the least
amount of information you need to get the job done? How much
do you actually need to know? Comparing the styles of two recent
presidents is instructive here. Bill Clinton managed his office with
a wealth of information at his fingertips, often immersing himself
in every detail of policy that crossed his desk. This had the unin-
tended result of sometimes making decisions and new policy delib-
erations take much longer than anticipated, such as the proposed
health care policy of his early administration. But George W. Bush
takes a very different approach to the running of his administra-
tion, delegating most of the decision making to agencies and
staffers. Although this approach has allowed Bush to focus only on
his most important priorities and to move legislation along quickly,
even allowing time for his famously reasonable schedule, it has
sometimes thrown his administration off balance, as evidenced, for
example, by the times he seemed unaware of statements made or
positions taken by his EPA administrator.

This illustrates the difficulty of maintaining a balance between
micromanagement and undermanagement. You may succeed for a
long time with a particular management style that relies on a cer-
tain level of information and then suddenly fails. If you obtain too
much information, you may be inundated with needless detail; if
you have too little information, you risk being taken by surprise by
an unanticipated policy outcome.

Thinking small about your information needs is necessary but
not sufficient. You must also attempt to anticipate the day-to-day
work involved in completing your assignment. Keep in mind that
your ability to obtain and interpret data is quite limited. One trap
to avoid is overindulging your own desire for data, requiring so
much reporting that your staff does not have time to complete its
work. Remember that requiring your staff to report is an act of great

consequence; by asking for one bit of information instead of another, you are signaling your priorities. It is only when you ask for information that matches your actual priorities that reporting can serve management. You should also expect that greater staff effort will go into the tasks for which you have requested information. We have found that some managers believe that with the World Wide Web and e-mail, the cost of requesting, sending, receiving, and absorbing information has been reduced, and it is acceptable to ask for any information that comes to mind. In fact, the advent of the Web has made information more ubiquitous and has increased the need for managers to be strategic about information.

Projecting Information Needs to Obtain, Explain, or Defend the Organization's Tasks

Previously, we used the matrix presented in Table 8.1 to structure our thinking about the information needed to get a job done. The matrix can also be used with the aim of identifying the information we need in order to market or defend an organization and its work. Projecting the type of information needed to sell an organization is different from projecting the type of information needed to run an organization. However, the projections should ultimately converge because some types of information fulfill both needs. For example, information on a policy problem is needed to provide a baseline for measuring a program's progress. The same information could be used to convince a legislature that a serious problem requires additional resources. Different segments of the data might be used and the data might be presented differently, but the same reporting system could support both internal and external needs.

Securing an assignment for your organization requires information about the nature of the problem. In addition to data on the problem's objective dimensions, you must present dramatic, emotion-stirring images that reinforce the urgency of the problem you have identified. Therefore, both quantitative and anecdotal information is required.

Explaining your organization's tasks to an outsider involves summarizing the administrative details in nontechnical language with a minimum of jargon. This type of information should be the easiest type for you to project and obtain. If you understand your organization's tasks well enough to manage them, you should have more than enough detail to be able to explain them to an outsider.

In contrast, projecting the type of information you need to defend your performance can be quite difficult. Developing a strategy for presenting a problem usually involves making choices from existing data. Tracking your organization's output and impact measures is not easy, and it is difficult to anticipate the type of accomplishments that will impress outsiders. Predicting probable lines of attack may be impossible. The best way to project the kind of information you will need to defend yourself to outsiders is to be in constant communication with customers, the media, legislators, elected officials, opinion leaders, academics, and the general public. What type of accomplishments are they expecting from your organization? What are their priorities and needs? How might you effectively communicate the trade offs you are making and the rationale behind your decisions? Although it will never be possible to please all of the outside interests monitoring your program, it is certainly prudent to anticipate their arguments. You can then routinely collect and present information that addresses outsider concerns.

A poorly thought-out strategy for disseminating information outside the organization can greatly impair a program. The performance of the George W. Bush administration in its early days is a case in point. Many of the initial agency policies put forth did not adequately consider public reaction. Consider the pronouncements on the environment, coupled with the new energy policy. Prior to releasing the new energy policy, the White House and the EPA made several new policy recommendations that emphasized the probusiness agenda of the administration over any environmentally sensitive policies they may have been planning. They took this step without considering what facts might have minimized the perception of being antienvironment. In reducing the requirement for arsenic levels in public

water, for example, the EPA did not demonstrate what research they had done to make this reduction a valid public health risk.

Because of these missteps, the reaction to the new energy policy focused on the probusiness aspects of the policy, such as drilling in the arctic reserve. The reaction was much more negative than the administration surely wanted, and the chances of some of the provisions passing Congress (such as the artic drilling) dimmed after the adverse publicity. Had the administration had a more strategic plan for communicating their overall policy, which they continued to insist was balanced, they would have had more luck in generating a positive reaction from all sides (Seelye, 2001; Jehl, 2001).

How to Influence the Flow of Information into Your Organization

If you wait for the information that will "naturally" pass across your desk, you will get a great deal of useless information and not enough of the information you need. Worse, you will become a repository for other people's agendas. If you hope to control your organization and its mission, and take reasonable entrepreneurial risks, you must actively pursue information.

The Aggressive Pursuit of Information

Typically, pursuing information involves developing information antennae and networks, getting out from behind your desk, and encouraging your staff to get out of the office, too. The nature of your organization's information network depends on the type of work your unit performs. All organizations need well-developed internal networks to take advantage of the organization's informal organizational and communication patterns. As discussed in Chapter Five, only a small fraction of an organization's information is communicated through formal hierarchical channels. Therefore, to be well informed about your organization's activities and direction, you must develop a network of informants throughout your organization. Developing

a network can actually be one of the more pleasant tasks in organizational life. Through your activities in work groups and task forces, through informal social contacts, and through the normal mobility within an organization, you can develop a wide range of internal contacts. You should work on developing and maintaining these professional and social relationships.

Sometimes, in the crush of day-to-day business, it is easy to neglect human relationships. In the long run, such neglect can be costly. Social interaction makes work life more interesting and can also provide you with the back channels often needed to accomplish important tasks. Bear in mind that networking is important for virtually every member of your staff, not just for senior management. Sudden changes in mail room procedures can have as great an impact on your organization as unanticipated changes in policy direction. As a manager, you can encourage information seeking by asking for information, verification, and the rationale behind formal decisions. You can also signal the value you place on good intelligence and on information that advances your organization's effectiveness. For example, if a staff member completes a successful informal negotiation with another organization or obtains a particularly useful piece of intelligence, publicly praising this staff member will communicate the value you place on such communication.

If your work involves a great deal of contact with legislatures, interest groups, or the media, you can develop a similar external network. Even if your job does not involve very much external contact, you should still develop an outside network. External contacts are important reality checks. If too much of your professional or social network is within a single organization, your information base is likely to be quite limited.

There are some problems associated with aggressively pursuing information. First, it is often difficult to change deeply ingrained behavior patterns. The members of your staff may be quite comfortable sitting behind their desks, and they may prefer to remain in the relative safety of the office environment. Some people enjoy work routines and find it stressful to change those routines by trav-

eling even locally. Cultivating external contacts may be perceived as talking out of school or working around one's own management structure. A more subtle problem is how to draw the line between gossiping and networking. If a staff person is an excellent source of organizational intelligence but does not seem to get any work done, his or her pursuit of information may be too aggressive. In other words, he or she may be an unproductive gossip.

Screening and Filtering Information

Once you have developed routines for bringing information in, you must then develop procedures for keeping information out. You must filter and prioritize the information you receive. More important, you must teach your staff people to prioritize the information they focus on and the messages they send to you. One of the most difficult problems you will face is the tendency of large organizations to sanitize information and obscure problems. Most organizations tend to value "can-do" employees—those who have positive attitudes. Although the person who brings a problem to a manager's attention is sometimes (perhaps subconsciously) blamed for that problem—and no manager wants to face a steady diet of problems and failures, it is important that you encourage the reporting of both successes and failures. This is particularly important in an organization attempting to use the principles of TQM. Without accurate information about current levels of performance, it is impossible to know whether changed work processes improve performance.

The information you obtain is directly related to the reward structure you establish for bringing information to your attention. Many managers are cautious about allowing bad news to be presented in writing because of the potential for it to travel and be misinterpreted. This is a legitimate concern, and the manager wishing to learn the truth about a problem area should never rely entirely on formal written communication. Although you need to let your staff know what information you need to make management decisions and to develop standard operating procedures

(SOPs) to obtain and filter that information, you should never expect to get bad news through formal channels. However, you can establish standard processes to ensure that you receive bad news. These processes can take the form of regularly scheduled social events, off-the-record breakfasts, field travel, and any number of other occasions for informal nonwritten exchanges.

You will also need to sift through and distill the sheer volume of information that is directed toward and obtained by your organization. You must let your staff know the type of information you consider to be necessary for decision making. You must also identify for your staff those information sources that cannot be ignored, such as important interest groups, legislators, and your boss. These patterns will naturally evolve in the life of an organization, but they must be monitored for inadvertent and dysfunctional biases. For example, you may be taking cues from an interest group that once had an important constituency but no longer enjoys meaningful support. There are no how-to books or clear steps for developing and implementing SOPs for filtering information. This is largely a matter of clearly communicating your organization's operational objectives, real work, and the information you personally find useful in decision making. If you have excellent staff people, they will use their understanding of your organization's needs to filter information and, one would hope, make the right choices when deciding what information should be presented to you. Your main task is to seek out bad news and encourage the continuous reevaluation of information and information sources.

How to Organize the Flow of Information Within Your Organization

You are not the only person within your organization who needs information; therefore, you must be concerned with the entire flow of information throughout your organization. Information circulation in an organization is as important as blood circulation in a human being. Fortunately, information and responsibility tend to be linked. Information about a task tends to flow toward those with

responsibility for performing that task. Often, difficulties seen as problems of information flow are really problems of poorly designed organizational structure and inadequately constructed assignments. Probably the most common examples of poor information flow are evident when one part of an organization is unaware of what another part is doing. The carpet cleaners may arrive one day before the carpet is ripped up and replaced. This is not simply a matter of a message not being sent or received; it's a matter of the organizational unit's assignments having been defined so narrowly that important questions are not being asked. When the rug cleaners arrive, they do not even notice that the rug is worn and might be a candidate for replacement. If the rug cleaners were part of— and therefore identified with—a larger, more general mission, such as building maintenance or, at least, floor maintenance, they might have made a quick phone call before beginning their cleaning.

Developing a Good Flow of Information

If the information flow in an organization is positive, important information is prioritized, shared, and rapidly transmitted throughout the organization. Good information flow is not a set of procedures and technologies. Although effective procedures and technologies can be helpful, good information flow is the result of an attitude toward work that drives staff members to ask the right questions. It also comes through managers who do not see information as a source of power but as a tool for accomplishing work. Some managers believe that information is a resource to hoard in order to enhance control over "opponents." This approach may have limited relevance in dealing with people external to your organization, but in most cases it makes no sense to keep information from your own staff.

Standard Operating Procedures and Mechanisms for Enhancing Information Flow

As previously noted, the essence of good information flow is staff and management attitudes toward seeking and sharing informa-

tion. However, improved technology and procedures can facilitate the flow of information. But although information technology is very exciting and dynamic, it is often a distracting waste of time and money. Electronic mail, cell phones, voice message systems, and management information systems are four of the major technological toys of the information age. Since the early 1990s, these technologies have become common throughout the developed world. Information technologies can make organizations more efficient but can also increase the flow of unimportant information. Many senior managers find it necessary for staff members to review and filter their electronic mail and voice mail messages. Many offices have added staff members just to distribute fax messages to other staff members. Like other tools, if properly used, technological tools can be helpful. However, it is important to understand that these technologies are not magic. They do not automatically make an organization work better. You and your staff must think about how to adapt these tools to your organization's work.

Electronic Mail. Electronic mail (e-mail) is simply sending messages to another person's computer. Although the technologies vary, the concept is fairly simple. An office or person is assigned an electronic mailbox, or a computer code, to which people can direct written messages. Usually, this is a storage space on a mainframe computer that a staff person accesses with a terminal or a personal computer and a modem. In some systems, a signal appears on your computer when a piece of e-mail has been sent to the mailbox. E-mail is a convenient way to bridge geographic distance and to save the time of physically transporting written communications. Electronic acknowledgments can be built into the system to assure the sender that the message has been received, and security systems can help prevent e-mail from being pirated by unauthorized users. Single written messages can be sent or broadcast simultaneously to multiple parties. Documents can be attached to e-mail in draft form.

One benefit of e-mail is that, unlike voice message systems, the user can easily scan messages and decide which ones to read first or in detail. Written messages also have the advantage of providing

important and time-saving records of departmental operations and allowing employees to make necessary intraoffice communications without tying up phones. A problem with e-mail is that once a message is sent, the sender loses control over who receives it. Messages can also be edited and forwarded to look as if they were composed by the originator, when they have in fact been modified in the forwarding process. One impact of the immediacy of e-mail technology that we have noticed is the tendency for e-mail messages to be sent before they have been carefully considered, composed, and edited. This can result in problems within organizations. On the positive side, e-mail can help ensure that all employees are included in departmental communications. Currently, e-mail facilitates employee access to people whom organizational hierarchies would otherwise make inaccessible, although we suspect that with the volume of e-mail increasing exponentially, this "democratizing" feature is evaporating. As the novelty wears off, most senior managers need to have their e-mail screened just as they have other information filtered. Nevertheless, it is this image of access that has made e-mail a popular symbol of the "information superhighway."

During the 2000 presidential campaign, the accessibility of the candidates and their staff via e-mail was a major difference from earlier campaigns. Public relations staffers initiated e-mail barrages highlighting positive and negative information, campaigns sent broadcast e-mails to supporters searching for donations, and candidates themselves conducted media interviews via e-mail. Furthering the electronic vibe of the campaign, each candidate maintained a Web site with information on views and positions (Wayne, 2000).

Cell phones and portable e-mail devices make it possible for information and messages to follow staff wherever they go. At meetings, you now see staff reading and sending e-mail messages and stepping out of the room to answer cell phone calls in a distracting display of multitasking. These technologies provide staff with a constant stream of information. Some of it is useful, but little of it is urgent or requires immediate attention. The impact of this infor-

mation and the effect of its rapid transmission on organizational life is unclear. We expect to see new organizational norms develop regarding the proper time and place to receive these messages.

Voice Message Systems. Voice message systems became a widely adopted technology in the 1990s. During that decade, the university at which we work spent $15 million to install a telephone system that featured a voice message system with fiber-optic data transmission. Essentially, voice message systems are centralized answering machines. A mainframe computer is used to operate answering machines for every phone in an entire institution. If you do not answer your phone, or if you are speaking on your phone to another person, your call is answered by the voice message system. If you have left a personal message on your machine, your caller may learn where you are and when you may be reached and can then record a message for you. When you arrive back at your desk, a light on the phone will flash if messages have been left for you. You can play back your messages from your desk or call in and receive your messages from any other push-button phone. As with e-mail, it is possible to broadcast single messages to multiple receptors. It is also possible to send a message you have received to other parties. Essentially, you have an electronic mailbox for spoken messages.

A voice message system can be a wonderful resource for staff people without clerical support. And it allows a staff person to temporarily turn off a phone and remain in touch with the work environment. It greatly encourages oral communication because you are guaranteed at least indirect access to the person you are trying to reach. The disadvantages of this system are not intrinsic to its use but arise when it is misused. At a certain organizational level, a senior manager will receive so many voice mail messages that he or she could spend an entire day listening to them. Unlike a human secretary, a voice message system cannot prioritize messages; nor can it can it be scanned visually in a few seconds. Similarly, it cannot interpret the urgency of a message, ask questions, or call a manager out of a meeting. When used properly, voice message systems

can be an expensive but useful enhancement to an organization's communication system; they can increase, and probably improve, information flow.

Management Information Systems. A management information system (MIS) is the fourth computer-based information technology now available to public managers. A well-designed, well-managed information system can improve an organization's ability to track both its own activities and the principal components of its environment (Andersen and Dawes, 1991). A computerized MIS is simply an electronic reporting system. Staff members can record their activities and accomplishments either on a paper form, with the data later entered into a computer, or directly into a form that appears on a computer screen. Periodically, the information entered into the system is aggregated for presentation to the managers. These reports are available in paper or electronic format. The greatest difficulty with MIS is that system designers often attempt to create rational, comprehensive systems that are beyond an organization's capacity to maintain. An organization can only gradually increase its capacity to report or interpret information. Frequently, too much staff time is needed to input information into the system. Sometimes, the information requested is simply unavailable or the system's reports are unreliable or inaccurate. At other times, the system's reports are too complicated to be used in management decision making.

A major management consulting firm once spent $1 million of taxpayers' money and a year of development to design a fairly elaborate MIS, which was initially ignored and ultimately discarded. In its place, the government tracked its field activities by using a secretary, who sat at a word processor next to a phone. Each week, the secretary phoned the agency's field offices, entered fewer than a hundred pieces of data onto a screen on her word processor, and produced a brief report tracking the organization's progress. The preformatted screen was part of a custom-designed software package that aggregated the field reports and then produced a series of very simple reports. It took less than a month and considerably less

than $10,000 to design this simple MIS. The point is that a well-designed, simple MIS can greatly improve the flow of information within an organization. In an effective MIS, the bits of data that management considers vital for tracking an organization's progress are summarized and widely disseminated. However, for MIS to work, management must prioritize its information needs, separating essential from nonessential information. When the task is delegated to an outside consulting firm, these hard choices rarely need to be made.

Each of these technologies—e-mail, portable communication devices, voice message systems, and MIS—can be useful if properly implemented. However, they are not magical technological fixes, and they can be expensive and extremely wasteful. A well-placed answering machine may be more cost-effective than a voice message system, a good filing system and a periodic, hand-calculated report may be more useful than an elaborate MIS, and the post office may sometimes serve your needs better than e-mail does.

In addition to these technologies, there are a number of simple, low-tech activities that can improve information flow—such as holding staff meetings that have written agendas and produce recorded minutes, increasing the circulation of critical memoranda, producing in-house newsletters, and holding retreats. And regularly taking individual staff members or small groups to lunch (or breakfast or dinner, or for drinks) can facilitate communication. Encouraging informal staff interaction can sometimes do more to improve information flow than a dozen networked PCs. Your own attitudes and leadership will set the tone for sharing information at the staff level. Therefore, it is important for you to hold as little information back from your staff as possible. You should constantly search for opportunities to interact with and report to your staff members, and you should actively encourage the informal sharing of information among them. Your access to your organization's external environment will be greater than that of your subordinates, and if they are to understand the world that surrounds the organization, you must share your understanding of that world. Your efforts will establish a

pattern that legitimizes constant informal communication. The aim is to make information sharing contagious within your organization.

Detecting and Preventing Information Breakdown

Information breakdown occurs when staff people do not receive information essential to the performance of their jobs. If the information exists but is only available outside the organization, the problem may be one of inadequate external networks and an insufficiently aggressive effort to obtain information. This is not a problem of inadequate information flow within an organization but of inadequate information acquisition.

Inadequate information acquisition is a serious problem; however, the most embarrassing examples of information breakdown occur when an organization acts without considering essential information that it already possesses. For example, a police department receives a tip that a demonstration is about to take place at the airport. But just before the police are dispatched to the airport, the protest group calls the media and announces that the demonstration has been moved to the mayor's office. The police chief hears this on the radio but does not pass the information to his dispatcher. The mayor then wonders why all the cops have gone out to the airport, leaving her trapped inside her office.

Poor response to available information can contribute to an image of incompetence. If your staff is constantly acting without considering available information—or if a request for information is met with old data—then your organization has an information breakdown problem. Detecting information breakdown is a matter of analyzing your organization's failures and near failures. If many of them are attributable to information breakdown, you should employ some of the correctives previously described. Once again, these include (1) the increased use of informal devices—ranging from brown bag lunches to office softball games—for improving communications, (2) the improved use of appropriate information technology such as e-mail, portable communications devices, voice

message systems, and computerized MIS, and (3) the modification of standard operating procedures to encourage sharing rather than hoarding information.

How to Control and Improve the Description, Synthesis, and Analysis of Information

Your need and ability to assess information will vary according to your organization's size and function. If you manage a policy and program analysis unit, assessing information is at the core of your function. Program management units collect and analyze information about an agency's internal operations, and policy analysis shops analyze external trends and problems. These types of organizations are designed to assess information.

Creating the Organizational Capacity to Assess Information

Line organizations, not inherently designed to assess information, frequently require such organizational capacity. If you manage a line operation responsible for delivering a service, you have a great need to judge the reliability of an extremely narrow range of information. Although you may not have the ability to devote significant resources to analysis, you still need to assess data pertaining to your organization's performance.

The least-cost method of developing this organizational capacity is to borrow it. If your agency has a program management shop that tracks performance, ask it to design and maintain a more detailed tracking system for your organization. Other options include asking your boss's staff to take on the task of assessing program information. Of course, you may not be too crazy about the idea of letting outsiders take a close look at your dirty laundry or your performance errors; such reluctance is understandable, and you might favor developing some of your own analytic capability.

Just as senior executives have added analytic staff members to their immediate offices, many line organizations have found it

necessary to hire analysts simply to communicate with their superiors. Defending resource allocations increasingly requires the capacity to track and price an organization's activities. If you decide to build an analytic staff, it is best to think small. If you can, send one of your current staff members to be trained in management systems and program analysis. If that is not feasible, try to hire a mid-level staff member from one of your agency's analytic offices. Hire an entry-level master of policy administration graduate, and you have a lean analytic unit. Use consultants to help design your management systems, and attempt to entice a graduate program in public policy to lend you some free or inexpensive student assistance.

Although it is important to develop some staff capacity to analyze and present information, in today's staff-lean environment, the best way to develop this capacity is to hire personnel in your line operations who can analyze data. And though you may need to have a lead person responsible for this function, that person should have other work as well. With some modest analytic capacity in place, you are then ready for the next step.

Developing an Information Management Strategy

Earlier in this chapter, we discussed projecting information needs, answering the question, "What kind of information do I need?" Then we discussed how to obtain the information you need. The remainder of this chapter concerns how to organize and analyze the information you obtain and how to use information as a management tool.

At the heart of an information management strategy is a system that provides information essential to decision making. Outside the system of management information, your organization will also need the informal communication links described earlier in this chapter. The key to an information management strategy is to prioritize your information needs and carefully analyze the costs of reporting and organizing information.

In the information needs matrix presented in Exhibit 8.1, objectives are prioritized before information needs are identified. You may

determine that your MIS can only provide systematic data on your organization's top two or three priorities. Remember that the more complex a reporting system, the greater the chance for error in reporting or processing. It is also easier for field staff members to participate in a reporting system that serves a clear purpose and serves both field and management needs.

Many of an organization's information needs are difficult to predict precisely. An important legislator may have a pet project that requires special tracking. A changed political, economic, or organizational environment can alter the reporting needs for a project. Considerable staff time goes into meeting ad hoc requests for information from organizational superiors or outside notables. Some of the time spent in searching for information can be reduced by having well-organized reports and files, but these need not be computerized. Inevitably, time is wasted meeting these inherently unpredictable requests for information. The key to successful information management is organization and agility. Try to avoid getting locked into a huge, inflexible management information system. Keep your reporting systems simple and capable of adapting to rapid change.

Regular Reporting: Its Uses, Abuses, and Limitations

A system of regular reports that track key management indicators is an essential tool of public management. A public manager cannot depend on a bottom line to reveal whether a risk has paid off or if a bet should be hedged. If you are out on a limb, it is nice to know how far from earth you are dangling. Therefore, a realistic set of program measures is necessary. This is particularly important in a new program area, where political support must still be recruited. As we noted earlier, reporting requirements tend to influence staff behavior. If an organization is being judged on a few visible performance indicators, resources tend to flow toward the activities being most closely measured.

Regular reporting—though it can help track and direct resources toward an organization's central missions—has two major limitations:

(1) it cannot accommodate rapidly changing missions and tasks and (2) it is difficult to verify the quality of the accomplishments reported. Management indicators are designed for tracking routine tasks. A government organization is judged not only by its ability to deliver established services but also by its ability to perform for its political masters during times of crisis. If the issue of homelessness is featured in the news every day, a politico does not want to face the media equipped only with long-term data on the number of public housing apartments being built each year. He or she wants to be able to claim that clean, safe emergency shelter was arranged overnight. There is no time to argue about appropriate measures of program effectiveness or to write the software for a new MIS. Success in this arena is defined as getting the homelessness issue off the front page.

Much of the work of public organizations, and certainly most of its highly visible work, involves these quick turnarounds. Regular reporting does not help you manage these situations, and your professional reputation will in large measure be based on your performance of high-priority emergency tasks. The challenge is to maintain established functions while heroically and visibly responding to crises. One major problem in public management is the tendency of an organization's most talented people to move herdlike toward the most visible, glamorous tasks. It is difficult to balance this tendency against the need for sustained productivity. Regular reporting can create an artificial sense of crisis that simulates the crisis created by the demands of politicos. If a reporting period is ending and a key indicator is down, a crisis is created and the herd may move in the direction of solving this routine problem.

However, management information systems are vulnerable to the problem of garbage in/garbage out. The accomplishments recounted in the regular report may mean one thing to the analysts at headquarters and something very different to the field person reporting those accomplishments. Ultimately, the accuracy of the report depends on the accuracy of data input. There is a wide variety of causes of misreporting. At one extreme, there is outright fal-

sification of data. At the other extreme is a genuine disagreement over the definition of a completed task. In either case, management will not receive an accurate picture of actual accomplishments. Therefore, regular reporting must be seen as a tool for tracking organizational performance but never as a substitute for a genuine working relationship between program managers and program implementors. As Kaufman (1960) points out, a manager must establish a variety of procedures for "detecting deviation from preformed decisions" (p. 126). According to Kaufman, these include personal visits, training, several forms of reporting, and stimulating the will to conform with management policy.

When developing indicators, we also need to consider the degree to which we are monitoring process without regard to the impact of that process. Simply put, we need to focus on how clean the streets are instead of on the number of workers deployed, trucks on the road, or route miles traveled.

At the federal level, this change in focus began with the passage of the Government Performance and Results Act in 1993. The act requires at least ten federal agencies to develop annual performance plans that specify measurable goals and report on progress. After modifications based on these pilot efforts, all agencies must produce five-year plans with measurable outcomes, beginning in fiscal year 1998 (National Performance Review, 1993).

Periodic Reviews of Management Indicators

Another danger of regular reporting is that the indicators used to track accomplishments can become outmoded. But this can be avoided through regular modification of indicators—balanced against the worthwhile goal of tracking accomplishments over time. Long-term tracking, however, is usually not as important as changing dysfunctional organizational behaviors that are stimulated by inappropriate indicators. Generally, we suggest an annual submission of an organization's performance indicators, along with an assessment of levels of improvement. More frequent change

detracts from the credibility of the indicator; less frequent change risks long-term performance failure.

The Problem with Numerical Targets

We do not favor setting numerical performance targets. We believe it is better to track performance and focus attention on improvement from current levels of performance. Cohen and Brand (1993) note:

> One of the underlying problems with numerical targets is the games that organizations play in setting these targets. A dynamic is established where those who do the work attempt to underestimate what they might accomplish and those not responsible for the work, but higher in the hierarchy, attempt to set higher goals. Goal setting becomes a political process where the unit with the most control over the goal setting process sets the goals. The workers attempt to utilize their control of information about current performance and the nature of the real work to drive the goal down. Management attempts to drive the goals up through simple assertions of authority [pp. 50–51].

The target is not based on an honest assessment of what might be possible. And even if it were, it is difficult to see how the future can be predicted with such precision. Rather than setting targets, we find it more useful to work on improving the day-to-day performance of work processes. This attacks productivity at its root. If productivity can be improved, it will be improved through analysis and experimentation, not through exhortations to produce more. In our view, numerical targets are the functional equivalent of such management exhortations.

The Limits of Information and Analysis

Information and analysis are important aids to management, but they are only pieces of a larger puzzle. Intuition, guesswork, wisdom, and experience are also requirements of effective management.

During the Vietnam War, Defense Secretary Robert McNamara relied on inappropriate management indicators such as counts of dead bodies to measure success. Unfortunately, the body counts were highly inaccurate, and the Viet Cong were a determined opponent willing to suffer extraordinary losses to win the war. McNamara's overreliance on quantitative analysis was costly for his president, his country, and the Vietnamese people. Both Allison (1971) and Steinbruner (1974) note that President John F. Kennedy relied on guesswork and intuition to resolve the Cuban Missile Crisis of 1962. Kennedy guessed that if he backed down and allowed the Soviet Union to place missiles in Cuba, he would be impeached. As the crisis developed, the United States received two letters from the Soviet government. The first was a personal, conciliatory letter from Premier Khrushchev; the second was a harsher letter that came from the Soviet Union's collective leadership. Kennedy correctly agreed with his brother Robert's guess that he should respond to the first letter and ignore the second letter, a strategy that ultimately resolved the crisis.

In many cases, you simply do not have enough information to base your decision on certain facts. In such cases, you should rely on the wisdom of older hands and on your own intuition. Of course, information can help reduce uncertainty, but ultimately we operate in a world of imperfect information. You must weigh your analysis of the information you are able to collect against the factors for which you have not collected information. If you base your analysis on 25 percent of the information pertinent to your subject, your analysis may seriously mislead you.

How to Control and Improve the Flow of Information from Your Organization

Chapter Eleven provides details on methods of dealing with legislatures, interest groups, communities, and the media. Therefore, most of the issues relevant to an organization's external relations are addressed in that chapter. Here, we briefly touch upon the effect

of internal management decisions on external information flow. In particular, we focus on the formal and informal release of information from an organization.

The Inevitability of Leaks

Every organization releases information when interacting with its environment. In a large bureaucracy, you may be one of several offices involved in a carefully orchestrated, formal release of a decision or policy. Other efforts at information dissemination are less complicated and more routine. No matter how simple the task of releasing information, the probability of mistakes is high. It is nearly impossible to isolate an organization from its environment, so it is nearly impossible to prevent an important piece of information from being leaked to the media. If you are disseminating routine information, the problem of leaks is less serious.

Getting your audience to notice your message is much more problematic. If the information you are planning to release is important, the media are quite good at finding someone in your organization willing to leak the story prematurely. The only way to prevent such leaks is to limit the number of staff people with access to information. This contradicts the advice given earlier, which was to encourage sharing information among staff members. The issue you must confront is how open your operation should be. What information must be closely held, and what information can you share? There are occasions when information must be kept confidential. There are situations where the risks of premature disclosure far outweigh any benefit gained by sharing information. However, many managers hold onto information as a way of wielding their power or influence.

Any decision to withhold information from your staff should be made with great care. People omitted from the information loop may feel left out and possibly powerless. These are not emotions

that build loyalty or stimulate productive effort. If you hold back information sparingly and explain the rationale for excluding your staff after the fact, you can minimize the negative impact of secrecy. If you judge that the benefits of secrecy outweigh the costs, be prepared for leaks. In general, we believe that premature disclosure of information is less dangerous for an organization than the appearance of secretiveness or covertness.

Managing the Release of Information

The fact that leaks may be inevitable on hot political issues does not mean that the release of information is uncontrollable or necessarily chaotic. It is possible to coordinate and organize your external communication processes to maximize the probability that your message will be successfully received. This requires clear rules regarding who is permitted to release information.

You must also become personally involved in the framing of external messages. As the head of your organization, however large or small, you are the one who is in most frequent contact with its environment. You are also most directly accountable for the messages that are transmitted. Your challenge here is to place yourself in the path of outgoing messages without becoming a bottleneck.

One tool for organizing information for external release is to establish a system for prioritizing the urgency of outgoing messages. Unfortunately, such systems often break down because of confusion over the meaning of an emergency and the tendency for everything to become a priority. Scientific systems for managing information are not a substitute for teaching your staff your own style for communicating with the outside world. You must convey your concept of how that outside world works and how your organization's messages are likely to play in that world. The key to managing external information flow is to train your staff to be aware of these factors.

Chapter Nine

Mastering the Budgetary Process

The single most effective tool for influencing organizational behavior is the budget. Since few of an organization's activities are voluntary, little happens unless it is paid for. In general, the budget works better as a negative rather than a positive control mechanism. Although lack of funding can prevent activities, the presence of funding is never a guarantee that activities will take place. In larger government organizations, budgets are developed and implemented by a virtual priesthood of budget analysts who speak a special language and operate on their own calendar.

For the public manager, the budget process is both an opportunity and an obstacle. It is a means of control and a means of being controlled. Every budget process requires the public manager to accomplish three distinct tasks: (1) obtain resources, (2) distribute these resources among the organization's divisions, and (3) track spending to ensure that resource allocation decisions are honored.

This chapter focuses on the culture of budgeting and how to select and evaluate budget staffers. Suggestions are provided as to how to justify budget requests. External and internal political factors that influence resource acquisition are considered, and methods for estimating and projecting resource needs are also provided. Next, we examine the ways in which resource allocations may be used to influence an organization's activities and how financial control systems can help track and evaluate those activities. Finally, this chapter looks at how financial control systems can influence and distort organizational behavior.

For the effective public manager, the issues of resource acquisition, distribution, and management are critical. If a person develops a reputation as an effective manager of the public's resources, he or she will probably be entrusted with additional resources. Such resources are the capital needed for entrepreneurial innovation, and they enhance the odds of successfully implementing a change-based strategy. If a program is truly experimental, it is quite possible that mistakes will be made initially. If resources are too tight, the innovation or experiment may not have enough time to mature and may fail for that reason alone.

Some innovative managers believe that resource issues are secondary. They consider themselves professionals in particular issue areas such as health care and education and are more focused on program results than on program administration. However, demonstrable program results are usually the product of effective administration. No government is wealthy enough to ignore consideration of the cost-effectiveness of a public program. An innovator who is unable to deliver the goods at a reasonable price will eventually be denied the opportunity to innovate, but a public manager who is budget-conscious will be able to acquire the resources needed to experiment. A manager who understands financial management will be able to use financial controls to influence organizational behavior.

In San Diego, former chief administrative officer Lawrence B. Prior III is an example of a public manager who used the budget process to impose discipline and control over a large and complex organization that was teetering on the brink of bankruptcy. The 1995–96 county budget projected a $65 million deficit, had only a few million dollars in reserves for a $2.2 billion operating plan, and was covering both debt service and operating losses from a publicly financed and operated resource recovery program.

Prior's first priority was to solve the solid waste crisis. By August 1997, Prior had a deal to sell the system the county lost money operating for $184 million to Allied Waste Management (Eimicke, 2000). County liability for future losses and debt from the system

were strictly limited. Provisions were made to keep user fees afford-able and the county retained the power to regulate the industry. Perhaps equally important, proceeds from the sale funded an envi-ronmental trust fund, built budget operating reserves to a safe and responsible level, and enabled the county to finance a zero-deferred maintenance infrastructure investment program. No proceeds were used as one-shot revenues to close the county's operating budget deficit. With the county's fiscal affairs in order, Prior was able to provide venture capital to innovative public managers with ideas to enable public agencies to operate as if they were an efficient pri-vate enterprise.

State and local governments across the United States are seek-ing to link the budget process to program performance objectives. By 2001, forty-seven U.S. states enacted performance budget requirements, most of which have been enacted since 1995 (Melk-ers and Willoughby, 2001). Cities are also moving toward perfor-mance-based budgeting—overhauling the traditional budget process that often rewards public managers for poor performance (for example, if the streets are dirtier, the sanitation budget is increased). Upon taking office, Mayor John Norquist of Milwaukee determined that the most effective management tool available to him was the budget process, and he chose a new performance-based system to achieve his objectives. Success would now be measured according to outcomes instead of inputs. Managers and the mayor agree on five strategic objectives for each agency and the agencies are evaluated on the degree to which they achieve those objectives. For example, the road maintenance department is evaluated based on the smoothness of the streets rather than on how many miles they travel, how many person hours they work, or how much money they spend (Eggers, 1993).

The use of budgeting as a management tool is not a new strat-egy. When Robert Kiley first arrived at the Massachusetts Bay Transportation Authority (MBTA), he removed responsibility for the budget from its traditional organizational home and placed it in a new office of budget and operations analysis, which was under

his direct control. By doing this, Kiley greatly increased his ability to closely scrutinize departmental budget requests and expenditures, and he was able to reduce spending in his first year of leadership. Prior to Kiley's chairmanship, the budget process was fairly loose and was characterized by frequent requests for additional "supplemental" allocations. This open checkbook style of budgeting ensured that budget decisions would not influence the behavior of line managers. By tightening the rules of the budget process and sticking by those rules, Kiley was able to transform the budget from a joke into an important management tool. The MBTA's increased ridership and Kiley's later recruitment to run New York City's mass transit system were in part the result of effective financial management (Hitchner and Hitchner, 1979).

However, despite a long history of trying to link budget priorities to performance targets, the results are at best uneven. The state of Oregon was a leader in establishing program benchmark goals for its public agencies in the early 1990s, but it was never able to effectively link its benchmark program to the budget decision-making process (Osborne and Plastrik, 1997). The city of Sunnyvale, in California, and the government of New Zealand have been more successful in linking performance management and budget process. Nevertheless, performance budgeting remains more of a theoretical objective than an applied reality.

In these early years of the twenty-first century, nations are using the budget process to assess the proper role of government in society. Responding to the demands of a global economy, public dissatisfaction with government performance, and economic downturns, central government budget makers are considering macro strategies, including

- decentralization of authority and devolution of service responsibilities to regional and local governments
- privatization
- contracting out
- discontinuance of nonessential programs

- user charges
- tax incentives
- franchising
- subsidies to private entities
- public-private partnerships
- deregulation

Some governments—particularly the city of Indianapolis and California's San Diego County—have used competition between public and private providers of services to simultaneously reduce budget expenditure pressures and enhance the quality of public service delivery. In the United Kingdom, New Zealand, and the United States, public employees can even receive incentive pay if citizen satisfaction with the price and quality of public services is high enough (Abramson and Kamensky, 2001; Osborne and Plastrik, 1997).

How to Obtain Resources

To obtain adequate resources for your organization, you need more than an important mission and dedicated staff. You also need to have a firm understanding of your organization's budget process and you need capable budget staff members who understand how to provide the detail and documentation needed to justify funding requests.

How to Select and Evaluate a Budget Staff

The first step in obtaining resources is to develop or maintain the professional staff needed to play the budget game. Budgeting is a critical function that line managers frequently misunderstand or try to avoid. It is frustrating because budgeting operates on its own logic and schedule, and it often seems disconnected from the production of government services. In staff offices, managers sometimes believe that protection by the high-level executives they serve exempts

them from the need to engage fully in the budget game. In our view, the budget is too critical to ignore. In both line and staff organizations, resources are needed to operate and innovate.

Budget staff members must understand the functions and objectives of their own organization and must also have a firm technical grasp of the budget process. An effective public manager develops a clear understanding of the budget process and is thereby able to judge the effectiveness of his or her budget experts. Although, typically, a general manager is not required to develop the same expertise as his or her expert professional staff, budgeting is a form of management expertise that the manager ignores at great peril. At a minimum, you must learn the general rules of the budget process and you must study budget strategies and understand enough to direct and defend your organization's budget submission.

Assuming that you have a general understanding of budget formulation, implementation, and audit, you then need to find or retain a budget staff. While there is no single ideal budget person, there are a few attributes usually present in the best budget staff member.

- Attention to detail—the budget is a complex document, and a misplaced decimal point is rarely trivial
- Patience—the budget process is long and convoluted, and the budget staff must be willing to draft and redraft
- Technical knowledge—of financial management, spreadsheet programs, mathematics, economics, and revenue projection models, as well as an understanding of your organization's goals and purpose
- Loyalty—to your organization rather than to the mores and norms of budgeting
- Discretion—the ability to keep sensitive budget allocations, projections, and data confidential
- Endurance—particularly during the budget season, when the working day lasts long into the night

Budget staff members must work closely with budget analysts or reviewers from internal and external overhead organizations, they must respond rapidly to modifications in budget justifications and computations, and they must use interpersonal skills to establish long-standing productive working relationships with their colleagues in the budget process, particularly those in the central budget office.

Revenue, expenditure, and allocation data are subject to wide and rapid variability. Information must be communicated informally in order to be timely. Budget staff members are not simply number crunchers who can be placed in a corner with their personal computers and spreadsheet software packages. They are negotiators as well as analysts. When you are searching for budget staff people, it is important to keep the full range of functions in mind. When assessing the quality of their work, you should focus on the technical, political, and interpersonal aspects of the job.

You should also evaluate your success in the budget process. You should not ask whether you got everything you requested but, rather, you should ask whether you lost budget battles because of inadequate preparation or poor communication. Obviously, political and economic factors will be the primary influence on budget results. However, talented budget specialists can influence close decisions. You can judge the quality of your staff by observing members' professional reputations and by noting whether other offices attempt to hire them away.

The Culture of Budgeting

Budgeting/financial management is a profession. In some respects, it is similar to accounting, whereas in other aspects it resembles the legal profession. Norms are attached to acceptable budget justification, estimation, and presentation. A central value in the "culture of budgeting" is the appearance of precision and the perception that details are fully mastered. Budget analysts strive for internal consistency in their documents and deliberations: Do the columns

and rows add up? Budget personnel must deal with budget reviewers who will be looking for items to cut and who frequently will not have detailed knowledge about the organization's programs (Rubin, 2000; Mikesell, 1986).

To assert their authority and obtain the information needed to make intelligent resource trade-offs, budget analysts must cut your organization's budget request. This forces you to provide additional data on program operations in order to defend the budget. This pattern of budget cutting and defense (or pass back and appeal) will happen within your agency, when your budget is reviewed by the central budget office, and again when your entire agency's budget is reviewed by an external office of management and budget or bureau of the budget. Although in some smaller local governments this review process may be less formal, no public manager enjoys the luxury of an unexamined budget.

The budget reviewer's need to cut is partly a requirement to justify his or her existence and partly a critical function in the administrative system. Without a budget staff, there would be little downward pressure on expenditures in the budget process. The importance of the budget staff is not limited to the bureaucracy. In Congress, budget committees are needed to impose fiscal discipline on subject matter committees, which are often willing to authorize more spending than budget committees are willing to allocate. In the bureaucracy, budget staff members play the same role that legislative budget committees play. Their spirited questioning of agency spending proposals inspires agencies to develop detailed budget justifications and estimates. In some local governments, budget review and restraint is a function of the professional city manager.

Budget analysts require agencies to explain the purpose of a particular expenditure and to defend a budget's cost estimates. They will search for any justification to reduce a funding request. This built-in conflict between those who make budget requests and budget reviewers is mediated in part by the fact that at different levels in the hierarchy a budget reviewer must become a budget advocate. All budget staff people have a stake in completing the work of

developing the budget, and generally an atmosphere of compromise and consensus emerges.

This norm of consensus is, of course, placed under greater stress when resources are being cut. Although most budget decisions can be appealed—from the staff level to the political level, professional staff members try to avoid allowing conflicts to be mediated at higher levels. When conflicts are left to high-level political players to resolve, professionals lose their power to influence outcomes. In addition, the political-level compromise may be worse than the outcome originally appealed.

How to Justify a Budget Request

You can use a variety of approaches to justify a budget request. First, it is essential that the form of the justification be proper. When a budget process begins, those managing the process always send a detailed set of instructions and formats to those responsible for budget preparation. If the format is incorrect or the required supporting data and analysis are not provided, your request may not be granted. The strength of your argument does not matter; if you have not adhered to the correct budget format and style of argumentation, your case will not be credible.

Budget justifications are fairly standard throughout government. First, you describe your current or baseline programs and resource use. Next, you describe the additions or cuts you are recommending, along with justification for your suggestions. Your justification might include changes in authority or executive policy, changes in operations or technology, changed environmental conditions—such as economic or demographic changes, and additional knowledge gained from increased experience. Finally, you must include in your justification the expected results of the changes you have proposed (Mikesell, 1986). A variation of this process is target-based budgeting, under which the budget office sets, from the beginning, firm ceilings for departmental expenditures (based on revenue estimates and executive-level policy decisions on program priorities). It is up

to the department to allocate the funds available among its spending categories (Rubin, 2000).

As in most policy discussions, it is best to rely on hard, quantified data from respected and verified sources. Linking resources to results has been a hot topic in Washington for the past two decades. The Government Performance and Results Act provides the structure through which performance measures can influence budget decisions (Abramson and Kamensky, 2001). If such data are not available, and frequently they are not, you must find credible substitutes. Estimates, extrapolations, and other forms of statistical creativity should certainly be attempted. Expert testimony, "best professional judgment," and exhortations about administration policy are weaker but certainly worth trying. Anecdotal information is weaker still, but it is usually better than nothing.

In defending a budget, it is best to keep in mind the essentially conservative nature of the budget process. Large cuts and large increases are the exception, not the rule. Therefore, the best arguments tend to be those that assert that items traditionally considered part of an organization's budgetary base either cost more, must be provided to more clients, or must be changed to maintain traditional levels of effectiveness. It is never wise to justify an expenditure by saying, "We really do not have the slightest idea of how to solve this difficult problem, and this experimental program is the best guess we could come up with."

Political Factors That Influence Resource Acquisition

A most instructive assessment of public budget strategies is provided by the late Aaron Wildavsky. In his book (1974), Wildavsky identifies what he terms "ubiquitous" and "contingent" strategies. He comments that "strategies to gain confidence and clientele are ubiquitous; they are found everywhere and at all times in the budgetary system" (p. 60).

Contingent strategies vary with budget circumstances. If your budget base is being cut, your strategy might be to threaten to end

a visible and popular program. If you are trying to increase your budget, you might claim that the increase is only temporary or is needed to deal with an emergency (Mikesell, 1986). Your ability to carry out contingent strategies will be influenced by your clientele support and professional reputation.

The political factors that influence resource acquisition can be derived from Wildavsky's strategy considerations (1974). Clientele support, professional reputation, and the general climate or market for your agency's services influence the politics of resource acquisition. If a powerful interest group supports your request, your professional reputation and the general level of political support for your request may be irrelevant. The interest group's strength may carry the day. The case of tobacco subsidies is a good example of a program with little popular support but a strong enough clientele group to dominate a budget process. Clientele support is critical, but developing such support is often a difficult and sensitive undertaking. Your freedom to develop client support will depend on your level in the hierarchy, the political sensitivity of your issue to elected leaders, and the openness of client groups to informal influence.

If you are not at a top level of your organization—or are involved in external constituency building—your budget politics will be principally internal, limited to influencing members of your own organization and perhaps some officials in the budget office. You may not be given permission to lobby individuals outside your organization and otherwise engage in external budget politics. However, internal budget politics can be as important as external budget politics, since it may be your only chance to influence the budget.

In many respects, internal budget politics creates the highest level of conflict. Even during cutback eras, there is always the possibility that a political case can be made and that more resources will be allocated to your mission. Typically, internal budget politics involves dividing up a relatively fixed pie. When the budget is being proposed, the agency usually has some target funding level within which it must stay. Legislatures work within similar constraints based on revenue projections, but these projections can fluctuate widely

and additional revenue can always be raised for absolutely essential needs. Also, trade offs between specific budget items are less apparent in a large multiagency budget than in a single agency's budget. In internal budget politics, you tend to know who your competition is. In external budget politics, you are not always competing against other specific programs but, rather, against the budget as a whole.

Professional reputation is a factor in external budget politics, but it is far more important in internal budget politics. It is less likely that external decision makers will be aware of your reputation. In addition, in external budget politics, the symbolic value of allocating funds and the political value of appeasing interest groups are more important than whether the funds will be used effectively. In internal budget politics, however, your professional reputation will be considered in assessments of the accuracy of your budget projections. Your reputation will reinforce the credibility of your budget justifications and will enhance or impair the probability that senior managers will back any new initiatives you propose.

There are a number of specific strategies you can use when attempting to influence budget politics. A typical ploy is often referred to as the "nose of the camel in the tent." Through this strategy, the proposing agency seeks minimal funding for the first year of a new program, anticipating that success will lead to major increases in future years (Anthony and Herzlinger, 1980). A variation on the theme is to characterize the new program as a limited "pilot" initiative—one that may or may not be renewed after the first phase of one or two years.

Another typical budget ploy is called the "football team strategy." When you are asked to cut your budget, you cut a very popular and visible program such as the football team or perhaps the school bus program. Although this is a high-risk strategy, it can focus the political agenda on spending that is widely supported. An example of a ploy "primarily for supervisors" is to "make a study"—that is, "defer approval of a proposal on the grounds that it is inadequately supported . . . [and you] ask for further justification" (Anthony and Herzlinger, 1980, p. 353).

A deceptive ploy may impair the credibility of your budget submission and backfire in the long run. In the late 1980s and early 1990s, the U.S. Department of Housing and Urban Development's unwillingness, or inability, to provide Congress with accurate data on the future financial consequences of Section 8 subsidy commitments prompted Congress to respond by cutting the agency's staffing levels and funding an outside consultant to develop a top-down study of the financial and management systems (U.S. Department of Housing and Urban Development Office of Inspector General, 1993.) After the destruction of the World Trade Center on September 11, 2001, New York governor George Pataki submitted a $56 billion disaster recovery proposal to Congress that included upstate New York projects—far removed from Lower Manhattan. This ploy failed and generated political resistance to legitimate recovery needs.

How to Distribute Resources

Before you can distribute resources, you need to first estimate how much it costs to perform the tasks your organization must complete. It is also useful to think about how resources can be used as incentives to encourage the completion of tasks you consider to be a priority. It is critical to remember that the budget process usually involves the allocation of scarce resources to priority projects that inevitably require more funds than they are originally allocated through the regular budget decision-making system.

How to Estimate and Project Resource Needs

A budget is a type of plan—a projection of how managers of an organization expect to spend money during a given period of time. The best predictor of future spending is usually past spending. In most cases, budget preparation begins with current spending, or what is termed the "budgetary base." In government, there are many budgets. The budget an agency proposes is not the budget

that it eventually implements. After an agency proposes a budget, it is submitted to the political executive's budget office and an executive budget is formulated. This executive budget is then submitted to the legislative branch for negotiation and final approval. The budget enacted by the legislature is signed into law by the political executive, and it then becomes the authorized budget under which the agency operates. In addition to such operating budgets, many states and localities have a capital budget of items that will be purchased during one year but used over many years. The federal government has no capital budget—unless you consider the national debt a form of capital budget.

The foregoing discussion illustrates the complexity of resource estimation. It is important to first understand the type of budget you are preparing. Is it an initial wish list or is it in an opening, a midpoint, or a final bargaining position? Is the budget an actual spending plan to which you and other managers will be expected to adhere? A fairly simple rule of thumb in resource estimation is to assume uncertainty and to attempt to retain as much personal flexibility as possible. Often, this means overestimating your organization's resource needs. Resource estimation is essentially a search for comparisons. What did we do that was similar to this, and what did it cost? We usually begin our resource estimates by asking the following questions: How much staff time should it take to complete this task? How much elapsed or calendar time should it take to do this job? What kinds of skills are needed to do this work? What are the other than personnel costs involved in completing this task?

When projecting costs, we usually begin by asking what the lowest numbers are that we can imagine are practical, and what the highest numbers are that we believe we can justify. This sets the range for an estimate. For example, let us imagine that you are required to establish a telephone hot line for a new service your organization is about to start. You could estimate costs by consulting someone who now operates a hot line, asking him or her several questions: How much staff time went into setting up the hot

line? Is the service contracted? If not, how much does it cost to establish and maintain the hot line's equipment and facilities, and what kind of equipment is used? How many calls come into the hot line, and how much staff time is required to answer the typical call? How much staff time is required to research the issues raised by hot line calls?

You could then speak with staff members involved in external relations in the hot line's issue area and ask them to project the volume of calls the new hot line will generate. With this information, you could come up with an estimate of the amount of money and staff time needed to fund the hot line.

Of course, it may take too much time to develop such detailed cost estimates for everything your organization does. This is why existing programs are often folded into an organization's budgetary base, and costs are assumed to be relatively stable from year to year.

Budget estimates are frequently built on guesses about how much work is involved in performing a certain task. Suppose you discover that maintaining a hot line requires eighty hours of phone staff time per week and ten hours of research staff time per week. The hot line also requires three hours a week of management time to oversee the phone operation and four hours a week of management time to oversee the information given out to callers. The phone equipment needed to run the line can be leased at four hundred dollars per month. A decision is made to contract out the hot line, and you estimate contract costs as follows:

> Hours of contractor phone staff per year:
> (80 × 52), or 4,160, @$30/hr.[*] = $124,800.
> Hours of research staff per year:
> (10 × 52), or 520, @$40/hr.[*] = $ 20,800.
> Hours of contractor management time to oversee phone
> operation per year:
> (3 × 52), or 156, @$50/hr.[*] = $ 7,800.

*Including fringe benefits and overhead

You estimate that your contractor cost will be approximately $153,400 for labor, $4,800 for phones, and $10,000 for miscellaneous other-than-personnel-services costs (for a total of $168,200). You guarantee a profit to the contractor of 5 percent ($8,410) and include a performance bonus of another 5 percent, for a maximum cost of $185,020 ($168,200 + $8,410 + $8,410). In addition, you need approximately 208 (52 X 4) hours of agency staff time to manage the project and to ensure that the information given out over the hot line represents agency policy. Internal time is not computed in dollars but in full-time equivalencies (FTEs). If we assume an average work year of two thousand hours per person, 208 hours is approximately 0.1 of an FTE.

Another way of estimating costs is to allow the importance of a task to dictate the funds you will allocate. Particularly in new organizations, or in new issue areas, it may be difficult to find a useful comparison on which to base your estimate. Public sector budgets, unlike private sector manufacturing budgets, are quite discretionary. If you are building a piece of equipment in the private sector, the raw materials and labor needed to build it can be precisely computed. Although the quality and therefore the costs of raw materials and labor can vary, there is a price you cannot go below and a price you must not go above to make a particular product. Conversely, if you are responsible for analyzing a public policy problem, there is really no limit to the amount of funding you can use to enhance your service. In some cases, you set an artificial spending cap and simply say you will go this far and no further. You justify the level of your cap by citing the importance or relative unimportance of the issue area. In other cases, you will develop a feel for pricing similar projects and simply use these to justify your estimates.

How to Use Resource Allocations to Influence Your Organization's Activities

Budget allocations are among the most concrete expressions of an organization's priorities. If you oppose a program, you can end it by

denying funding. If you favor a program, you can increase its odds for success by funding it. By providing a number of organizational units with sufficient funds to perform the same task, you can virtually guarantee that the task will be accomplished.

However, as we indicated at the beginning of this chapter, the budget is a very blunt instrument of influence. A function can be starved or nourished, but it is difficult to use the budget to manipulate more subtle changes in policy direction. The budget is best used in concert with other management tools for influencing behavior. It is important to remember that although human behavior can be influenced, it generally cannot be bought and sold. People must be motivated to perform the tasks you request. You must exert leadership and provide incentives. When managers approach the top of a hierarchy, they sometimes become enamored of the "big picture." They see management as a macro-level game in which organizational units are pieces to be moved around as though on a chessboard. They can sit back, make "decisions," and change the organization's direction. This tendency toward management abstraction should be avoided, and budget allocations are best seen as the beginning rather than the end of an effort to influence an organization's behavior.

An example may help illustrate this point. In recent years, in some states throughout the country, highway bridges have collapsed, resulting in death and disrupted transportation. One answer to this problem appears to be more frequent and more detailed bridge inspections. A budget can be used to provide more resources for additional bridge inspectors, consultant assistance, and travel funds. Although this might generate additional activity, it does not guarantee that inspection procedures will be changed and made more detailed. New standard operating procedures must be developed, and staff people must be motivated to change their behavior and follow new procedures. Although additional funding helps make these changes possible, money alone is not enough. You can signal the increased priority of bridge inspection by providing increased funding, but you must then follow up with additional management initiatives.

How to Monitor the Use of Resources

Effective public managers understand that budgeting is not the only way to use resources to influence an organization's behavior. Of almost equal importance is the process of monitoring resource use. Financial tracking provides a manager with critical information on what activities the organization is funding.

How Financial Control Systems Can Help Track and Evaluate Your Organization's Activities

Financial control systems are methods for reporting and recording an organization's spending. A typical system follows an organization's responsibility structure. A responsibility structure is another name for an organization's formal arrangement of hierarchical authority and reporting relationships. Control structures are most effective when they match responsibility structures. This ensures that those with managerial responsibility have the data they need to make decisions. If the control structure does not match the responsibility structure, the reports emanating from the financial control system will not be useful. Managers will read reports on X, Y, and Z, although they only have authority over half of X and all of W.

A financial control system records all funding obligations made by authorized officials. Similarly, the financial control system records authorizations to expend funds within obligated limits. The system then provides a mechanism for releasing funds expended. In the federal government, this is an authorization for the Treasury Department to write a check. The system records all transactions and provides management with reports on spending. Fortunately, the reports provided by a financial control system are not random lists of expenditures but are instead carefully structured, well-organized compilations. A financial control system's recording and reporting of financial data are arranged by categories of expenditures and distinct organizational units. Broad categories can be aggregated "up" from specific categories, and reports may provide summary data on program or agency expenditures. Information may also be presented on specific line items such as personnel, travel, and equipment. Funding

obligations are made in each category of the financial reporting system, and actual spending or outlay levels are compared with these obligations. Periodic reports (weekly, monthly, or quarterly) are prepared and used to monitor spending trends. Although most agencies do not collect their own revenues, those that do have similar systems for projecting expected revenues and reporting actual receipts.

Management involves motivating behaviors. Effective managers monitor staff workers' behaviors in order to modify and improve their organization's motivational strategy. One way to monitor an organization's activities is to track resource use. Financial tracking provides an indication of organizational behavior. For example, if you have made field travel a high priority and only 10 percent of your travel budget has been used in the first quarter, you may need to reinforce your policy. But you may discover that the entire 10 percent was spent in the past month, and the low spending was due to a start-up lag. You might also discover that most of the unit's travel is projected to take place in a particular quarter because of a seasonal aspect of your program. An examination of financial data from previous years might indicate that the spending pattern you have discovered is typical.

Therefore, the financial tracking system could be used to explain an unusual pattern. But the financial tracking system might not be helpful in explaining the unusual spending pattern. You might need to consult a performance tracking system or other parts of a management information system to explain the spending pattern in question. You might also need to speak with the people whose performance you are monitoring. Financial control systems cannot always answer questions about performance, but they can frequently help managers identify questions that should be raised. Control systems can be used to pinpoint areas needing additional inquiry.

How Financial Control Systems Can Influence and Distort Organizational Behavior

"Gaming," or fooling a financial tracking system, is relatively easy. Therefore, you should never assume that spending data alone can pinpoint problems. One simple device for deceiving control systems is to

mislabel expenditures. If two organizational units are under your control and one is overspent in some category and the other is underspent, it may be possible to have one organization "pay" the costs of the other. The pace of obligating and expending funds can be used to create misleading impressions. You might deliberately hold back an expenditure in order to create a "planned" financial crisis. This can make it appear as if a sudden change in the organization's environment, rather than management policy, is responsible for the overspending.

The design of financial control systems can have significant implications. As Fred Thompson (1993) notes, the choice of *where* to control *what* is a much more obvious decision than determining *whom* to control *when*. The controls may be applied before or after the subject acts. Control structures must be designed to match the organizational behaviors being monitored. Thompson's research suggests that "mismatched controls add 5 to 20 percent to the real cost of supplying services [and] over-control can cost more" (p. 311).

In some organizations, obligation of funds—the binding commitment that permits the expenditure of funds—is the main financial indicator tracked. Actual expenditures are thought to lag behind but to more or less automatically follow obligations. However, one way of gaming a financial tracking system is to overobligate funds in a particular contract, even though you have no intention of allowing a contractor to expend all of the funds. Later in the fiscal year, you might "deobligate" these funds and assign them for another purpose. Managers attempting to track organizational behaviors through obligation data would obviously be misled by this practice.

Just as performance indicators in a management information system can distort organizational performance, so, too, can financial indicators distort organizational behavior. Despite efforts to contain spending in the final quarter of the fiscal year, many organizations still spend conservatively early in the fiscal year and engage in a spending frenzy at the end of the year. Managers attempt, in effect, to please financial control systems. They think about what type of data they want more senior management to see in financial tracking reports. The behaviors designed to make an

organization look good in financial terms may not be the behaviors needed to implement effective programs.

Unfortunately, the type of constrained, or bounded, rationality that emerges when managers conform to the dictates of a reporting structure can sometimes cause those managers to lose sight of program results. Management becomes process-oriented rather than goal-oriented because "results" have been redefined by inappropriate surrogate measures. The manager of a highway project may slow down construction to avoid generating an "exception" report that identifies spending that is ahead of projection. Another manager might decide to complete a task by using contractors—even when internal staff members could do the job—in order to demonstrate a continued need for contractor resources.

The possibilities for distorted management decisions are virtually limitless. A creative manager can design all sorts of creative contraptions to ensure that a project looks good on management reports. We firmly believe that any control system can be fooled. For a control system to work, those providing information to the system must have a stake in its accuracy. The system must help them in their work and be an important mechanism of internal control. The system cannot simply be a way to catch the mistakes of their subordinates. A financial control system is also never a replacement for a productive organizational culture and network of positive interpersonal relationships. It can, however, be a useful tool for a group of managers and staff members who work together and trust each other. Keeping track of obligations and expenditures is an essential managerial task. It must be done, and if it is done well, it can help an organization achieve its goals. However, financial control is a means and not an end.

There are methods to mitigate these distorting factors. First, customers, stakeholders, and employees can be involved in the design of the performance management system. Second, management should press for linking performance information to budget decisions. Finally, an effective performance management system should lead to the reallocation of responsibilities among agencies and individuals to create maximum efficiencies.

How to Use the Budget to Control Your Organization

We turn, then, to the following question: How can you use the budget to control your organization? At the outset, we suggest that you give up on the idea of controlling your organization. You should strive to influence rather than control. Human beings are not machines and ultimately are not controllable. They can be motivated and influenced. The budget is an excellent tool for setting broad programmatic direction. Budget allocations can be used to undertake a risky, entrepreneurial initiative. In that sense, you are influencing and possibly redirecting the organization through the budget. However, placing a bet on an experimental program is not the same as managing a risky enterprise. Once you have taken the plunge, you need to steer and direct the behaviors you are purchasing. Financial control structures are useful, if limited, tools for influencing or steering organizational behavior. When they are used in support of an organizational culture with shared values and a clear sense of purpose, financial controls can help identify problems. Even in less healthy organizations, they can provide a rough indication of the organization's behaviors. If the system is less than 100 percent accurate, it will certainly be more correct than incorrect. A cumbersome financial control system can delay and obstruct administration; therefore, efforts to improve the system are worth the effort.

In sum, the budget is a necessary but not a sufficient tool for influencing organizational behavior. An effective public manager must understand budget formulation and financial management. However, it is important to avoid relying exclusively on this powerful tool. It is easy to be seduced into believing that finance is management. Tracking expenditures is easier than influencing human beings to act in a desired manner.

For a controversial program to succeed, you must understand the risks involved, and you should always seek to reduce any unnecessary risks. Financial controls can help you closely monitor the costs and benefits of your pilot programs. Effective financial management can increase the probability of successful public management. It cannot guarantee success.

Chapter Ten

Shaping Organizational Goals and Strategies

Every effective manager must address two simple but central questions: Where should I take this organization? and What type of work should we do? The answers to these questions can substantially influence your organization's future success and, thereby, your own professional prospects.

This chapter begins with the issue of organizational strategy and addresses its definition, necessity, and importance. We also discuss how strategy is developed and implemented and how you can estimate what your organization is capable of doing. Your definition of success has implications for the resources needed and for the strategy formulation and entrepreneurial projects taken on by your organization. Developing a practical operational strategy and communicating a sense of purpose are key tasks of effective public managers.

The second part of this chapter discusses what you should do with the work you are given, and it poses the following questions: How do you evaluate whether an assignment is worth doing? How do you get out of bad assignments and attract good ones? What do you do if your situation is hopeless and your assignments are clear losers?

Finally, all government work has an ethical dimension. Inasmuch as ethical issues are particularly difficult to assess, this chapter concludes by discussing the following questions: How do you ensure that your organization's work is ethical? How do you assess the ethics of your assignments? How do you assess the ethics of your relationships with private parties? What do you do if you consider an assignment unethical?

Why Strategy Is Important

It is possible to manage an organization without an organizational strategy. It is also possible to project an image of competence without a coherent strategy. However, without a strategy, it is difficult to have much influence over your organization's agenda. If you are fortunate, you may inadvertently be involved in implementing a well-designed program. In that case, you may end up looking like you really know what you are doing. Some people are able to develop a positive professional reputation based only on good media relations and a lot of luck. For most of us, though, a well-thought-out organizational strategy provides a more likely path to success.

What Is Strategy?

Peter Drucker describes strategy as "actions taken today to meet tomorrow's objectives" (Mercer, 1991, p. 17). Others define strategy as the basic pattern of current and planned resource deployments and environmental interactions that indicate how an organization will achieve its goals (Hofer and Schendel, 1978). Strategic planning is rooted in the military concept of comprehensive preparedness for any and all eventualities in the course of battle (Sutherland, 1978).

Mark Moore (1995) envisions a strategic triangle for the public sector that simultaneously defines the organization's mission in terms of important public values, describes the sources of support and legitimacy that the organization can draw on to accomplish its mission, and explains how the entity will be organized to achieve its mission. In this way, the public manager is challenged to think beyond the more traditional challenges of implementation. It encourages public sector executives to look for opportunities to use their organization to create public value.

Strategy formulation begins with the identification of objectives and the determination of methods for reaching objectives. These objectives and activities are then scaled to fit within resource constraints. Each element of a strategy (objectives, activities, and resources) is constrained by political, social, economic, and envi-

ronmental variables. The objectives and activities of public organizations are constrained by the formal authority provided by statute. Formulating a strategy requires the following steps (see Cohen and Eimicke, 1998):

1. *Problem and opportunity analysis.* Scan the organization's environment to identify current constraints and possibilities. The organization's central mission must be drawn from this set of feasible options and must lead to a shared sense of purpose among the members of the organization. An effective means to accomplish this step is to develop or reassess the organization's mission statement.

2. *Identification of interested parties.* Identify the individuals and groups that interact with the organization, to assess their current interests, potential demands, and reasons for dissatisfaction with the organization.

3. *Historical analysis.* Determine what factors led to past successes and failures. To what extent was the result influenced by factors internal and external to the organization? Could the result have been different if the organization had responded more quickly or in another fashion?

4. *Organization and situation assessment.* Determine what the current capacity of the organization is. What is expected of the organization? How are external factors influencing the organization?

5. *Assessment of the impact of specific activities.* Determine to what degree these activities resulted in the accomplishment of specific objectives.

6. *Midcourse corrections.* Determine what modifications are needed in activities, resource allocations, or objectives to respond to changes in the organization's environment.

Why Do You Need Strategy?

Organizations can function without a clear strategy. If an organization responds effectively to demands made from its external environment, it will please those making the demands and will establish a

reservoir of support. However, without a plan, the organization runs a great risk of taking on missions that are in conflict, outstripping the resources available to it, and being unable to articulate a clear and coherent core competence. Without a clear strategy, it is difficult for an organization to justify its reason for being and continue to attract the resources it needs to survive.

You will do a great deal of work and accomplish very little. It is risky to step too far out in front and have too many self-initiated agenda items, but it is also risky to simply respond to the orders of your organizational superiors. In the end, the people who know best what your organization can and should accomplish are the people who currently work in the organization.

There are countless examples of strategic thinking in government. Throughout the 1990s, the federal government engaged in a broad-based experiment in strategy development called the National Performance Review (NPR). The NPR was led by the Vice President Al Gore and was based on the writing of David Osborne and the reinventing government movement. The NPR encouraged and enabled federal agencies to focus on customers, core competencies, and its overall mission. Although the NPR is not without its critics (Lenkowsky and Perry, 2000; deLeon and Denhardt, 2000; Rosenbloom, 1993; U.S. General Accounting Office, 1996), other analysts have given the initiative high marks for its strategic approach to procurement reform, customer service, and downsizing (Kettl, 1998; Lambright, 2001). A wide range of reforms were implemented in agencies as diverse as the Defense Department, Health and Human Services, HUD, the EPA, Veterans' Health Administration, FEMA, and NASA. Although the initiatives differed, all were accomplished through the use of the tools of strategic planning: mission clarification, environmental assessment, the matching of opportunities and resources, constant communication and engagement, and adjustment of the plan in response to changing circumstances.

At NASA, administrator Dan Goldin used strategic planning to cope with an unanticipated $5 billion cut in the wake of the

government cutback message of the congressional elections of 1994. Initially depressed by the size of the cut, Goldin used the cuts as an opportunity to revolutionize the agency—focusing the agency on its core mission and using the tools of privatization, decentralization, and downsizing to meet both budget and performance objectives (Lambright, 2001). The success of Goldin's efforts was symbolized by the July 4, 1997, landing of the Pathfinder spacecraft on Mars. Pathfinder cost $171 million, whereas its far less effective predecessor, Mars Observer, cost $1 billion. In the spirit of the NPR, Goldin had used strategic planning to shape NASA into an agency that was truly better, faster, and cheaper (Lambright, 2001).

How to Develop and Implement Strategy

A strategy is not just a written document. It is a way of thinking about your organization's work. A strategy helps connect objectives to activities and resource allocations. If you are operating without a clear strategy and wish to develop one, a good way to get started is to hold a retreat or even a simple brainstorming session to assess where your organization is heading.

A key element in developing an organizational strategy is to simultaneously take a long-term and a short-term perspective. Look at the programs and goals entrusted to your organization. How much progress will you make in the next several years? How will the problem you are working to solve change? How will the market for your program change? Who are your internal and external customers (those inside and outside the organization who use what you produce)? What do they want? Is it likely that resources may be cut in your program area? What highly visible and dramatic short-term accomplishments could your organization achieve to demonstrate your competence and attract additional resources? Who should do the work required to achieve your strategic goals? Should the work be contracted? How can you ensure that the work is done efficiently and effectively? Is competition feasible? Is it possible to use public organizations and reward good workers with "gainsharing"?

When the federal hazardous waste cleanup, or Superfund, program began in the 1980s, the EPA's management officials realized that they needed some quick victories to establish legitimacy. They understood that cleaning up hazardous waste sites would be a long, difficult, and complex process. In order to maintain public support, the EPA decided to focus attention on twenty waste sites that they would attempt to rapidly detoxify. The EPA's senior managers hoped that these quick cleanup actions would buy them the time they needed to develop a thorough and sophisticated program. Unfortunately, the strategically conceived plans of the EPA's managers were never carried out. The change of administration—from Carter's to Reagan's—interrupted the twenty cleanups. Reagan's new EPA administrator put Superfund on hold, pending a policy review. In many respects, the EPA never recovered from this early loss of momentum. Congress could never be convinced that the agency was serious about rapidly implementing the program. Halting the program to develop a long-term strategy impaired the EPA's ability to implement such a short-term strategy. It is usually not a good idea to stop a program dead in its tracks to reexamine its premises and develop a long-term strategy. Such a reexamination is often essential, but it must augment rather than replace existing activities.

In contrast with its experience in the Superfund program, the EPA was more successful in implementing its initial strategy for cleaning up leaking underground storage tanks. Here, the agency decided to focus its efforts on getting cleanup funds to state governments. In its first year, the EPA's Office of Underground Storage Tanks was able to fund tank cleanup programs in more than forty states. Rapidly funding state programs provided the EPA with a quick victory and bought it the time it needed to develop a long-term cleanup program.

In a similar vein, soon after taking office in 1993, HUD secretary Henry Cisneros addressed the same problem of getting housing funds out of the agency bureaucracy into the hands of builders while controlling for waste, fraud, and abuse. His strategy was based on simplifying HUD's decision structure, combining the agency's mul-

tiple programs into larger grants, and delegating the responsibility for selecting and monitoring grantees to the states. As with the EPA, rapidly funding state programs provided HUD with a quick victory and bought some time to overhaul a deeply troubled agency.

Small-scale, promising pilot projects are good candidates for quick victories. While you are attempting to develop or rethink your organizational strategy, small-scale experimental programs can (1) test your hunches about future program direction, (2) demonstrate your seriousness and sincerity, and (3) show rapid results in important program areas. As Peter Drucker (1999) argues, pilot projects are far superior to studies, market research, and computer models because they subject the new idea to the "test of reality."

The best strategies are built incrementally over time and are based on modest efforts to engender institutional learning. The objectives and activities of your strategy should not be major departures from your current programs and activities. If you envision a need for large-scale change, it is wise to think of incremental steps that could gradually bring about that change.

Charles Lindblom (1959) outlines the advantages of the incremental approach. In contrasting incrementalism with the comprehensive approach, he points out that incrementalism decreases the scope of planning analysis and allows the policymaker to gradually make policy adjustments by using information gained from the effects of past steps. Moreover, organizations, being organic creatures rather than mechanical devices, can only absorb a limited amount of change in a given period of time. The reason why many comprehensive plans end up on bookshelves collecting dust is that they attempt to accomplish too much in too short a time. The issue of organizational capability is central to the development of effective strategies.

Your organization's objectives and activities must be not only politically, socially, and economically feasible but also within your organization's ability to implement.

Effective innovation and entrepreneurship must be built on simple, manageable tasks. If you are taking risks by embarking upon

new programs, it is wise to be certain that your organization can actually carry out these new activities. Obviously, simple activities that are similar to current activities are the easiest to implement. Innovative, entrepreneurial programs are not made with magic tricks; they are built by persistent, imaginative people who, though not afraid to take risks, are well grounded in organizational reality. Move the organization forward as fast as you can, but continuously assess the feasibility of your plans.

How to Estimate What Your Organization Is Capable of Doing

The first step in estimating organizational capability is to make a frank assessment of organizational accomplishments. In order to improve performance, it is essential to measure your organization's current level of performance. What has this organization actually done? Have any environmental or internal conditions changed that might threaten the organization's continued performance?

The second step is to project what might be accomplished by the organization. This involves an assessment of individual and collective capabilities. Organizational structure is critical here. In his management classic, *Strategy and Structure* (1962), Chandler argues that organizational structure should follow organizational strategy. He believes that new strategies typically lead to administrative difficulties, declining performance, reorganization, and recovery. Organizational capability is not simply the sum of the individual talents of the organization's members but the creation of new combinations of talents and communication patterns. Reorganizations can create new working relationships better suited to a new strategy.

Although structure should be influenced by strategy, there are limits to organizational adaptation. It is also difficult to predict whether a new structure will result in more benefits than costs. As we indicated previously, reorganization disrupts informal communication patterns that may be subtle but essential to the organization's functioning. In addition, the individual talents of existing

staff members may be a more limiting factor in public sector reorganization than in private sector reorganization because public staff people are difficult to fire and in some cases difficult to transfer. Whereas in the private sector reorganization can signal major personnel changes and downsizing, a public sector reorganization may be limited to changing assignments.

This is why strategy formulation in the public sector is often better performed incrementally than comprehensively. If you develop a comprehensive organizational strategy and then hand it over to one of your organizational units that is incapable of implementing the strategy, you may have a colossal failure on your hands. If, instead, you encourage that unit to experiment with a small pilot project to test a new strategic concept, the downside risk is substantially reduced. You assess organizational capability by testing the organization's ability to perform new tasks. If the project fails, you then attempt to diagnose the failure by addressing the following questions: Was the concept wrong? Did the environment change? Was implementation flawed? Was the organization incapable of performing the necessary tasks? If so, why not? How could performance be improved?

Another element of organizational capability is the individual attitudes, values, and preferences of your staff. Strategy formulation should not be solely a top-down activity. Although you should have more knowledge of your organization's environment than any single member of your staff, the collective perceptions and knowledge of your staff can be a valuable input to strategy formulation. Recently elected New York City public advocate Betsy Gotbaum took over the New York City parks and recreation department during a severe budget shortfall. To cope with massive budget cuts, a hiring freeze, layoffs, and furloughs, Gotbaum pursued several strategies, including the implementation of TQM. She assembled planning and implementation teams of eight senior managers to oversee the TQM process. These management teams actively encouraged line managers and workers to make suggestions about the process, and in fact most of the initial projects came from

employees outside the management team (Cohen and Eimicke, 1994b, 1998).

Individual performance is an essential determinant of organizational capability. If an individual has contributed to strategy formulation and believes strongly in the strategy, it is more likely that performance will be enhanced (Golembiewski, 1990). When Donna Shalala (1998) took over the massive Health and Human Services Agency at the beginning of the Clinton administration, she deliberately made her first assistant secretary appointment from the ranks of the department's Senior Executive Service. She wanted to send a message to the agency's fifty-nine thousand employees that civil servants are important and that they would be part of her team.

Defining Success and Sequestering Resources for Strategy Formulation and Entrepreneurial Projects

It is not easy to gain control of your organization's agenda. You are being judged on your ability to manage the ongoing work assigned to your organization, and you will not be rewarded for trying to redefine that work. You take a risk in asking basic questions such as the following: Is this program actually succeeding in the real world? Who are our customers? How is success defined in this program? What are we trying to accomplish? In many public sector organizations, managers are not expected to ask such questions. They are expected to competently perform the work that they are assigned. For example, if the office you are taking over issued twenty-five hundred licenses last year at a cost of $10 per license, you will be successful if you can issue twenty-six hundred licenses at $9.75 per license. It does not matter if the licenses are relatively meaningless and no longer perform the function they were designed to accomplish. The absence of a bottom line makes it difficult to evaluate the success of a public sector organization, and success is therefore often defined in diverse ways. You can give the impression that you are a dynamic manager while accomplishing very little.

The effective public manager is interested in success in sub-stantive rather than symbolic terms. There is no point in risking the public's money and your own professional reputation for noth-ing. If your program's goal is to reduce hunger, then the number of meals served is one measure of success, but so, too, is the number of meals served to people who would not have eaten otherwise. Reducing the cost per meal is an important indicator of success—unless it is accomplished by providing poorer quality food or decreasing the quality of preparation.

A concern for quality may not be built into your organization. To develop such a concern within your own specific unit, you will need to continue the routine work while developing your own strategy for increasing quality. However, it is critical that a concern for quality and entrepreneurship be brought into the "regular work" as soon as possible. Initially, during a learning phase, you must fig-ure out some way of diverting resources and staff members from the regular work and allocating them to the development and imple-mentation of your entrepreneurial strategy or projects. This is an investment in organizational learning. However, if organizational learning is always divorced from regular work, the lessons learned will never by applied to routine tasks.

There is no magic formula for determining what level of resources you can safely divert from regular work to entrepreneur-ial and strategic projects. You should look for opportunities to rede-fine regular work as entrepreneurial or strategic projects. For example, work on your regular budget submission can be restruc-tured to include strategy development or pilot project design. A major study funded by your office can be reduced slightly in order to support a small-scale experiment. Entrepreneurial projects may be designed to pay for themselves.

The transition from an ordinary to an entrepreneurial organiza-tion can be difficult. Existing patterns of work processes can act as an almost gravitational pull, drawing staff members and funds away from new initiatives and new ways of working. You may find it necessary to establish separate task forces or to create a new organizational unit

to ensure that the new work and new work processes are not sup-
planted by the old processes and old objectives. You will also have to
devote considerable personal attention to the new work to ensure
that staffers adhere to your priorities. Ultimately, the work done on
special projects and by task forces must become your organization's
regular functions. If it remains unintegrated, you will end up sepa-
rating your organization's mind from its hands (Mintzberg, 1987).
The strategic modes of thinking that you develop should become
part of your organization's typical approach to doing business.

Identifying the Real Work That Must Be Performed to Implement Your Strategy

The key to effective strategy is to set realistic but important goals
and to maintain the connection between ends and means. Much
work in government, and in many other organizations, is performed
as a matter of habit. Even new assignments are followed in pre-
dictable steps. Basic questions often go unasked, such as, Who are
the customers? How does this task help deliver the product or ser-
vice? and Can any steps in this process be eliminated? Realistic
goals are goals that can be achieved by means of current or pro-
jected resources.

Let us assume that you are responsible for implementing a food
stamp program. The first step in formulating your strategy is to
develop a simple list or flowchart of the work involved in placing
food stamps into the hands of poor people. Having done this, you
should then talk to the people involved in service delivery to see
why they perform tasks the way they do and how they would change
the process if they could. Next, you should consult outsiders who
have been involved in similar programs (this practice is sometimes
called benchmarking) and outsiders who have been involved in
very different programs. Brainstorm and tap their imaginations.
Search for analogous situations or for ideas that might be attempted
in your program. Undertake some small-scale projects to experiment
with new ideas. Keep in mind the goal of delivering food stamps,

and analyze the work required to achieve that goal. Modify your flowchart to simplify the steps involved in delivering the service.

Focus on the customer—the recipient of the food stamps—and try to design a program that makes it easier for that customer to receive your service. Do not merely focus on simplifying the process of delivering your service (your work), but also examine service delivery from the perspective of the consumer: Does service delivery respect the dignity of the recipient? Is the process of receiving the service as quick as possible? Is the recipient made to feel like an important customer? When you focus your strategy on the "real work," you are able to draw boundaries around your organization's activity.

Many public organizations develop a huge variety of internal processes, such as policy review processes, budget processes, priority-setting procedures, personnel performance appraisals, and legal reviews. You can find yourself so wrapped up in these internal processes that you have little time to perform your real work—those tasks that are directly related to delivering products or services to your client. Although you must be a player in these internal processes and in the politics they generate, it is crucial that you not confuse bureaucratic housekeeping with the real work.

The Role of Leadership in Strategy Implementation

Implementing strategies requires leadership. Leadership is not a mystical quality possessed by charismatic individuals; rather, it is a function of management. Chester Barnard's *The Functions of the Executive* ([1938] 1968) and Philip Selznick's *Leadership in Administration* ([1957] 1984) are among the best social science works on leadership. Together, these books provide a clear picture of the meaning of organizational leadership. In thinking about this model of leadership, you may find it useful to think of a manager standing on a platform. Above the manager is the organization's environment and below is the organization's staff. The manager performs functions that involve looking "up" to the environment and looking "down" to the organization.

Looking up to the environment, the manager has two basic functions: (1) to obtain resources and (2) to defend the organization's distinctive competence. Resources the manager must obtain include money, staff members, authority, and turf. Defending distinctive competence means ensuring that the organization is perceived as being uniquely capable of performing a given set of tasks. An essential activity of administrative leadership is to promote the organization's work to the legislative branch, throughout the executive branch, and with interest groups and the public. Looking down into the organization, the manager has four principal functions: (1) to infuse the organization with value, (2) to develop the organization's distinctive competence, (3) to distribute incentives, and (4) to structure and mediate internal conflicts (Selznick, 1984; Barnard, 1968).

Infusing an organization with value involves defining an organization's mission and role and adapting that mission to the needs of organizational survival. It requires a leader to define a core set of objectives and operating principles and then to constantly communicate these values to the members of the organization. In order to infuse a sense of values, a leader must convince members to adapt and essentially absorb the organization's precepts.

Naturally, such a communication process is not a one-way street. Both manager and staff must modify their behavior and preferences in creating a living, breathing organization. The organization is transformed into a social grouping valued by its members for its own sake, exclusive of its productive purposes. Evidence of this transformation is the organization's concern for self-maintenance. Like any living being, the organization is attempting to survive. The organizational manager must nurture this organism and steer it toward productive purposes. In a healthy organization, staff members share a sense of common purpose and mutual values. In an efficient organization, this social energy is transformed into marketable products and services. The manager must be in touch with the informal social forces at work in the organization and attempt to understand and influence those forces.

The second "downward," or internal, role of the manager is to *develop the organization's distinctive competence*. This is the creation of marketable services and products. In the public sector, this translates into programs that generate political support. It requires that an organization be uniquely capable of performing some task valued by those who distribute resources. Infusing the organization with value is the process of stimulating an organization to share the same goals and attitudes.

Gordon Chase (Chase and Reveal, 1983) describes how, when he first became a health administrator, he would ask his commissioners and senior managers what they had been doing. Initially, some of his senior officials would answer by telling him how many meetings they had attended, how many memos they had written, and how many staff members they had hired. Chase would respond, "But whom did you make healthy today? Did you make anyone in New York healthier—and how do you know?" (p. 177) Chase's goal was to redirect his senior officials' perspectives toward the services they were to provide. Developing distinctive competence stimulates the organization to behave productively. This is achieved by setting realistic goals and developing standard operating procedures.

The third internal role of the manager is to *distribute incentives*. Incentives are used to motivate the organization's staff to act in desired ways. A manager must direct incentives with an understanding of an individual's talents and preferences. Selznick ([1957] 1984) considers one primary function of leadership to be the understanding of an organization's informal social structure. By understanding your staff's values, preferences, communication patterns, and relationships, you can direct incentives and stimulate productivity.

This is why leadership cannot be practiced from behind a desk. You must get out and learn about the social organism you manage—in order to influence it. Tom Peters and Nancy Austin (1985) advocate "managing by wandering around" (p. 8). Robert Behn (1988) has adapted this notion to the public sector; he writes about "management by groping along" (p. 64). They all note that it is difficult to manage if you sit around waiting for adequate information

to come to you. Peters and Austin (1985) point out that "hard-data-driven information is usually a day late and [is] *always* sterile" (p. 6), Peters and Austin's italics). By spending at least 25 percent of the time with staff members and customers, a manager can be in touch "with the first vibrations of the new" (p. 7). Your primary source of influence is your power to direct incentives. Successful strategy implementation requires an assessment of the incentives available to stimulate organizational change.

The final internal role of the manager and another way to exert influence is to *structure and mediate internal conflicts*. The manager plays a unique role in an organization's social structure. Disagreements and conflicts among staff members are brought to the manager to resolve. Mediating conflict is cost-free for neither organizational managers nor staff people. Employees lose influence over the final decision by allowing conflicts to percolate up the organizational ladder. Managers risk alienating some workers by deciding in favor of their organizational opponents. This final function of leadership also involves setting up processes for identifying and resolving conflict. In general, leaders should approach conflict with care. The chances of failure are great because before a conflict gets pushed up the hierarchy for resolution, positions harden, egos are engaged, and emotions are exposed.

Leadership is an important factor to be considered when you formulate and implement strategies. You need a management philosophy that works, and you need to develop the ability to listen to, learn about, and observe your environment. Bear in mind that you are never writing your strategy on a blank piece of paper. All organizations, and in fact all human enterprises, bring with them both a history and a trajectory. You must understand where the organization has been and where it is headed if you are to steer its future direction.

Even the best-laid plans often fail, and you should be modest in assuming that what you are attempting will work. It may be trite to say, but the key to recovering from failure is to learn quickly from your mistakes. In government, it is often very difficult to identify failures, and because goals are so broad and vague, it is often possi-

ble to avoid responsibility for failure. For example, if our goal is to clean up the groundwater, it is difficult to say whether our program is working if we do not know how contaminated the water is in the first place.

Nevertheless, there are certainly failures. An effort to keep graffiti off certain subway cars may not work. A municipality's effort to keep a local factory from moving may fail. A program to process licenses might fall short of its goal by 15 percent. These types of failures are inevitable. Our personal view is that failures must be quickly and explicitly identified, analyzed, and absorbed. By *absorbed*, we mean that the lessons learned should be internalized and a new effort should be launched to overcome the failure. It is critical that the staff involved in the failure not be punished for failing. Instead, focus your negative incentives on those who attempt to hide failure or are unwilling to learn from their mistakes.

How Strategy Can Help You Wake Up a Sleepy Organization

One of the greatest dangers that organizations face is that a process orientation can begin to dominate their actions. Redefining an organization's objectives, activities, and resource allocations can help combat such organizational ossification. You must remind people why they joined the organization in the first place. Get them to focus on the real work rather than the fake work that develops out of organizational habit.

The Importance of a Sense of Purpose

As we mentioned in Chapter Three, one of the primary motivators of public sector employees is their desire to be involved in critical missions. It is important to build on that predisposition and explicitly connect the work of your organization to important objectives. When staff members do not understand how their work fits into the accomplishment of larger objectives, their work can deteriorate

into ritual. A sense of purpose elicits extra effort. People realize the consequences of nonperformance and share in the rewards of collective accomplishment.

There is something thrilling about the articulation of important public policy goals. Think how motivating it is to hear recordings of Martin Luther King Jr. describe his dream for his children to live in a world of racial equality. People are still inspired when they watch the video of John F. Kennedy telling Congress that the United States should set the goal of reaching the moon by 1970. Connecting ends to means, or strategy formulation, is a never-ending task. Objectives and activities must be constantly redefined and reinvigorated with new life and renewed energy.

Communicating Higher Expectations

To wake up your organization, you may need to shout, stomp on the ground, and rattle the foundation. You will need to communicate your organization's mission and its strategy for accomplishing that mission. This is a continuing process of teaching, listening, and communicating with the people who work for you and with you. You must learn how to use your organization's purpose to motivate work. Simultaneously, you must develop the sensitivity to listen to and learn from the people who work for and with you. Understand what they expect from you. Try to perform up to their expectations or try to change those expectations.

Turning an organization around is a collective enterprise. Managers who consider themselves better than their staff members are usually unsuccessful in communicating higher expectations. The process of communicating higher expectations requires mutual respect. When such respect is established, it becomes easier to use the organization's mission as a means of motivation. Without mutual respect, the communication rings hollow and seems manipulative. Under such circumstances, it tends to fail. The point here is that simply articulating missions and strategies is necessary but not sufficient. The manager must engage the organizational organ-

ism and develop communication channels and relationships in order to facilitate the dissemination of managerial messages and the feedback of staff preferences.

What to Do with the Work You Are Given

Since most public managers report to somebody, few are able to take on assignments simply because they seem interesting. Work is assigned to you by your boss, and your organizational strategy is constrained by the nature of the assignments. We know a senior manager who operates by a fairly simple rule: she never does anything the first time she is asked to do it. Her theory is that if the task is important enough, it will generate a second request. If it is not, it will die a silent death in her in-basket. We would not recommend this approach, but it is easy to understand the time demands that generated it.

How to Evaluate Whether an Assignment Is Worth Doing

You can evaluate most assignments according to three criteria: the source of the assignment, the importance of the task, and the formality of the assignment. If the assignment comes from a person to whom you are directly accountable and if it appears to be a priority for this individual, it is probably worth doing. If the assignment fits within your organizational strategy or can be made to fit within the strategy, it is also worth doing. If, however, the assignment seems irrelevant or unimportant, it may be wise either to avoid the assignment or to provide a symbolic or partial response. Finally, if you receive a written order with an assignment number in some sort of tracking system, you will probably want to follow through on the assignment. Conversely, if you receive a casual request from a disorganized person three levels higher than you in the organizational hierarchy, it may be safe to ignore the request.

In general, it is important to be responsive to high-priority requests. However, to do this you must be able to judge the impor-

tance of an assignment. Logically, if you do not prioritize assignments, you must treat them all equally. If you treat all assignments equally, you will devote the same effort to low-priority tasks that you devote to high-priority tasks. Your professional reputation as a manager depends on your ability to complete important assignments, which you will not be able to do if you do not occasionally shed assignments you judge to be less important. Nearly every manager goes through the process of prioritizing and shedding assignments. Some prioritize and shed work explicitly, whereas others do it almost accidentally. Generally, it is politically unwise to advertise the fact that you are ignoring "orders." However, it is important to keep a record of the assignments you have ignored: you should maintain a sufficient paper trail to defend your decision to ignore or "delay" an assignment.

Determining the priority of the work you are assigned requires that you study your organization's work and your manager's preferences. It also requires that you have a vision and a strategy. If you are simply a repository for other people's priorities, you will have no basis for deciding which work to seek and which to avoid. The firmest basis for deciding whether an assignment is worth doing is whether it fits into your overall organizational strategy. There are other reasons for undertaking tasks, but in the long run there is no substitute for a sense of organizational purpose. Most assignments are the result of interaction between you and your colleagues; they are not formal orders. If you have a clear sense of purpose, you can prevent some assignments from ever being given, and you can modify other assignments before they are finalized.

How to Get Out of Bad Assignments and Attract Good Ones

How do you get to Carnegie Hall? Practice, practice, practice. Attracting good work is simply a matter of producing good work. We are certain that there are a variety of political games you can play to attract plum assignments, but if your performance is inade-

quate, you will not attract interesting work. Political posturing is relatively useless in the long run, whereas engaging in internal politics is a necessary part of your job. You must advertise your organization's success and capabilities. Senior managers are too busy to look for you; you must tell them what you have accomplished.

Getting out of bad assignments is a bit trickier. Every organization must accept some portion of the government's drudge work. Good organizational citizenship requires that you do some work that does not fit directly into your mission or adhere to your priorities. It is a matter of degree. If you believe that your organization has been given too high a proportion of bad assignments, you should attempt to shed some of them. One approach to getting out of bad assignments is to do your other work so well that you can afford to fail at a bad assignment.

Another strategy is to force senior management to trade a bad old assignment for a bad new assignment. This keeps your collection of unimportant work at a steady state. Another strategy is to pressure management to trade an assignment you know it values for an assignment you wish to discard. Finally, you can simply ignore the bad assignment.

Generally, the best approach to a bad assignment is to grin and bear it. If possible, reduce the level of effort devoted to such tasks. Generally, however, it is risky to give the appearance that you think you are too good for certain types of tasks. Projecting a can-do attitude is extremely important. You compromise that image by attempting to get out of undesirable tasks.

What to Do If Your Situation Is Hopeless and Your Assignments Are Clear Losers

If your assignments are obviously losers, find a new job immediately. If that is not feasible, develop a turnaround strategy. Analyze your agency's work and look for important tasks that are falling between the cracks; if your organization has the capability to undertake these tasks, just do them. In addition, project new markets about to

open and move into them. Naturally, you will be limited by your organization's legal and budgetary authority as well as by the policy priorities of your superiors. However, within those constraints, it is possible to identify new work that could be used to turn your unit around. While some senior managers will feel threatened by your initiatives, others will support you. At a minimum, your work life will become more bearable. Assuming that you cannot be fired, the worst that could happen is that you might be transferred to another organization.

It is also important to examine your own assessment of the hopelessness of your situation and the relative worth of your assignments. It could be that the work is important but not visible enough to gratify your ego or the collective ego of your staff. It could also be that the work is being done so poorly that assignments that could be winners are perceived as losers. In short, your real problem might not be your organization's mission but its attitude.

How to Ensure That Your Organization's Work Is Ethical

Public management is a public trust. You have been given the tremendous responsibility of carrying out the public's business. Therefore, it is your responsibility to ensure that you and others in your organization behave in an ethical manner.

How to Assess the Ethics of Your Assignments

It is not easy to analyze the ethical dimensions of public programs. There are few absolute, universal rules of morality; however, you must still judge the morality of the work you are given. Although some clear ethical principles exist and it is generally considered wrong to get involved in stealing, lying, and killing, governments are always engaged in all of these practices. Therefore, you must make personal value and moral judgments about the type of activities you are willing to perform. These judgments should not be

made casually, and when taken seriously, they can require profoundly disturbing choices. The best public managers develop an acute appreciation of the ethical dimensions of public decisions.

Ethics in government does not typically involve consideration of new issues. Ethical issues are deeply rooted in the development of human civilization and are addressed by all of the holy books of Eastern and Western religions. What is justice? What is appropriate charity and social responsibility? What is correct or moral behavior? What is legitimate authority? Public servants face these and other ethical issues all the time. They are recurring themes. In Henrik Ibsen's classic drama *An Enemy of the People* (1903), a community notable faces the choice of either revealing his knowledge that a town's public baths are contaminated or keeping the information private to protect the town's economy. The analogy to modern environmental and public health policy is obvious, although we suspect that many contemporary environmental managers would relish the prospect of such a clear-cut trade off. Typically, ethical issues are far from black and white. In the mid-1980s, Oliver North lied to the Congress of the United States. He believed that his actions were justified by the higher cause of national defense. Franklin Roosevelt certainly deceived Congress with the same justification during World War II. Of course, FDR was fighting a declared war and a widely acknowledged threat from Japan and Nazi Germany. North was fighting what he perceived to be the subtle threat of worldwide communism. North was also acting despite a specific prohibition by Congress. Although we find it easy to agree with FDR's ethical choice and easy to disagree with North's, we do not believe that these are simple or clear-cut ethical issues.

Assessing the ethical content of your assignments requires that you project the likely effects of your actions and then analyze those effects according to your own concepts of morality. It might sound frightening to have each individual apply a personal definition of morality to public actions, but we have little alternative. We will simply have to hope that we share enough common values and moral precepts to make sensible, consistent, and ethical

public policy. We believe that the greatest danger is not deliberately unethical government policy but *inadvertently* unethical public policy. In the crush of fast-moving events, ethical reflection is considered a luxury. Managers are not rewarded for taking the time to seriously consider the morality of their actions. Nevertheless, it is essential that managers weigh the ethics of the programs and policies they set in motion (Bowman, 1991).

How to Assess the Ethics of Your Relationships with Private Parties

Public servants live an official and unofficial life. We all have friends in and out of the profession. We sometimes exchange gifts and we sometimes pick up each other's tab at a restaurant. If you work in government and there is *any* chance that a gift could be perceived as a bribe, *do not accept it.* If you are at a restaurant with a vendor or a regulated party, pay your own way. If you are making an investment, be certain that it has no relationship to your official responsibilities.

If you work in government, do not expect to make a lot of money. If you need more money, leave government work. The expertise and skills you have developed in the public sector will probably be marketable in the private sector. Once you have left government work, do not recontact your old agency until ethics rules permit. Corruption often starts small—say, with a free lunch or a bottle of scotch at Christmas. If you do not draw an absolute line, soon you may be rationalizing larger and less subtle payoffs. By refusing all gifts, you avoid the need to analyze which ones to accept. We realize that this may force you to be less sociable than you might prefer, but it is simply the price of public service.

What to Do If You Consider an Assignment Unethical

Albert Hirschman (1970) identifies three choices you have if you disagree with an assignment: you can leave the organization (exit), you can go public with your opposition (voice), or you can mute

your opposition in order to retain your influence within the organization (loyalty). Essentially, the same choices are open to you if your disagreement is based on ethics. It is true that operating in the real world involves compromise and accommodation, but every individual must draw the line somewhere.

The Nuremberg trials of Nazis charged as war criminals after World War II demonstrated that individual public servants are accountable to universal ethical standards. If you believe an assignment is wrong, try to reverse the decision; if you fail, then you must weigh the three options Hirschman (1970) identifies. There is no prescription we can offer for weighing these ethical choices. You will not last long in any organization if you see every decision as an ethical choice. But you will not sleep well if you violate your own code of morality.

Some Ethical Guidance

We have devoted a great deal of time and writing to providing practical and specific ethical guidance for those working in public service (Cohen and Eimicke, 1996, 1999; Cohen, Eimicke, and Perez-Salazar, 2000). Lengthy ethical statutes and detailed booklets from ethics commissions often get mired in advising what one should not do, providing little useful advice regarding the best course of action in a difficult situation. What follows are five guidelines that have stood the test of time and effectiveness for us. We hope they are equally viable for you.

1. *Seek justice under the law*. We have struggled with this first principle. Obeying the law seems an obvious first step toward ethical professional conduct. Many important public ethics documents begin with this directive (Locke, 1952; Lewis, 1991; Wilson, 1993; Frederickson, 1997). Yet as we contemplate obeying the law, our thoughts immediately turn to Nazi Germany's laws against Jews and the disabled, the Jim Crow laws against African Americans, the Apartheid laws of South Africa, and the caste system in India.

Sometimes, it takes public servants with ethical principles to find a way around a bad law to achieve justice. Nevertheless, if your preferred course of action requires breaking the law, it probably needs to be rethought.

2. *Serve the public interest.* Locke (1952) defined the public interest as the will of the majority. Most decisions cannot be delayed until a public opinion poll is conducted. However, public hearings on major public projects and Internet feedback questions are often feasible. We also recommend a reflective self-analysis of a course of action, according to Walter Lippmann's criteria of "what men would choose if they saw clearly, thought rationally and acted disinterestedly and benevolently" (1955, p. 42).

3. *Ensure thorough analysis.* Experts in the bureaucracy are often the only public officials with the knowledge and tools to accurately assess the expected outcome and impact of public decisions. Civil service protections and the absence of political ambition contribute to this more reasoned decision-making process. Still, the connection between competence and the morality of public policymaking is not always made. Carol Lewis (1991) suggests that incompetence be treated as an abuse of office. We agree. Making a decision without the appropriate level of technical skill and knowledge is a dereliction of duty. Exercising such incompetence at the public's expense is a violation of the public's trust, an abuse of office, and a breach of ethics.

Even when public servants have unimpeachable motivations, public projects can still be plagued by cost overruns, faulty fiscal analysis, and deficient planning. In the current environment of privatization and outsourcing, these problems are exacerbated as public administrators negotiate with private business people who have much more information and access to technical expertise than they do. This asymmetry of information is probably unavoidable. However, the effective public manager can mitigate these challenges by following a few simple rules: don't be afraid to make mistakes of commission, follow the lessons of past experience, and negotiate contracts that permit modification as better information becomes available.

4. *Act with compassion and empathy.* We believe that ethical public behavior extends beyond compliance with the law, professional competence, and attention to the will of the majority. Otherwise, popularly elected tyrants could convince civil servants to enforce laws that repress unpopular minorities. To protect against this, we recommend that public officials seek to administer laws and regulations with compassion for those affected. Frederickson (1997) characterizes this quality as benevolence—"a disinterested love of others" (p. 202).

5. *Take personal responsibility for decisions.* Ethical public administrators must accept personal responsibility for their decisions and the impact of those decisions over time. We have identified a simple test to assess whether you are accepting personal responsibility for an official action. Before making a difficult public policy choice, envision your decision and the process that led to your making it as the lead story in tomorrow morning's leading newspaper and on the top television and radio networks. If fair coverage of your action would make your family, friends, and colleagues proud, or at least unconcerned, then proceed. If the story presents the prospect of sleepless nights, stop where you are and immediately seek the advice and assistance of your superior.

Chapter Eleven

Dealing with the Media, Legislative Bodies, and Interest Groups

Keeping the public informed is one of the duties of public officials in a democracy. This duty applies to appointed as well as elected officials (Lee, 2000). Communication with the public falls into several categories. First, there is public reporting—post hoc communication by a public agency on its activities to the public at large. Historically, this type of communication often came in the form of a written annual report. Today, it might also include periodic informational mailings, public posters and kiosks, and an Internet Web page.

Another type of public agency information might come in the form of efforts to increase citizen participation in public policy formation. Public hearings and forums are often held to inform the public and gauge public opinion on an important and potentially controversial public policy decision—for example, a fare increase for public bus and subway riders or the siting of a homeless shelter.

A third form of public information seeks to improve public service to the citizen and customer. The message might focus on new and easier ways to renew drivers' licenses, pay parking tickets, or to access free flu shots. Television and radio public service announcements, billboards, posters, fliers, and newspaper stories also inform the public about fire safety, availability of flood insurance, free child health care coverage, business tax incentive programs, and the dangers of lead-based paint.

Today, the most common and controversial form of public information involves responding to requests for information from the media. As television has come to dominate the news media, the focus on government tends to be on elected officials—particularly, chief

executives. With the ever more intense competition for an audience (and the advertising dollars that follow the eyeballs), crime, disasters, and other types of bad news are more often the focus of reporters. It has also been observed that the prevailing media attitude toward government has shifted from skeptical to cynical (Carter, 1996; Lee, 1999). Typical media stories about government highlight incompetence, fraud, abuse, and arbitrary, uncaring attitudes among bureaucrats.

Some public managers have extensive dealings with the outside world and others have very little outside contact. Those involved in local service delivery, such as police services or garbage collection, often find themselves directly on the media firing line. However, even those managers with little external contact occasionally find themselves in the public eye. Unanticipated public exposure can be a terrifying experience.

Well-managed agencies have very specific standard operating procedures for dealing with the media. All inquiries from the media should be referred to the public information office, and that office is responsible for official statements to the media and the public. Even with the best procedures in the world, you may find yourself cornered by a media professional who assures you that he or she is on the side of the agency and that everything you say will be off the record and not for attribution.

This chapter is designed to help you cope with the world outside your agency by providing some guidance on media relations as well as dealing with legislatures, overhead agencies, and interest groups. Your relations with the public (as a consumer and citizen) can also play a role in determining your success as a public manager. Although the best advice is to leave these responsibilities to your agency professionals, an innovative and effective public manager should have solid communications skills.

How to Deal with the Media

The mass media is often the public manager's most effective method of communicating with the public. This is particularly true for organizations that are not in regular contact with the public, such as reg-

ulatory agencies, overhead agencies, agencies serving special populations, and the armed forces. Community leaders and decision makers from the public, private, and nonprofit sectors monitor the work of government organizations through the print and electronic media. It is very difficult for an agency to obtain political support and resources if it has a negative media image. Dealing effectively with the media is critical to organizational survival.

The Best Defense Is a Good Offense

The best way to stay out of trouble is to take an activist approach to media relations. Unfortunately, bad news seems to be more marketable than good news. No one wants a bad news story, but public managers must learn to deal with the reality that some bad news, along with some good news, is better than no news at all. As recent surveys by the Council for Excellence in Government suggest, an open and accessible policy toward the media will prove beneficial over time (Michaels, 2001; Linsky, 1986b).

In taking an activist approach, you not only get more coverage, you also have more control over that coverage and can increase the probability that the coverage will be positive. When an agency does not cooperate with the media, there is a natural tendency to believe that the agency has something to hide. In addition, the media have an interest in providing news stories. That is what they are paid to do. By avoiding comment, or making it difficult for them to learn about what your organization is doing, you make it harder for them to do their job. If you make their life more difficult, you increase the odds that they will make your life more difficult. If, however, you go out of your way to provide them with access and handouts that make it easier to report your activities, you just might receive a slightly more positive tilt in their coverage.

Just as important is the fact that bad news does not improve over time. Faced with the reality of a bad story, getting all the news out as quickly as possible may minimize the number of days the story is in the headlines. The more reporters know about the complicated problems of policy issues, the more likely they are to see

that you are doing the best that can be done in a bad situation. And the sooner you get your story out, the better chance you have of shaping public opinion regarding the situation rather than having others shape that perspective for you.

There are also issues a public agency seeks to generate public interest in through a public service campaign (Lee, 1998–1999; Weiss and Tschirhart, 1994; Rice and Atkin, 1989). Public service campaigns have been waged for a wide range of issues—such as preventing forest fires, discouraging smoking and drunk driving, advocating recycling, and conserving energy. The media can be passively involved in these campaigns through the required airing of public service ads. Electronic and print media can also be actively involved in assisting public interest campaigns through the development of news stories on such issues as healthy babies campaigns, regular checkups for breast cancer, and on-site coverage of holiday roadside sobriety checkpoints. Obviously, the media are involved in helping this public agency discourage drunk driving. However, whether you as a manager choose to take an activist or a reactivist approach, you should be aware of some fundamentals of media relations.

Over the longer term, agencies that are successful in dealing with the media approach the public information function strategically. These agencies identify goals for their public relations functions and pursue them methodically. To do this successfully, agencies should also focus on enhancing the oral and written communication skills of all employees—particularly those of staff members directly responsible for external relations. In the jargon of modern political communications, "spin" is the term often used to describe how a spokesperson for an organization interprets a story attracting media attention. An effective spin practitioner, or "spin doctor," is able to effectively frame a problem or issue for the media and the public.

An example might be the management of the public housing issue during the Clinton presidency. Although a triumph of positive public policy during the Great Depression and Second World War years, public housing projects were overwhelmed by overcrowding, poor maintenance, loss of inner-city jobs, antifamily wel-

fare policies, segregation, drugs, and crime during the sixties, sev-
enties, and eighties. President Reagan's HUD secretary, Jack Kemp,
made some progress on the issue, advocating community develop-
ment, tenant ownership, and more economic integration. How-
ever, the media image of HUD, generally, and public housing,
specifically, remained very negative.

During the Clinton years, HUD secretary Andrew Cuomo and
his staff successfully spun the issue so that they were fighting against
the long-established policies of their own agency. Major housing
projects were evacuated and demolished, which provided excellent
photo opportunities. The already-established policies of low-rise
development, home ownership, community development, and
economic integration were repackaged, polished, constantly rein-
forced, and effectively implemented. Although the public housing
stock still requires major attention, because the Clinton adminis-
tration effectively managed public information regarding this trou-
bled program, it received credit for solving the problem rather than
being blamed for a program that could have been seen as a failure.

Why the Media Are Interested in Your Organization

Public management generally involves spending the public's
money and conducting activities that the public considers impor-
tant. As we indicated in Chapter Two, government's failure to
enact, for example, national health care legislation might attract
widespread media attention, whereas the failure of a private busi-
ness is generally not news. It is typical for the media to be inter-
ested in your organization when the public is. When policy issues
enter the political agenda, they bring with them media attention.

Some issues, such as crime and the economy, have persistent
agenda status—probably because of their dramatic content and
because such issues materially affect the quality of life for a large
percentage of the media outlet's audience. Other issues, such as
global trade, terrorism, information technology, income inequality,
international human rights, homelessness, global warming, and

AIDS, are relatively new agenda items. All of these issues share a scope and nature that requires that government participation be effectively addressed.

With the rise of television as the primary source for news, there has been a dramatic shift in news content toward visuals, drama, and spectacle (Lee, 1999). As broadband and access to the Internet expand rapidly, the competition for "new" news will likely intensify. Whereas television network news has created the "thirty second news item," the Internet may create a market for more news—in more depth and on a range of issues—with narrow but global audiences. And stories on the Internet potentially have a much longer shelf life. However, in television, six-hundred-channel cable and satellite packages are creating more opportunities for news.

The media play a central role in our political process. When public opinion is undecided, the rhetoric and face of the issue can have a profound impact (Kelman, 1987). The administration of President Ronald Reagan used dramatic physical settings to create a positive association, with the policy initiative being championed by the president. Former senator William Proxmire used the imagery of his Golden Fleece Awards (such as the four-hundred-dollar hammer purchased by the Defense Department) to focus public attention on what he believed to be wasteful public spending.

Media coverage of government is often negative. Therefore, it is not surprising that most public managers wish the media would simply disappear and let them do their jobs in peace. However, when the media are interested in your organization, it is because it is their job to be interested. As a public servant, your role is to understand the key role the media play in a stable democratic process and, where possible, you should help them do their job. Sometimes, the results might even be beneficial.

Why the Media Sometimes Distort What You Say

In general, the media are concerned with communicating to the largest possible audience. In order to accomplish this goal, information is condensed, details are omitted, and a very simplified ver-

sion of an event or issue is reported. This is especially the case with television news coverage (Lee, 1999; Jamieson and Campbell, 1992; Linsky, 1986a). Television news items do not attempt to explain an event or even to present a complete account of it. TV coverage is structured around short news items that attract attention and do not try to explain the complexities of an issue. The goal is a sensational and popular story. This incomplete presentation of facts is most noticeable in television reporting, but print media coverage is becoming less comprehensive as well. It is often rationalized that this phenomenon is due to intense competition among an ever-expanding number of media outlets, including the Internet and, increasingly, the mobile Internet.

Whereas investigative reporting often presents more detail on a particular story, most newspaper articles are only brief, condensed versions of actual events. Furthermore, the degree of bias within the story will vary according to the type of article. Commentaries and editorials admit a point of view, whereas "straight news" stories are supposed to simply present the facts. Too often, you have the feeling that controversy makes the story. When the reporter calls, the story is completed, except for the blanks where your quote will verify the conclusion or represent the reporter's yeoman attempt to represent all sides of the issue (Carter, 1996).

Even if a reporter attempts to write a complete and unbiased story, any quotation or opinion stated out of context can appear to mean something different from what it was intended to mean. Reporters work under extraordinary time constraints and deadlines. Yesterday's newspaper's only value is lighting a fire or wrapping a fish.

Media distortion can also result from a reporter simply not understanding what you have said. Reporters are generally communications specialists and issue generalists. Miscommunication can easily result from their lack of technical knowledge or your assumptions regarding prior knowledge and general understanding of industry jargon. Reporters also make mistakes. So do government managers. The effective public manager takes the long view on media relations, seeking to get the facts right and create a positive public image of his or her agency and its mission. And in the

end, you and the reporter may have very different priorities. Reporters need to make news. And the making of news can be your worst nightmare.

Knowing the Rules of the Game

To ensure the best possible press coverage of your organization, it is helpful to treat journalists as colleagues. This type of relationship can be a key to achieving successful press relations. Linsky (1986b) notes, "If policy makers know the conventions of the press, they will be better able to develop their own ways of dealing with journalists so as to maximize their chances of achieving their policy goals" (p. 205).

If you accord people in the media the same respect you would other professionals inside and outside your organization, you will have conquered the most difficult task in media relations. Remember that, as professionals, media people have the same types of responsibilities you do: they have deadlines to meet, demands to satisfy, and bosses to please. And you are both ultimately accountable to the public. Therefore, it is mutually beneficial for you to work well together. Moreover, if you do not learn to treat reporters with respect, they may very well try to present you in a less than flattering light.

To develop a solid working relationship with those in the media, show respect for their professional responsibilities. If you want coverage of an event or if you plan to hold a press conference, give ample notice. Provide members of the press with the information they need to cover the story. If possible, anticipate their needs and give them information before they ask for it. Treat all press representatives with equal respect. Do not exclude certain reporters or publications for ideological or personal reasons.

Ethics, integrity, and our personal experience suggest that honesty is always the best policy. Do not try to withhold or distort information. The media will often have more information than you give them, and they can use it to your detriment. These basic rules

of the media game are generally applicable to any organization operating in the public arena, whether the legal structure is public, private for-profit, or private nonprofit.

Learning the Tricks of the Trade

To understand the importance of media relations, it is crucial to understand how much influence the media can have on your organization's everyday operation and also to understand the role the media can play in "building and sustaining support inside and outside the government" (Linsky, 1986b, p. 11). The media can play a key role in presenting the story as you want the public to see it. The most important aspect of your press strategy is to maintain close communication with your press contact people. Give them the information they need in good form, and this will help in getting information presented the way you want it to be. A well-written and carefully constructed press release has a good chance of being quoted verbatim. It also saves the press precious time in writing. Making yourself available at a press conference or at a specific time in your office to talk with media representatives is another way of facilitating the coverage you want. Always try to give reporters as much time as they want. It never hurts to put a bit of thought into what might make a catchy sound bite on your issue, too.

When you are providing the press with the information you want them to have, it is very important to be well informed about issues that relate to the information you are providing. If the issue is complex, develop or have others develop a notebook with questions and proposed responses. Your press person should have ready and rapid access to subject matter experts. You should be able to anticipate questions about the drawbacks or negative aspects of your program and be prepared to present a rational and clear defense of it. Be circumspect when you release information and speak to the press. You should not systematically exclude any media outlets from obtaining access to your information, but you may want to provide early "exclusive" access to your story to a specific

outlet in order to influence first impressions of your story's presentation and reach key opinion makers in the best light possible.

Try to anticipate the reaction your information will elicit from your boss, key interest groups, legislators, and the public. It is important to avoid careless statements, and it is also important to avoid vague, euphemistic language. Television in particular has a way of making you look like a criminal if you appear even slightly reluctant to discuss an issue.

Following all of these tips on media relations should help you avoid misrepresentation of the facts. However, if you feel that the media have treated your organization unfairly or misinformed the public, you should have a strategy for dealing with this situation as well. Bill and Hillary Clinton dealt with wide-ranging criticism of their health care reform package from insurance industry representatives, the medical profession, Congress, and a number of media analysts. They directly confronted the criticism in a variety of ways, including giving presentations to friendly forums around the country, which were sure to attract substantial local coverage regardless of the subject matter. They and their administrative surrogates appeared on numerous talk shows and even on MTV to speak to the public without a media analyst filter. They even went so far as to appear on a network television comedy show to spoof one of the most effective paid media campaigns against their program. Less important than whose facts were right was the fact that the administration had specific mechanisms for responding to what they claimed was unjust coverage. These responses are good examples of how you can react if you feel the media have been unfair to your organization. They exemplify an aggressive strategy that takes media messages seriously and works hard to correct the media when they are wrong.

Finally, the public manager should consider the potential impact of using the media as a marketing tool. Although this strategy requires a lot of effort and a very strong press operation, it may be the best way of communicating important or even urgent messages to the public. Increasingly, citizens learn about important

social issues through the mass media, and they decide how to act toward the issue, based on what they see and read (Moore, 1995). Therefore, many public agencies seek to modify public behavior through public education marketing campaigns aimed at combating such problems as drug and alcohol abuse, smoking, and AIDS.

The most important trick of the trade is to be clear and honest when communicating through the media. Take the function of media relations seriously and as a routine job of your agency. If your office does not have the luxury of being insulated from the public and is involved in hot issues, you should cultivate an informal professional relationship with reporters. If you find yourself in over your head, do not hesitate to call on professional press relations staff people for advice. If dealing with the media becomes so time-consuming that you cannot get your other work done, establish or contract with an organization to manage and possibly conduct your media relations.

Preparing Information for the Media

One of the most effective strategies for obtaining positive media coverage is to provide reporters with information in a form that is ready for their use. To do so, your agency must be in constant contact with media representatives. Press and television jobs tend to be characterized by rapid turnover, and contact people change regularly. Always know, or have a press person who always knows, who the current contact person is for your particular media concern. When sending out information, make sure it is directed to the correct person, or it may never see the light of day.

Keep yourself informed of specific formal requirements for information you submit to the media. Most press releases and public service announcements (PSAs) must meet certain criteria. For example, PSAs often cannot be longer than thirty seconds when read aloud. The most common oversight in written submissions to the media is the failure to include basic information such as the date, time, and place of an event, as well as the name of the person in your

organization who can provide further details. Keep the information simple and to the point.

Equally important in getting the message out is being aware of the media's schedule. Find out how long in advance a release must be received in order for the media to provide coverage. Many organizations send out press releases months in advance of an event and then wonder why the event does not get coverage. Others are equally confused when they deliver releases the day before and the event is not mentioned in the next day's paper. Each station or publication will have its own deadlines, and you must keep on top of them. As a general rule, the earlier in the day you provide the information, the higher the probability that it will be covered. The closer the photo opportunity is to the newsroom, the greater the chance that a camera crew will be dispatched. Weekends are slower news days, so the chance of coverage is greater, but the audience will often be smaller. Finally, always follow up on any written submissions to the media with a phone call. This not only draws attention to your issue but also allows you to provide any missing information or further details. By catering to the media's needs in this way, you show that you care about the coverage and thereby increase your chances of at least getting evenhanded treatment.

Keep in mind that many times the issues you believe are important are not covered because the media does not consider them newsworthy. Of course, the media can make mistakes and miss an important issue. You know more about the issue and have a deeper appreciation of its significance, but you are so close to the issue that it can be difficult for you to judge how the average person might react to your story. It may be useful to discuss your story with a reporter; doing so may identify the "angle" that makes your issue worthy of scarce media time or space.

In many public organizations, media relations must be cleared through a central press office. Often, these offices are staffed by experienced media professionals, and they can be a real asset when you are dealing with the media. Although these staff people may not be experts in your field, they generally have a good general

understanding of your agency and the priorities of senior management. They also have experience and relationships with the media organizations that cover your agency. You and your media person must become a team in effectively communicating the significance and detail of an issue that has attracted the media's attention.

The Importance of Media Relations

In some public organizations, you will find that you are too low in the hierarchy to be permitted to deal with the media or in too obscure an issue area to attract media attention. Most public programs have the potential to develop into salient political issues. If you are in a hot-issue area, media relations can be a matter of organizational survival. It may be easier to be anonymous at the federal level than at the local level. In any event, you should be prepared to deal with the media if you attract their attention, and you should consider using the media to communicate with your customers. In some respects, no media coverage is only slightly better than bad media coverage. At the very least, media criticism implies that what your organization is doing is important. Overall, public relations will be easier if you take an activist approach in dealing with the media. As Kelman (1987) observes, "what generates good (or bad) attention in the media is generally whether people have sought to do the right thing or whether they have instead acted selfishly" (p. 253). (See also Linsky, 1986b.)

How to Keep Legislatures, Overhead Agencies, and Interest Groups Satisfied

Legislatures, overhead agencies, and interest groups are organized groups that, though external to the public manager's organization, can nevertheless have great influence on its daily operations. Of the three groups, legislatures have the greatest direct ability to influence an agency's operation through the budget approval process and legislative review or oversight, which is often exercised

through the mechanism of public hearings. These external organizations, along with private sector contractors and partners, are increasingly sophisticated and demanding of public agencies (Emmert, Crow, and Shangraw, 1993).

The Importance of Outside Organizations

Legislative committees, appropriations committees, and committees on government operations monitor the administration of programs (Fesler, 1980). They review the operation of agencies and have the authority to set budget and staffing levels. Furthermore, by enacting legislation that affects an agency's programs, legislatures help direct the agency's substantive focus. The legislative committee with oversight over your agency is second only to your manager's direct superior in terms of the attention you must pay to accountability (Moore, 1995). In reality, this sort of direction setting is an interactive process that involves bargaining among career professionals in the agency and in the legislature and among elected officials and politicians throughout the executive and legislative branches. They may have legal authority over your agency, but your agency has the knowledge and capacity to deliver goods and services to the public. You need each other.

Overhead agencies and special interest groups have an indirect but often significant influence on an organization's operation. Overhead agencies in some jurisdictions are enormously powerful players in government operations. Budget offices at the state level often determine whether a program authorized by the legislature will actually be implemented. The federal Office of Management and Budget not only reviews and approves agency budget submissions but also approves federal regulations before they are promulgated. Other overhead agencies are perhaps less visible but are equally important to government management. They are responsible for functions without which your organization could not operate. They include the budget office and personnel, as well as what is often called general services, which includes maintenance

and purchasing functions. Overhead organizations are important because they directly control the resources you require to get your job done.

Interest groups differ from legislatures and overhead agencies because they are organized entirely outside the government. These groups represent public interests in specific areas, and they are often divided in terms of single-issue interests, citizens' organizations, and professional associations. Single-issue interest groups tend to be very committed to their cause. As a result, they can be difficult groups for agencies to deal with. Citizens' organizations usually have a less direct focus and are concerned with overall governmental operation and broad policy issues, such as tax rates or increases in government spending for social welfare. Professional associations may have a connection with the public manager's employees from the employees' education or practical training and are concerned with the process, quality, and standards of program and service delivery. Interest groups are important because they influence an agency's performance on behalf of particular concerns, and they are the most common means of contact between the public manager and the public.

Interest groups are an important channel of information and a source of innovative policy proposals. They can help you identify entrepreneurial opportunities and assist you in conducting and evaluating small-scale pilot projects. You should be aware of the ability of interest groups to influence elite perceptions of your competence and performance. They can provide the important political support and lobbying assistance you may need to obtain resources or authority. If interest groups oppose what you are doing, they can make it very difficult for you to implement your programs efficiently.

These external organizations have varying degrees of influence on public agencies. A study conducted at the state level shows that although the influence of legislatures, clientele, and professional associations differs according to agency type and size, "the legislature exerts a consistently high level of influence[, whereas] clientele

groups and professional associations manifest successively less influence" (Brudney and Hebert, 1987, p. 203). This study also indicates that larger agencies are better able to isolate themselves from the influences of these outside organizations.

As an effective public manager, you need to make a concerted effort to understand the patterns of influence and the power position of specific legislators, legislative committees, and legislative staffs. Equally important is a solid understanding of the operation of the overhead agencies. Finally, you should pay close attention to the methods, political clout, and constituencies of the interest groups active in your policy area. These organizations are the key players in your organization's external environment. It is possible for them to destroy the work of your organization and in fact destroy your organization. In a more positive vein, your ability to successfully take entrepreneurial risks will depend on your ability to elicit the support of these outside groups.

What Outside Groups Are Trying to Accomplish and What They Want from Your Organization

Relations with groups outside your organization will go more smoothly if you remain aware that their mission is separate and distinct from yours. Simply put, they are not primarily concerned with programs and services. Legislators generally want to get reelected. To do this, they seek to assure that public services important to their constituents are delivered and that they get credit for that delivery in the local and national press. Some legislators also have political or ideological principles and wish to influence policy.

Overhead agencies such as budget divisions and general service units focus on economy and efficiency—doing more with less. In simple terms, they seek to please the taxpayer persona of the public. They are less concerned about what your agency does and more focused on getting your agency to perform as cheaply as possible.

Personnel offices want to ensure that hiring and promotion are based on merit. These offices are very process-oriented. They will press you to advertise widely for available positions, interview a wide range of candidates, document compliance with affirmative action and equal opportunity requirements, and choose a candidate that best fits the job description. You will often feel that they are slowing you down, but you should also appreciate that they are making sure that you comply with the law and that the hiring process is as fair and open as possible.

Special interest groups want their issues to be the focus of government attention and they want to ensure that financial contributions continue to roll in. They want you to adopt their policy position, but, in many respects, access is as important as impact. It is extremely important for these groups and their representatives to show the necessary clout to meet with the public manager in charge of their policy area. Meeting with them on a regular basis can protect you from attack, even if you do not modify your policies to meet their objectives.

In every case, these groups want credit for your agency's success when it will help them achieve their respective goals. If legislators can use your program to gain popularity or visibility with their constituents, they will be more interested in your program and will work to provide you with additional resources. They will be particularly attentive if you provide a service that is currently a hot issue or enjoys a high demand in their district—such as health care, housing, or transportation. They want to appear to be involved in satisfying their constituents' demands for service.

Overhead agencies are also extremely interested in visible agencies—those with larger budgets, more employees, and high administrative overhead expenditures. They gain recognition from curtailing growth in government and keeping total spending down. If your organization has the potential for making productivity improvements, overhead agencies are more likely to pay attention to you. This can be particularly frustrating because it is through your initiative that productivity improvements are achieved, but

overhead agencies may be quick to take credit. They may also be quick to pocket any savings you generate.

Cultivating Outside Groups

You should work hard to cultivate outside group support for your mission. Developing a working relationship with each of the three groups mentioned here can put your agency in a very favorable position. You can build a very beneficial relationship with some very simple actions.

Legislatures have the most influence over your organization and thereby represent the most important opportunity for your organization. Legislators often demand special treatment, and in many respects they are entitled to such treatment. They are elected by the people and you are not. You need to let them know that you think they are important. When they need information from your organization, treat their requests respectfully and answer them quickly. At most federal agencies, congressional requests are centrally tracked and carefully monitored by senior management. The competence of an office is in part judged by its ability to deal with "congressionals" effectively and efficiently. Perhaps the best way to impress a legislator is through positive contact with his or her constituents. If legislators do not hear complaints or, even better, if they hear positive remarks about your service, they may be satisfied that you are doing your job well. It is most important to keep legislative representatives informed about your organization's activities. They should never have reason to suspect that you are doing something behind their backs, and you should ensure that they are never taken by surprise by hearing about your organization's activities from another source. In the process of keeping legislators informed, you can develop useful outside contacts, and your staff can form working relationships with legislators' staffs while exchanging information. If an issue involving your organization arises in the legislature, you want to be certain that the legislative staff feels comfortable calling on your organization for information

and assistance. It is far better to view legislative staff members as colleagues than as opponents. Certainly, you have a mutually dependent relationship. You need their political support to survive, and they need your programs to deliver constituent services.

Overhead agencies have tremendous influence over the day-to-day operation of your organization. Their rules and operating procedures are perhaps the most difficult to understand and often seem unreasonable. For the most part, managers of public programs perceive budget, personnel, and general services agencies as a nuisance. These organizations can interfere with your operations, and they rarely understand what you are doing. They make work for you by requiring you to justify your needs for space, people, money, and equipment. They also slow down the process of obtaining these resources. However, you generally need them to acquire the basic materials of service delivery, such as space, computers, telephones, and furniture.

Often, the overhead agency process seems purposely designed to annoy managers. When employees are transferred between offices, they are sometimes assigned to a new office space without furniture. The common practice is to move their own furniture from the old office to the new office. Problems arise when the yearly furniture inventory is taken, and managers are held accountable for the furniture that has been moved to distant areas of the complex. If the managers are unaware of a system such as this one, their lives can be made miserable as they try to follow the rules, searching for missing furniture and missing pieces of their sanity. Merely being informed of the rules ahead of time makes relations with the agency much easier. In such situations, informal contacts can be very valuable. As a manager, you can use personal contacts to learn about changes in rules and informal methods of breaking bottlenecks. If you develop a working relationship with the overhead agency, you have a much better chance of being forewarned of unexpected situations.

Interest groups can be both the easiest and the most difficult outside organizations to deal with, depending on whether they support your organization's activities. In many ways, interest groups

should be treated similarly to legislatures. They will appreciate being informed of an agency's activities, with particular attention being given to new initiatives. They want to know that you take their concerns seriously and respect their interests. If you develop a solid professional working relationship with interest groups, you may be able to avoid the more public tactics they often use to attract attention. If these groups resort to media events and demonstrations to communicate with you, there is a good chance that you will lose control of the situation. However, be careful not to cater too much to special interest groups. Your organization has its own mission, which may or may not coincide with an interest group's goals. Unlike legislatures, these groups do not have any authority over your agency's operations. Although it is to your advantage to take their concerns seriously, you must avoid the perception or the reality that you are controlled by an interest group.

Informal contacts with interest groups that favor your programs can be very helpful in developing public support for those programs. These groups usually have access to sectors of the public other than those you have access to, and they can help you stay close to your customers. Interest groups can publicize an agency's programs and services as well as help identify the needs of their community. They can also help monitor the effect of your program on the real world.

Preparing for an Outside Review or Hearing

In the course of relations with the legislative branch, an agency typically encounters oversight and review sessions. Sometimes, these are routine exchanges; at other times, they are highly contentious. To be prepared, it is vital that you have some idea of your organization's standing with the reviewing body. If relations with outside agencies come to the point of a contentious review or hearing, your attempts at achieving a special working relationship with them have failed.

As William Gormley (in Lane, 1999) observes, state legislatures "discovered" the power of oversight as a form of bureaucratic con-

trol during the 1970s. The exercise of this authority became easier as state legislators became full-time professionals and their staffs expanded. Mechanisms such as sunset provisions of agency authority and legislative review of administrative rules and regulations made legislative oversight routine and pervasive in many states.

The potential for damage to your agency escalates if a routine review is replaced by an investigation. Gordon Chase (Chase and Reveal, 1983) describes legislative investigation as "war." Basically, an investigation is a situation in which the legislature has control and the game is played in its arena. To make matters worse, this is a political game at which most public managers have little experience. The proceedings allow little opportunity for the manager to present factual information from an administrative or policy perspective.

When an outside investigation or review is conducted, it is a statement that the ongoing oversight process has not been successful. It is a given that there is some procedural problem within your agency. Thus, the best preparation for a public hearing is to be well informed of the activities of your agency that are in question and to be honest, clear, and straightforward in making statements about them. Do not volunteer damaging evidence, but be prepared to speak when asked. Investigative hearings are not an opportunity to educate the public or to present a substantive defense; they are an opportunity to try to calm and satisfy the public and to reinforce the credibility of your organization.

Dealing with Conflicts Involving Outside Organizations

The public manager's first instinct, when conflicts arise with outside organizations, is to avoid these organizations. In some cases, this is possible. If your organization is not currently involved in any controversial issues, legislatures and interest groups may not be very interested in your operations. However, it is nearly impossible to avoid dealing with overhead agencies—although you can sometimes avert conflict by deferring purchases or hiring for a short time. If temporarily avoiding these outside organizations is

a possibility, it may help to keep conflicts from escalating. However, you will eventually have to interact with all or some of these outside organizations, either to obtain their services or because of their demands on you. Remember that relations with such groups can be the key to your success, so try to deal with conflicts in a professional manner.

If you must go to war with an outside organization, recruit allies and attempt to develop a rough estimate of the relative power or resources of each side of the conflict. You may hold enough cards simply to oppose an outside organization and get away with it. Some interest groups may be so weak that you can oppose them with little fear of reprisal. You may have so much credibility with your chief elected officials that you can win a battle with your budget office. But it is unlikely that you will have the power to win a conflict without any cost to your organization. Therefore, it is far better to work out compromises and seek some basis for accommodation.

When a serious conflict arises, suggest mediation. Attempt to recruit a third party to negotiate a settlement. Interest-based bargaining, developed by the Harvard Negotiation Project, advocates a focus on problems rather than people, and on interests instead of positions. Pick up a copy of *Getting to Yes* (Fisher and Ury, 1983) or Ury's *Getting Past No* (1991). Better yet, send copies to your opponent. Remember that public management involves an extreme degree of interdependency. Today's enemy might be tomorrow's ally or even tomorrow's boss. Preserve the capacity to work with your opponent on another day. If conflict is unavoidable, work very hard to keep it from becoming personal. In fact, go out of your way to reassure your opponent that your problem is with his or her position and not with his or her personality. Managing relations with outside organizations is a delicate balancing act between protecting your organization's interests and catering to theirs. You must internalize the demands of outsiders that influence your political support and resource base. At the same time, you must make certain that your organi-

zation does not lose its identity or its ability to produce its essential programs.

How to Stay Out of Trouble with the Public

The best way to stay out of trouble with the public is to pay attention. The public has a right to know what government is doing and it has a right to be heard in the decision-making process. A government agency has a responsibility to keep the public informed about what is going on and to welcome feedback about how things are going.

Dealing with the Public: Why and How?

If you work as a line manager in a state's motor vehicle department, interaction with the public is a large part of your job. However, a significant number of the twenty million employees at the various levels of government in the United States rarely interact with the public. You may come into contact with the public so infrequently that it may seem possible to avoid dealing with it at all. However, although the public may not be an immediate presence in your organization's activities, your role as a public manager is that of a public servant, and you are accountable to the public for the services you produce. Consumption of your services keeps your organization in business. If your customers are unhappy with your product, they will eventually find a way to voice that view within the political process.

Beyond your interest in the public's role as consumer, you should be aware that the public has the ability to affect your organization's activities in ways similar to those of interest groups. Members of the public influence government decisions through organized community efforts and often have close contact with the legislatures that represent them. Being aware of the relationships between public groups and their representatives can help you win support for your organization. If you develop good working relationships with community groups, they may be able to use their influence to support or oppose legislation on your behalf. In addition, some theories of public

opinion suggest that it is not public opinion that shapes government policy; rather, it is government policy that shapes public opinion (Kingdon, 1984). In this case, you can use public encounters to develop support for your agency's programs. The public can also provide you with valuable feedback on your programs, help you define and monitor quality, and recommend improvements.

You also need to deal with the public because it is easy to generate political opposition if members of the public feel that you are ignoring them. If it appears as if you are acting without consulting a community, you can generate intense and widespread opposition because of your lack of manners. Even if you must oppose the positions taken by a community's activists or elite, it is amazing how quickly you can generate opposition even among potential supporters if you give the appearance of not consulting the people affected by your program.

Finding Out What the Public Wants from Your Organization

The first issue you must address is, who is the public? Public participation scholars speak about many publics. The public is most commonly organized around communities. These communities most often have a geographical basis, as in the case of urban neighborhood or block associations, but they can also be organized according to ideological or policy interests.

Demographics often play an important role in the community organization. For example, neighborhoods may represent a certain ethnic or religious background. Civic organizations and community groups have a wide range of concerns—from business interest in economic development to services such as education, health care, and public safety, to problems such as homelessness, crime, or drug trafficking. Becoming familiar with these local community groups and their respective concerns will help you anticipate what the public wants from your organization.

In general, each public group will want you to deliver services or accept its policy perspective. It will also want you to pay atten-

tion to its specific needs and demands and solve any problems that it identifies. Various groups will also want you to confer legitimacy on their demands. This is a resource that government agencies have by virtue of their official position, and it can be a very easy resource to deploy. People will have more sympathy for the constraints under which you must act if you demonstrate empathy with their concerns. Showing members of the public that you take them seriously will greatly facilitate public relations. This is important in all cases, but it is particularly important when you are dealing with ad hoc groups active on hot local political issues. Often, these local groups include citizens who are typically apathetic and unskilled in normal political processes. They are active because a local issue is having a direct effect on their homes or families. Such issues are often central to their personal identity and survival.

People depend on community services on a daily basis in order to lead normal lives. Because community services address such fundamental needs, well-organized community groups are usually the most vocal and straightforward in getting their interests heard. Thus, you will probably not have any difficulty in finding out what the active members of the public want from your organization; keeping yourself informed of their fundamental concerns will be helpful in deciding how to deal with them. One problem with responding to active citizens is that their views may not be representative of the views of the general public. There is a strong, positive correlation between political participation and socioeconomic status (SES) (Milbrath, 1965; Verba and Nie, 1972). This means that the most active citizens may make demands that average citizens would not make. Although SES is a good predictor of political participation, it certainly is not an ironclad law. If the stimuli are strong enough and those who have been apathetic are motivated and educated to participate, poor and working-class people will participate in politics. During Jesse Jackson's first presidential campaign, a large number of low-SES African American citizens registered to vote and participated in the electoral process for the first time.

When Steven Cohen was developing the community relations program for the EPA's hazardous waste cleanup Superfund program, he commissioned case studies of citizen-government interaction at twenty-two hazardous waste sites (ICF Inc., 1980). That study provided solid evidence that when working-class homes were threatened by toxic waste, individuals with relatively low SES became active participants in local politics. We learned, however, that these groups used nontraditional political tactics. Rather than practice the clubby, nonconfrontational politics of the elite, they favored dramatic, visible public events. These events were a very painful way of learning what the public wanted from the government.

Explaining Complicated Issues to an Uninformed Public

When you attempt to meet public demands and convince people that you are working in their interest, you will be dealing with a wide range of sophistication about your organization's work. It is not uncommon for community organizations to rely for representation on the abilities of a few individual activists who are informed of the issues and capable of rallying public support. The general public is rarely as informed or knowledgeable about the intricacies of specific issues as these representatives are. When you deal with the general public, you should expect its members to have a limited understanding of the complexity of most issues. Even community leaders, who may be well informed about the issues, are probably not well informed about your agency's other responsibilities, internal structure, or the overall effect of your programs.

For these reasons, explaining issues to the public may be difficult. However, although it may be tough, there is no issue that cannot be broken down into its essential elements and explained to a general audience. Although some experts believe that their work is simply too complicated to explain to the general public, that is merely the excuse of someone not willing to take the trouble to talk to average people. The primary rule here is never to overestimate your audience's specific knowledge or underestimate its intelligence.

The best approach is to keep information simple. Prepare clear and direct statements about your organization's position on an issue and your plan of action. Avoid bureaucratic jargon, acronyms, and vagueness. It is not necessary that the public understand all the elements of an issue. Your responsibility is to identify the most important aspects and educate the public about them. Nothing is too complicated to explain to the public.

Preparing for Public Meetings

Public meetings serve two general purposes: to inform and involve the public in an organization's activities and to make that organization more accountable to the public. Public meetings are an opportunity to gain support for your activities. The first step in preparing for a public meeting is to do your homework. Learn about the program you are planning to talk about, and prepare visual aids to help you explain it. Ensure that meeting preparations are competently handled. Little things such as chairs, heat, light, sound, visuals, and publicity must be properly managed if a meeting is to succeed. Most important, be well informed about the public's particular interests and the issues that are likely to be raised during the meeting. Be prepared to respond to those issues. If possible, present simple statistical data and use examples to illustrate your points. Critically evaluate your own speaking skills. Have yourself videotaped. If you are a poor public speaker, get training and improve.

One form of public meeting—the public hearing—is an attempt to involve the public in government programs and to increase accountability. A case study of the federal government's general revenue-sharing program was conducted in order to determine the effectiveness of public hearings in achieving the objectives of involving the public and increasing accountability. This study indicated that public hearings had a significant impact on public interest and involvement in local affairs. Furthermore, the more hearings that were held, the greater the level of public involvement and the greater the impact on programs. However, when studied over time, this impact was shown to

have only short-term policy implications. Thus, the study found that public hearings had more influence in raising citizens' awareness than in affecting policy outcomes (Caputo and Cole, 1984).

Although hearings may not have much influence on your program's direction, many state and federal laws require public hearings in the course of program implementation. Since you will find yourself devoting time and energy to these activities, it makes sense to attempt to derive some benefit from them. You can use public meetings to generate support for your organization and to create a perception of openness and competence.

Planning and Managing Community Relations

Planning community relations involves becoming familiar with the views and operating styles of different community organizations. This can help you predict which groups will be most likely to cause trouble, and it can help you develop strategies for dealing with them. Thus, it is probably wise to pay attention to the views of the activists. Devote some resources to gathering political intelligence about community or interest groups most affected by your program. Keep track of what your organization is doing that might be of interest to these groups, and try to predict when public action might be likely on the basis of the past record.

You often cannot avoid conflict, but identifying probable causes of conflict can help you develop a strategy for mitigating its worst effects. The most important rule in community relations is not to let public conflicts escalate. Furthermore, try to establish working relationships with the leaders of well-organized public interests. These individuals are your most valuable resource in avoiding public confrontations and in arriving at mutually acceptable solutions.

As in your relations with special interests groups, it is to your advantage to have the public on your side; however, this may not always be possible. Your organization may have a mission that is in conflict with the mission of specific community groups. If they are reluctant to compromise, your job is to uphold your organization's mission, and so conflict may be inevitable. In this case, be prepared

to suffer through public outcries, insults, and demonstrations while supporting your program goals. Do not try to hide from this public attack, keep your activities from the public, or pretend that your organization is doing something other than what it really is doing. Going about the business of your organization in a professional manner is the best strategy in dealing with the public, and in some cases you may even be surprised by your own performance.

Dealing with the "Not in My Backyard" Syndrome

We think that the best conclusion for a section on community relations is a discussion of the "not in my backyard" (NIMBY) syndrome. A common problem in local community relations is attempting to find a place to locate necessary services or facilities that have undesirable or unpleasant characteristics. Negative reaction to facility siting has become the most difficult obstacle in planning for new programs. Siting issues are often addressed with court action that slows down program implementation and impairs an agency's ability to perform. Two examples provide a clear illustration of this problem. In 1998, the city of New London, Connecticut, developed a plan to revitalize its blighted Fort Trumbull neighborhood. The redevelopment plan was initiated when a large pharmaceutical company decided to build a research and development headquarters adjacent to the neighborhood. At the same time, the state decided to restore a nearby old fort as the centerpiece of a new state park. Three years later, the city was in state court, defending itself against a suit by seven Fort Trumbull property owners. The property owners contended that the city plan was unconstitutional, as the properties acquired through condemnation were to be turned over to private developers to build an office, a hotel, a conference center, and an apartment complex (Mansnerus, 2001). The city argued that their planning process was in full compliance with state law and that it provided maximum benefit to the neighborhood, the city, and the state. The plaintiffs argued that the benefits of the revitalization would go to the private developers. The bottom line was that the program was delayed by court action.

After years of educating the public about the need for additional waste management capacity and acting under the leadership of a committed governor, Georgia's Hazardous Waste Management Authority began its search for a new facility in 1987. Seeking to avoid confrontation, the authority solicited bids from counties willing to accept the facility with the associated jobs and a percentage of gross revenues. Only four of 159 counties responded and three subsequently withdrew. The remaining county—poor, rural Taylor County—offered the authority a large tract of land without notifying adjacent property owners or the general public. Resulting community opposition effectively doomed the project (Heiman, 1992).

These are just two examples of the effect that a single group can have on service provision to the general public. The problem of locating undesirable services is one of the most difficult to overcome, which is evidenced by the fact that this problem remains unsolved in so many areas. In the case of the Fort Trumbull redevelopment, it seems that the project might have been possible if the community had been presented with the plans and if compensation had been fully negotiated before condemnation began. Basically, those involved must address these problems by working closely with the community leaders. Like special interest groups, community leaders will appreciate being informed of your activities and being treated professionally.

Although your goals and the community's interest may seem to be at odds, cooperation will be more constructive than confrontation in attempting to achieve service delivery while recognizing the community's concerns. Having said all this, there are some NIMBY problems that will not be solved without a forceful display of political power. Other problems will require bribes or side payments to communities to dispose them toward accepting a noxious facility. For example, the proposal to install an incinerator can be made more attractive by offering to add a park. As the population increases and the American landscape fills, NIMBY is likely to continue. One job of the effective public manager will be to develop innovative strategies for dealing with this incredibly difficult public policy problem.

Chapter Twelve

Surviving and Thriving in Public Service

In this first decade of the twenty-first century, government continues to undergo fundamental change. Public service careers increasingly involve careers in government and in private nonprofit and for-profit organizations. Government organizations are becoming leaner, with fewer staff and middle-management positions. Public service in the twenty-first century requires public managers trained in e-government, contract management, and management innovation, as well as in all of the traditional functional management tools discussed in the original (1988) edition of this book—budgeting, human resources management, political management, and information management. As society faces ever more complex problems— from the global economy to global terrorism—the need for highly educated, flexible, and imaginative managers continues to grow. In the months after the attacks on the World Trade Center and the Pentagon, the need for government became more obvious and the image of public service was enhanced by the sacrifice of American firefighters, soldiers, rescue workers, and police officers.

The Costs of Public Sector Careers

As the preceding chapters indicate, managing in the public sector is difficult and frustrating. This gives rise to an obvious question: Why bother? Public sector careers pay less than those in the private sector, they can be affected by political factors beyond your control, and they require you to interact with a host of semicomatose organizations to get your job done.

Several structural features of public organizations can make public management very frustrating. Because public organizations do not live and die by the bottom line and because civil servants are difficult, if not impossible, to fire, some public organizations and some civil servants are lazy and nonproductive. Of course, failing private organizations that have noncompetitive environments exhibit similar characteristics. However, it is presumed that most of these organizations are eventually driven out of business by more aggressive competitors.

In the public sector, nonproductive organizations that manage to obtain the financial resources needed to survive can remain in existence long after their productive lives are over. In the private sector, when the bottom line is red and the lines of credit have run out, employees cannot be paid and the organization dies. Although there is a connection between a public organization's performance and its success in the budget game, the relationship is rarely one-to-one. This means that at times during your career, you may be asked to manage a nonproductive organization. And because it is always difficult to turn such an organization around—given the constraints of the civil service and procurement system, the vagaries of politics, and the rigidity of governmental budgeting processes, you may be faced with serious management problems and very little flexibility in framing a response to those problems.

If you are fortunate enough to manage a competent organization, you may find that you must constantly deal with less competent organizations to get your work done. You may also find it difficult or at times impossible to adequately reward your organization's excellent performers. Then, too, you may find that the rewards you are receiving are not commensurate with your accomplishments. Perhaps even worse, you may find that your organization's best work, judged as excellent by any reasonable professional standard, is misperceived by the media, the public, or the legislature and considered second-rate. In some cases, you might even be punished for performance that by any reasonable measure is truly excellent. A related factor is society's less than positive image of the govern-

ment bureaucrat—which is one of the bumbling bureaucrat (see Chapter Two). No matter how hard you work or how effective you are, you may be stigmatized by your attachment to the public sector.

The Benefits of Public Sector Careers

Despite the problems just noted, excellent people are still attracted to the public sector. In large measure, they come because they believe the mission of public organizations is important. They want to deal with the vital problems of the day and help craft solutions to those problems. Some people are attracted to the possibility of receiving greater responsibility sooner than they would in the private sector. The salary caps in public organizations are a two-edged sword. On the one hand, they force talented senior staff members to leave government if they wish to earn a high salary. On the other hand, these departures mean that senior management positions are frequently vacated and potentially opened to talented younger people. Of course, the counterargument here is that the exodus of talented senior managers to the private sector causes a brain drain that leaves mediocre, security-minded people in charge of large public organizations. Undoubtedly, both of these phenomena take place. We are merely arguing that salary caps create some opportunities in public organizations that do not exist in the private sector. Where this potential exists, excellent young people are attracted by the challenge and the possibility of personal power that the public sector offers.

Unquestionably, a public sector career can cause you to be branded a bumbling bureaucrat. However, it can also place you within an exciting community of colleagues interested in using the government to promote society's welfare.

We have discussed "sense of mission" in the abstract; let us get a bit more personal and specific. The most exciting work Steven Cohen was ever involved in was helping to create the federal hazardous waste cleanup (or Superfund) program. When he was a graduate student in Buffalo, New York, some very strange things

had begun to happen in a working-class subdivision in nearby Niagara Falls. It started with a spring thaw that pushed toxic chemicals out of their resting place in an abandoned canal and turned the canal into a toxic waste dump. Local and state governments and, finally, the federal government became involved in an effort to understand and clean up the environmental and public health threat at Love Canal. It soon became clear that there were thousands of Love Canals all over the country. A crash program was needed to study and clean up the worst of these toxic dump sites. To Cohen, Superfund was not simply a big federal program to move around some chemical barrels and prevent the spread of toxic contamination; rather, it was an attempt to answer the pleas of worried parents, such as the young mother at Love Canal who screamed at a state health official at a public hearing, "Why did you poison my baby?!" To Cohen, the challenge of building a program to deal with toxic chemicals was simply more inspiring than moving capital from one place to another or developing a new way to sell toothpaste. The chief benefit of public sector careers is the importance and scope of government's tasks.

William Eimicke had a similarly challenging and rewarding experience when he was chosen as the deputy commissioner to manage New York City's exploding portfolio of foreclosed housing stock in the late 1970s and early 1980s. In a two-pronged strategy to increase property tax collection rates and to better preserve its aging low-income housing, the city ended its practice of revolving-door auctions of occupied foreclosed apartment buildings and instead embarked on a strategy of community group and tenant management, rehabilitation or consolidation (based on the extent of deterioration), and selective sales to proven tenant groups, community-based organizations, and responsible private management firms.

During the transition, the city built up a huge portfolio of over a hundred thousand units with forty thousand occupants, spread out among four thousand buildings in five counties. Trying to provide essential services—particularly during the cold-weather months—to buildings that had been abandoned by their owners as

many as three years prior to foreclosure meant a regular schedule of fourteen-hour days, six days a week, for most of Eimicke's nearly four-year tenure.

The rewards included being able to provide a seventy-year-old widow with heat and hot water for the first time in two years and, only a year after taking over, selling the first five buildings to tenant-owned cooperatives. Today, Eimicke frequently walks past an entire city block (adjacent to the Columbia University campus) of what were once foreclosed buildings, which were rehabilitated and converted to cooperatives during his watch. Nearly two decades later, these cooperatives are still viable, owner-occupied apartments, and there is now talk of privatizing the portfolio, which has more market value now as a result of the city's intervention.

Another reward is that public managers contribute to the common good. In the final analysis, the goal of the public sector is to make it possible for average people to do ordinary things. Our goal is to make the extraordinary daily life we are so fortunate to have here in the United States of America continue and help it develop wherever else it is desired in the world. Family, friendship, work, love, play, nurturing, joy, learning, spiritual and artistic fulfillment, and even sadness—those things that we treasure in our private and personal lives—are the important values that the public sector must enable and protect. Public service is not about building monuments or engaging in collective enterprises for their own sake; rather, it is about making it possible for individuals to lead their lives with freedom and choice. The paradox is that without government, these private worlds cannot survive, and without effective public managers, government cannot survive.

Why Be a Risk-Taking Public Entrepreneur?

It is possible to accept the argument that public sector careers are worth pursuing and, at the same time, reject the argument favoring public entrepreneurship. The argument for public entrepreneurship, which we advanced in Chapter Two, is that the issues faced

by public organizations are growing in scope and complexity and that creative, agile managers and organizations are needed to address those issues. In short, effective public management requires risk-taking, entrepreneurial public managers.

There are those who argue that government managers do not have any right to take risks, that such risk taking usurps the power of elected leaders and the public. We strongly disagree. We are not saying that public managers should experiment with policy direction or even overall implementation strategies; these are the prerogatives of elected leaders. When public entrepreneurship requires such risks, the effective public manager must advise elected leaders to authorize such risk taking. If the elected leaders refuse, the public manager must explore alternative approaches.

However, most of the entrepreneurship that we are suggesting does not require such authorization. Most of it has to do with methods of managing programs well within the control of the typical public manager. Whereas you might accept this argument for the entire system, it still does not answer the far more personal and important question of why you should be a risk taker. The argument for being a risk taker in government is that it is not possible to be goal-oriented in the public sector without taking some chances. The normal pattern in large public organizations is to steadily execute standard operating procedures (SOPs) and to passively react to new stimuli. Yet if conditions change as rapidly as we project they will, a premium will be placed on those organizations capable of quickly developing and implementing new SOPs. Managers who are capable of crafting new strategies in response to information they have obtained from small-scale pilot projects or by "wandering around" will be eagerly sought.

As we indicated earlier, risk taking should not be confused with recklessness. The risks you take should be calculated and part of a realistic organizational strategy (see Chapter Ten). You should always take the initiative and reinterpret your mission and SOPs in light of environmental changes. If you wait for programmatic changes to be dictated from above or imposed from the outside, you

will never gain control of your organization's work. In addition, if your organization's distinctive competence is to implement the programs you are assigned, presumably you know more about these programs than anyone else. External redefinitions of your mission and tasks will tend to be a little bit off the mark. This is one reason why agency staff members work so closely with legislative staff members in framing legislation. The bureaucrats simply have more information about the day-to-day operation of a program than anyone else. To be effective, you should be constantly involved in defining and redefining your mission and activities. You must stay in close touch with your field staff and customers and factor their views into the design of the programs your organization administers.

Any effort to redesign an ongoing governmental program involves an element of professional risk. You have to stick your neck out and assert that your understanding of the situation is superior. You have to make educated guesses about the direction in which you want to take your organization. It is less risky to sit back and wait for events to develop and orders to come from above. Your career may be safer if you act cautiously and carefully measure the direction of prevailing opinion. However, your chances of accomplishing very much are greatly diminished by such passivity.

The Need to Defy "Organizational Gravity"

Let us be honest: in large organizations, if managers do not take risks and fight the tendency toward organizational paralysis, new ideas and creative environmental adaptations will usually be killed by naysayers. We are certain that you have seen the type of individual we are talking about. For every good idea that someone proposes, a naysayer can figure out fifteen plausible reasons why the idea will fail. Often, he or she can be very creative in spinning out negative scenarios. It is difficult for effective public managers to combat these arguments because the managers are often reduced to saying that it is their judgment that a particular initiative will work. It is often a debate between those who refuse to take risks and those who are

willing to do so. Keeping a new initiative alive requires effort. Without someone actively pushing and forcing the issue, organizational inertia will act like a gravitational force and the new initiative will crash to the ground.

The more we look at organizational behavior, the more we see the difficulty of creating and implementing new standard operating procedures (Cohen and Brand, 1993; Cohen and Eimicke, 1998). Yet the creation of such procedures is one of the most important jobs of management. The essence of management is to facilitate institutional learning—to develop new patterns of response to existing and emerging problems and to teach those new patterns to the people who make up the organization. As Franklin Roosevelt learned during the New Deal when he created the "alphabet agencies," it is easier to create a new organization than to change the ways of an existing one. Unfortunately, we do not all have the luxury or the power to create a new organization but must instead force-feed innovation into existing ones. If a public manager does not have an energetic and aggressive strategy to market and institutionalize a new initiative, organizational gravity will soon sink the new idea. The only way to defy gravity is to take initiative and take risks.

Entrepreneurship as a Professional Value

A creative, adaptive public sector is needed to respond to our rapidly changing environment. Risk taking is a necessary value for a creative organization, and it needs to be operationally defined and nurtured. We consider it particularly important that risk taking not be misperceived as wild or unethical behavior. A public manager must remember that the money being risked belongs to the public. Public entrepreneurship must fit within the essentially incremental context of public policy formulation and implementation. Unlike private entrepreneurship, the public variant must operate within the constraints of statutory authorizations, legislative appropriations, and political reality. Whereas private entrepreneurship must deal with the constraints of the market and the bottom line, pub-

lic entrepreneurship must deal with the more complex constraints of law, politics, the media, and public opinion. However, complexity and difficulty are not excuses for passivity. Aggressive, entrepreneurial risk taking is an appropriate value for the public sector. The ventures must be conscious and calculated to be effective. We must build structures and incentives in the public sector that facilitate and reward these types of gambles.

As managers, we must constantly focus our staff's attention on the service we are delivering and the customer we are serving. We should constantly reinforce the need to engage in the type of small-scale experimentation that contributes to institutional learning. We should constantly strive to build new SOPs to deal with the rapidly changing problems that government is asked to address. This means that we must learn from and even tolerate those failures that land us on the front page of newspapers. In fact, when a small pilot project fails, we should consciously seek to reward the public manager who promoted the experiment. Obviously, the party should not be as joyous as one celebrating a success, but if we want to nurture risk taking, we must reward even failed experiments.

Organizational structures should be developed to provide the capacity to take chances. Most organizations provide themselves with extra resources to perform administrative tasks and to deal with emergencies and "fire drills." Similarly, it should be possible to use an additional piece of an organization's resource base to provide for risk taking and institutional learning. It should also be possible to use standard personnel review procedures to promote the value of entrepreneurship. When developing your staff's individual annual performance standards, require each of your staff members to create, implement, and evaluate some set number of small-scale pilot projects. In addition, constantly redefine the work required to receive an "outstanding" (or the highest available) rating. If someone receives a rating of outstanding for a given body of work in year one, he or she must perform additional work to receive a rating of outstanding in year two. If you have learned anything, the second time you perform a task should be easier than the first time. You can

foster the value of entrepreneurship by requiring risk taking in performance standards and by signaling your employees that they will only receive high ratings if they learn from experience.

You can also use two other traditional leadership tools to encourage the value of experimentation: "jawboning" and leading by example. Jawboning is simply telling your staff that risk taking is important and pointing out entrepreneurial opportunities as often as possible. Jawboning alone is usually ineffective, however. Talk is often cheap, so it is important to lead by example. Thus, the most effective way to infuse and reinforce the value of taking chances is to take some yourself. Visibly and personally commit your organization to an entrepreneurial project. Demonstrate what you consider to be an appropriate degree of calculation, and gamble on a new venture with uncertain prospects. If the gamble pays off, you have an example of the benefits of risk taking. If your experiment fails, acknowledge the failure and identify the lessons to be learned from it.

We are certain that some of you feel that risk taking is unrealistic in your organization. We return to our point that these risks must be calculated. In some situations, the environment will be less conducive to experimentation than in others. In these less inviting situations, reasonable risk taking may involve only very small changes in the status quo. Nevertheless, there are no organizational situations in which entrepreneurship is completely out of the question.

Can the Public Sector Succeed?

In Chapter Two, we discussed the elements of public sector failure and argued that the American public sector is as competent as its private sector. There, we noted the deficiencies of both public and private management. In this chapter, we note the past successes of American industry and government—successes that were enjoyed despite the deficiencies of management.

In the middle of the twentieth century, American industry created a consumer society that was the envy of the world. As compe-

tition with foreign industry increased, we engaged in a revolution in private management to improve our ability to compete. Today our economy faces a great many problems, but the economic accomplishments of the past seventy years are difficult to deny. In a similar vein, although government is confronting a number of problems, ranging from environmental protection to fighting terrorism, the accomplishments of the past century are undeniable. The late Speaker of the House of Representatives Thomas P. "Tip" O'Neill (O'Neill and Novak, 1987) said it best when reviewing his fifty years in government:

> I often hear successful people talking about the "good old days." Their message is always the same: how wonderful life used to be when we had less government and fewer social programs and people were left to fend for themselves.
>
> But I came of age in those good old days, and I remember clearly what they were like. When I first entered politics, 50 percent of the population were living in poverty. A full 25 percent were out of work. Even if you were fortunate enough to have a job, life was still pretty tough. . . . For most people, the work week was six days long—and those were six long days. . . . For most Americans, health insurance was out of the question. If you became sick, your world collapsed. For the elderly, life was filled with uncertainty and fear. Only a lucky few had pensions, and social security was a brand new idea.
>
> That was the America I knew in 1936. And despite all the problems we now face, I can never forget how far we have come in fifty years. Today, everyone goes to high school, and close to two-thirds of our young people pursue some form of higher education. And although poverty has certainly not been eliminated, we were able to get the poverty rate down to 10 percent in 1980. Today, virtually all workers have some form of health insurance. Social Security has made it possible for people to retire with a small but steady income. Without this protection, half of the elderly would be living in poverty.

[Government has created] many other things, too, including housing and job programs, a thriving system of state colleges and universities, and a farm program that has helped make us the greatest agricultural nation in the world [pp. 376–377].

Understanding the Mythology of Failure

Despite the great successes that O'Neill (O'Neill and Novak, 1987) described, the federal government is generally associated with failure—such as that of the security system at U.S. airports, the performance of antimissile missiles, the conduct of the Vietnam War, and gridlock—for example, the gridlock that impeded the nation's attempt to develop national prescription drug benefits for the elderly. Accomplishments never seem to get the same degree of attention as failure. This is, of course, a natural outgrowth of a society that learns about itself from the mass media. It is also a natural product of the process of political-issue formulation in American democracy. Issues do not become politicized without conflict. Successes are generally not as interesting as failures.

In addition, public programs are built in response to problems that receive agenda status as political issues. That is, at a certain point, an issue is considered a legitimate item for consideration by government (Cobb and Elder, 1972). Issues do not receive agenda status unless they are difficult to solve and involve conflict between groups or segments of society. E. E. Schattschneider, in his landmark work, *The Semisovereign People* (1975), notes that an issue that gains status on the political agenda is one in which society has decided to expand the scope of conflict. If the conflict is considered unimportant, it is left outside the realm of government. If the conflict is considered important, it becomes socialized and is considered a legitimate subject for government action. In fact, according to Schattschneider, one of the main functions of government is to identify private conflicts that are too important to leave to the private sector and must be addressed by the larger society. Schattschneider notes that

> Democratic government is the greatest single instrument for socialization of conflict in the American community. . . . *Government in a democracy is a great engine for expanding the scale of conflict. Government is never far away when conflict breaks out . . . government thrives on conflict. . . . It is necessary only to mention political parties, pressure groups, the courts, congressional investigations, governmental regulatory agencies, [and] freedom of speech and press, among others[,] to show the range and variety of instruments available to the government for breaking open private conflicts. . . . Why is everything about public affairs vastly more newsworthy than private affairs* [pp. 12–13, Schattschneider's italics]?

Put simply, government programs are born out of conflict. They are often created with inconsistent goals. Their purpose is to deal with social problems that cannot be addressed through the capitalist market. If a program is successful in dealing with a problem and the issue remains important, the program will probably hum in the background and receive incremental increases in its resource base. It will never attract much attention. This stands in contrast with the media attention paid to failed programs. If a program is not making progress on the problem it was designed to solve, it will remain on the political agenda and in the media's eye. This media attention will enforce the myth that government cannot accomplish anything. The myth of government's incompetence is a natural by-product of the role of government in our society. Government's job is to socialize conflict and then to implement programs to resolve the conflict. This means that the new, media-genic missions that government takes on will be among the most difficult work our society can create. These new problems, whether they be reducing incidents of teenage pregnancy or cleaning up toxic dump sites, will be the kind of problem that no one has figured out how to solve. Government will be forced to wrestle with these problems in a media fishbowl until solutions become routine. When problems become relatively easy to solve, they disappear from the public's view. These old issues are soon replaced by a new

generation of political issues. American bureaucrats are then expected to wrestle with this new set of issues, while receiving little credit for resolving the old ones. Thus, Tip O'Neill's fifty-year retrospective (O'Neill and Novak, 1987) can point to stunning successes in the public sector, but the myth of bureaucratic incompetence will persist.

Diagnosing Failure

Unfortunately, not all public sector failures are myths. In Chapter Two, we described five ingredients for public sector failure: (1) accepting the negative image of public management, (2) using the constraints of the public sector as an excuse for nonperformance, (3) allowing caution to become inertia, (4) hiding behind ambiguity, and (5) forgetting that people matter. Most of these ingredients are what we consider correctable management failures. However, management deficiencies are not the only causes of failed public programs. Additional causes include (1) design failures—programs with a poor match between goals and authorized activities, (2) resource inadequacies—programs without enough money or staff to succeed, (3) political opposition—programs that are implemented without the political support needed to secure the cooperation of influential elites, and (4) corruption—unethical public servants more interested in the success of their personal finances than in the success of their program.

In Chapter Ten, we discussed strategy formulation. One crucial element of an effective strategy is a realistic diagnosis of your organization's current and projected status. There is an understandable tendency in government to avoid evaluating or acknowledging program failures. A negative written assessment of a program might be leaked to the media. A news story on an internal assessment of failure can cost an organization more than it gains by conducting such an assessment. Your political support may be threatened, and any hope of developing an image of competence may be destroyed. You will probably not receive credit for your effort to learn from

your mistakes; instead, you will be identified with your mistakes. Nevertheless, it is impossible to develop a realistic organizational strategy if you do not continually conduct candid evaluations of your organization's capability and accomplishments. Although it might be wise to avoid major written organizational studies, it is still possible to conduct less formal assessments. Results can be communicated through oral briefings and informal conversations.

Frequently, you will find yourself drafting carefully crafted statements about your organization's accomplishments. These documents will protect you politically and help you obtain resources. It is easy to forget that these organizational advertisements are not meaningful descriptions of reality. In short, do not get taken in by your own hype. Continue to critically assess your organization's performance. Every organization can improve. The ones that tend to get worse are those that are smug and self-satisfied and fail to exploit opportunities for improvement.

Public Sector Successes and Their Replication

Although public managers have been faced with an amazing variety of impediments to success, many have overcome them. As the quotation from Tip O'Neill (O'Neill and Novak, 1987) indicates, government enjoyed some important successes during the second half of the twentieth century. Our interstate highway system represents one of the largest public works programs in the history of the world. Established in the late 1950s, the system took about twenty years to complete and made rapid intercity car and truck travel a reality. The food stamp program was begun in the mid-1960s and has dramatically reduced the problem of hunger in the United States. The Internet itself was started by the U.S. government so that computers at defense laboratories could be linked. Project Head Start helped stimulate a revolution in early childhood education. The development of this nation's public high school and university systems is a little-acknowledged public sector accomplishment of profound consequence. The EPA's multibillion-dollar grant program

for the construction of sewage treatment plants has improved water quality throughout the United States. An entire era of waterfront development in major American cities would never have begun if our rivers had remained the open sewers they were before the 1970s.

The successes of local government have been equally impressive. In the city in which we live, New York, we have seen a mass transit system on the edge of extinction transformed into a viable operation. Every day, in thousands of governments throughout the United States, similar acts of management excellence can be found. The emergency response by New York City's government to the destruction of the World Trade Center on September 11, 2001, saved many thousands of lives, and the inspirational leadership of New York City's mayor Rudolph Guiliani was felt throughout the world.

Although a wide variety of factors contribute to successful public programs, certain elements are common to most of them. Some of these elements involve external relations, whereas others involve effective internal organizational management. This book has been principally concerned with internal management, but as Chapter Eleven indicates, external relations can be critical. External factors contributing to program success include political will—or the support of the political elite (principally elected officials), the support of the socioeconomic elite, a positive image in the mass media, and a relative absence of significant opposition among members of the general public. Internal factors contributing to program success include a workable program design, organizational capability—or the human and financial resources needed to implement a workable design, effective leadership, and an organizational culture that supports the value of overcoming bureaucratic constraints.

It is difficult for a public program to succeed if it does not have the support of elected leaders and other political players. These political actors control the budget process that provides resources to public programs. In addition, oversight hearings can be used to harass the managers of an unpopular program. Defending your program from attack can occupy much of your time and can cause your staff to devote insufficient time to internal program management.

Similarly, you may fail if your program is opposed by key opinion leaders and powerful business interests. Such leaders can directly block your program by denying you their cooperation and participation, and they can indirectly block your program by stimulating the opposition of the political elite.

Your organization's image in the mass media is also critical. It is easy for your program to be misperceived by the media if your organization has poor presentation capability or is unwilling to pay attention to media concerns. If the media dislike you, it will not be long before your elite and broad public support will begin to evaporate.

Finally, though you may not need widespread support from the public to implement your program, intense or extensive public opposition will make your job very difficult. Elected leaders count their telephone calls and tabulate their e-mail. If you are managing a program that arouses tremendous popular opposition, it will take many acts of political courage to ensure your survival. Your organization's life will depend on acts of conscience by politicians. This is an unhealthy type of dependence and is to be avoided.

Program design is a critical variable affecting success. An effective program design is one that matches activities to goals. Public program designs are constrained by legislative authority, but agencies have a good deal of administrative discretion in selecting priorities and providing operational definition to programs. Poorly crafted legislation can lead to unimplementable program designs, but even a piece of legislation that is internally inconsistent can be reshaped by administrators into a feasible program. However, a beautifully designed program is meaningless if your organization does not have the capacity to deliver it.

We have known very few managers who did not believe that they could do a better job with additional resources. But it is not simply a matter of money; bigger is not always better. Organizational capacity is most often increased by effective deployment of resources rather than by absolute growth of resources. Some minimum level of resources is necessary to achieve a kind of institutional critical mass, but this is not usually the issue. More often,

organizations are unable to provide the capability needed to implement a program because their human resources are poorly trained, poorly motivated, or, in short, poorly managed.

This leads to the third internal factor contributing to program success: leadership. Our concept of the role of the administrative leader is drawn directly from Chester Barnard's *The Functions of the Executive* (1968 [1938]) and Phillip Selznick's *Leadership in Administration* (1984 [1957]), and that concept is summarized in Chapter Five. The role of leadership is to obtain resources and deploy those resources to motivate staff members to perform. It is also a leader's job to ensure that the organization's performance results in accomplishments that serve public needs. To do this, public managers must take entrepreneurial risks (Levin and Sanger, 1994). Societies and economies are changing so rapidly that it is increasingly difficult to respond to public needs. Effective public managers must continually attempt to interpret those needs and rapidly design creative responses.

The final internal resource needed to ensure a successful program is essentially attitudinal. A successful public organization has a can-do attitude. When a huge obstacle is placed in its path, such an organization develops a strategy to remove the impediment or, as a last resort, it figures out a way around the impediment. More important, the organization believes it can find a way around the problem and does not give up until a solution is found. More important still, the organization expects to find obstacles in its path and is realistic enough to provide the capacity to deal with these problems.

A can-do attitude, then, is not derived from some fairy-tale notion of the nature of public life or the importance of public missions. It comes from a realistic understanding of bureaucratic processes and the difficulty of managing public organizations. We are arguing for effectiveness that is built on a realpolitik of the public bureaucracy—a firm understanding of organizational interests and the organizational behaviors likely to result from those interests. If the external and internal resources we previ-

ously cited are available, as, many times, they are, public programs can succeed.

Concluding Thoughts: Toward a Profession of the Public Service

We believe that public service—and that includes work in non-profit and public-oriented parts of private organizations—is a critical profession. We also believe that it is our highest secular calling. We both remember watching John F. Kennedy exhorting us to ask what we can do for our country. Having witnessed Vietnam, the Civil Rights movement, the Great Society, Watergate, the Reagan revolution, the Iran Contra scandals, the Clinton-Gore effort to reinvent government, and the Bush administration's war on global terrorism, our belief in the centrality of government remains firm. We believe that public service professionals have an obligation to build a strong social service and to improve the lives of less fortunate members of our society.

Although the private sector has certainly provided the principal vehicle for developing the vast material wealth that the United States enjoys, it has been left to the public sector to deal with the problems that cannot be handled by the free market. It was government that stabilized the agricultural economy during the 1930s and stimulated a food production system that is the envy of the world. It is government that provides insurance for the unemployed, the aged, and the sick and provides food stamps for the hungry. It is government that builds roads, sewers, and water lines. It is government that has begun to protect the air and water and tries to keep us out of the path of toxic chemicals and wastes. It is government that protects us from the threat of global terrorism. We rely on government to protect us, maintain the economy, and defend us from enemies abroad.

Yet, as we all know, government does not always perform its tasks efficiently or effectively. That is why we desperately need entrepreneurial public managers. For most of this century, students

of public administration have sought to make government work better. Some have attempted to come up with magic answers. Some analysts were concerned with the stability of government and hoped that better constitutions would make for a better government. Others felt that changes in organizational structure would help and therefore created "superagencies" such as the extinct U.S. Department of Health, Education, and Welfare and New York City's Human Resources Administration. Some, like former secretary of defense Robert McNamara, placed their faith in systems analysis and instituted planning, programming, and budgeting systems. Former president Jimmy Carter attacked government waste with Zero-Based Budgeting, which forced agencies to defend their entire budget every year. Bill Clinton and Al Gore attempted to focus on internal management processes in order to reinvent government.

Some of these ideas have helped government; some have not. But all were stimulated by an intense desire to make government work better. We add the following suggestion to this litany of reform proposals: improve government performance by enhancing the skills of those who work for government. We believe we need a new type of effective public manager, a more *innovative* public manager.

References

Abramson, M. A. (ed.). *Toward a Twenty-First-Century Public Service: Reports from Four Forums.* New York: PricewaterhouseCoopers Endowment, 2001.

Abramson, M. A., and Kamensky, J. M. (eds.). *Managing for Results 2002.* PricewaterhouseCoopers Endowment for the Business of Government Series. Lanham, Md.: Rowman & Littlefield, 2001.

Allison, G. T. *Essence of Decision: Explaining the Cuban Missile Crisis.* New York: Little, Brown, 1971.

Andersen, D. F., and Dawes, S. S. *Government Information Management: A Primer and Casebook.* Englewood Cliffs, N.J.: Prentice Hall, 1991.

Anthony, R. N., and Herzlinger, R. E. *Management Control in Nonprofit Organizations.* Burr Ridge, Ill.: Irwin, 1980.

Avery, G. "Outsourcing Public Health Laboratory Services: A Blueprint for Determining Whether to Privatize and How." *Public Administration Review,* 2000, 60(4), 330–337.

Bardach, E., and Lesser, C. "Accountability in Human Services Collaboratives: For What? And to Whom?" *Journal of Public Administration Research and Theory,* 1996, 6, 197–224.

Barnard, C. I. *The Functions of the Executive.* Cambridge, Mass.: Harvard University Press, 1968. (Originally published 1938.)

Bartlett, J. *Familiar Quotations.* (16th ed.) New York: Little, Brown, 1992.

Beam, G. *Quality Public Management.* Chicago: Burnham, 2001.

Behn, R. "Managing by Groping Along." *Journal of Policy Analysis and Management,* 1988, 7, 664–667.

Bellante, D., and Link, A. "Are Public Sector Workers More Risk Averse Than Private Sector Workers?" *Industrial and Labor Relations Review,* 1981, 34(3), 408–412.

Bernstein, N. "Waiting to Sleep: For Family in Shelter System, Living From Bench to Bench." *New York Times,* Mar. 25, 2001, p. A1.

Blank, R. M. "An Analysis of Workers' Choice Between Employment in the Public and Private Sectors." *Industrial and Labor Relations Review,* 1985, 38(2), 211–224.

Bowes, L. *No One Need Apply*. Boston: Harvard Business School Press, 1987.

Bowman, J. S. (ed.). *Ethical Frontiers in Public Management: Seeking New Strategies for Resolving Ethical Dilemmas*. San Francisco: Jossey-Bass, 1991.

Broder, J. M., and Henneberger, M. "The 2000 Campaign: The Vice Presidency; Few in No. 2 Spot Have Been as Involved in Policy as Gore." *New York Times*, Oct. 31, 2000, p. A1.

Bruder, K. A., and E. M. Gray. "Public Sector Benchmarking: A Practical Approach." *Public Management (PM)*, 1994, 76(9), S9–14.

Brudney, J. L., and Hebert, F. T. "State Agencies and Their Environments: Examining the Influence of Important External Actors." *The Journal of Politics*, 1987, 49(1), 186–206.

Brull, S. "What's So Bad About a Living Wage?" *Newsweek*, Sept. 4, 2000, pp. 68–70.

Butterfield, F. "Inmate Rehabilitation Returns as Prison Goal." *New York Times*, May 20, 2001, p. A1.

Campbell, G., and McCarthy, E. "Conveying Mission Through Outcome Measurement: Services to the Homeless in New York City." *Policy Studies Journal*, 2000, 28(2), 338–352.

Caputo, D. A., and Cole, R. L. "The Public Hearing as an Effective Citizen Participation Mechanism: A Case Study of the General Review Sharing Program." *American Political Science Review*, 1984, 78(2), 404–416.

Carter, S. L. *Integrity*. New York: Basic Books, 1996.

Champy, J. *Reengineering Management: The Mandate for New Leadership*. New York: HarperBusiness, 1995.

Chandler, A. D. *Strategy and Structure: Chapters in the History of the Industrial Enterprise*. Cambridge, Mass.: MIT Press, 1962.

Chase, G., and Reveal, E. C. *How to Manage in the Public Sector*. New York: Random House, 1983.

Chetkovich, C. *Winning the Best and Brightest: Increasing the Attraction of Public Service*. New York: PricewaterhouseCoopers Endowment, 2001.

Cobb, R. W., and Elder, C. D. *Participation in American Politics: The Dynamics of Agenda Building*. Needham Heights, Mass.: Allyn & Bacon, 1972.

Cohen, S. *Managing Workfare: The Case of the Work Experience Program in the New York City Parks Department*. New York: PricewaterhouseCoopers Endowment, 1999.

Cohen, S., and Brand, R. *Total Quality Management in Government: A Practical Guide for the Real World*. San Francisco: Jossey-Bass, 1993.

Cohen, S., and Eimicke, W. "The Overregulated Civil Service: The Case of New York City's Public Personnel System." *Review of Public Personnel Administration*, 1994a, 14(2), 11–27.

Cohen, S., and Eimicke, W. "Project-Focused Total Quality Management in the New York City Department of Parks and Recreation." *Public Administration Review*, 1994b, 54(5), 450–456.

Cohen, S., and Eimicke, W. *The New Effective Public Manager*. San Francisco: Jossey-Bass, 1995.

Cohen, S., and Eimicke, W. "Is Public Entrepreneurship Ethical?" *Public Integrity Annual*, 1996, *1*, 3–11.

Cohen, S., and Eimicke, W. *Tools for Innovators: Creative Strategies for Strengthening Public Sector Organizations*. San Francisco: Jossey-Bass, 1998.

Cohen, S., and Eimicke, W. "Is Public Entrepreneurship Ethical? A Second Look at Theory and Practice." *Public Integrity Annual*, 1999, *1*, 54–74.

Cohen, S., and Eimicke, W. "Assuring Public Ethics in Privatized Public Programs." Paper presented at the annual meeting of the American Society for Public Administration, San Diego, Calif., Apr. 1–4, 2000a.

Cohen, S., and Eimicke, W. "The Need for Strategic Information Systems Planning When Contracting Out and Privatizing Public Sector Functions." In G. Garson, (ed.), *Handbook of Public Information Systems*, New York: Marcell Dekker, 2000b.

Cohen, S., and Eimicke, W. "Managing Privatization: The Tools, Skills, Goals, and Ethics of Contracting." Paper presented at the annual meeting of the American Society for Public Administration, Newark, N.J., Mar. 10–13, 2001.

Cohen, S., Eimicke, W., and Pérez Salazar, M. "Ethical Public Entrepreneurship: Common Dilemmas from North and South America." *Public Integrity*, 2000, pp. 229–245.

Cohen, S., and Tipermas, M. "Superfund: Preimplementation Planning and Bureaucratic Politics." In J. P. Lester and A. Bowman (eds.), *The Politics of Hazardous Waste Management*. Durham, N.C.: Duke University Press, 1983.

Committee for Economic Development. *Improving Management of the Public Work Force*. New York: Committee for Economic Development, 1978.

Contino, R. A., and Giuliano, J. "Productivity Gains Through Employee Participation at the New York City Department of Sanitation." *Public Productivity and Management Review*, 1991, *15*(2), 185–190.

Cooper, P. J., and others. *Public Administration for the Twenty-First Century*. Orlando, Fla.: Harcourt Brace, 1998.

Cushman, J. "Post Office Is Full of Ideas to Survive an E-Future." *New York Times*, Dec. 18, 2000, p. C-12.

Danziger, J. N., Kraemer, K. L., Dunkle, D. E., and King, J. L. "Enhancing the Quality of Computing Service: Technology, Structure, and People." *Public Administration Review*, 1993, *53*(2), 161–169.

deLeon, L., and Denhardt, R. "The Political Theory of Reinvention." *Public Administration Review*, 2000, *60*(2), 89–97.

Deming, W. E. *Out of the Crisis*. Cambridge, Mass.: Massachusetts Institute of Technology, 1982.

Downs, A. *Inside Bureaucracy*. New York: Little, Brown, 1967.

Drucker, P. *Innovation and Entrepreneurship*. New York: HarperCollins, 1985.

Drucker, P. *Management Challenges for the Twenty-First Century*. New York: HarperBusiness, 1999.

DuBrin, A. J. *The Practice of Supervision: Achieving Results Through People*. Dallas: Business Publications, 1980.

Eggers, W. D. "A New Breed of Mayor." *Wall Street Journal*, Nov. 4, 1993, p. A14.

Eimicke, W. *San Diego County's Innovation Problem: Using Competition and a Whole Lot More to Improve Public Services*. New York: Pricewaterhouse-Coopers Endowment, 2000.

Emmert, M. A., Crow, M., and Shangraw, R. F., Jr. "Public Management in the Future: Post-Orthodoxy and Organization Design." In B. Bozeman (ed.), *Public Management: The State of the Art*. San Francisco: Jossey-Bass, 1993.

Fesler, J. W. *Public Administration: Theory and Practice*. Englewood Cliffs, N.J.: Prentice Hall, 1980.

Fisher, R., and Ury, W. *Getting to Yes: Negotiating Agreement Without Giving In*. New York: Penguin Books, 1983.

Fischer, R. J. "An Overview of Performance Measurement." *Public Management (PM)*, 1994, 76(9), S2–S8.

Frederickson, H. G. *The Spirit of Public Administration*. San Francisco: Jossey-Bass, 1997.

Frumkin, P. *Managing Outcomes: Milestone Contracting in Oklahoma*. New York: PriceWaterhouseCoopers Endowment, 2001.

Gibson, C. F. "Understanding and Designing Formal Organization Structure." Harvard Business School, Case 9–478–034. Boston: President and Fellows of Harvard College, 1978.

Goldsmith, S. *The Twenty-First Century City: Resurrecting Urban America*. Washington, D.C.: Regnery, 1997.

Golembiewski, R. T. *Ironies in Organizational Development*. New Brunswick, N.J.: Transaction, 1990.

Gordon, V. "Contracting and Negotiation: Effective Practices of Successful Human Service Contract Managers." *Public Administration Review*, 1998, 58(6), 499–509.

Gortner, H. F. *Administration in the Public Sector*. (2nd ed.) New York: John Wiley & Sons, Inc., 1981.

Green, J. "How Much Privatization? A Research Note Examining the Use of Privatization by Cities in 1982 and 1992." *Policy Studies Journal*, 1996, 24, 632–640.

Greenhouse, S. "Child Care, the Perk of Tomorrow?" *New York Times*, May 13, 2001, sec. 4, p. 14.

Gulick, L. H., and others. *Papers on the Science of Administration*. New York: Institute of Public Administration, 1937.

Hadden, S. G. "Intelligent Advisory Systems for Managing and Disseminating Information." *Public Administration Review,* 1986, 46 (special issue), 572–578.

Hammer, M., and Champy, J. *Reengineering the Corporation: Manifesto for Business Revolution.* New York: HarperBusiness, 1993.

Hammer, M., and Stanton, S. A. *The Reengineering Revolution.* New York: HarperBusiness, 1995.

Harrison, K., and Stanbury, W. T. "Privatization in British Columbia: Lessons from the Sale of Government Laboratories." *Canadian Public Administration,* 1990, *33*(2), 165–197.

Hays, S., and Reeves, T. Z. *Personnel Management in the Public Sector.* Needham Heights, Mass.: Allyn & Bacon, 1984.

Hays, S., and Whitney, S. "Reinventing the Personnel Function: Lessons Learned from a Hope-Filled Beginning in One State." *The American Review of Public Administration,* 1997, *27*(4), 324–342.

Heiman, M. K. "Public Authorities as Agents of the Not-So-Quiet Revolution in Hazardous Waste Facility Siting." In M. K. Heiman (ed.), *The Public Authorities and Public Policy.* Westport, Conn.: Quorum/Greenwood, 1992.

Heinrich, C. J. "Do Government Bureaucrats Make Effective Use of Performance Management Information?" *Journal of Public Administration Research and Theory,* 1999, *9*(3), 363–393.

Herzberg, F. *The Motivation to Work.* New York: Wiley, 1959.

Hirsch, W. Z. "Contracting Out by (U.S.) Urban Governments: A Review." *Urban Affairs Review,* 1995, *30*(3), 458–473.

Hirschman, A. O. *Exit, Voice and Loyalty.* Cambridge, Mass.: Harvard University Press, 1970.

Hitchner, T. R., and Hitchner, S. B., Jr. "The MBTA: Budget Process (A)." In *Kennedy School Case Study.* Cambridge, Mass.: Harvard University Press, 1979.

Hofer, C. W., and Schendel, D. E. *Strategy Formulation: Analytical Concepts.* St. Paul, Minn.: West, 1978.

Ibsen, H. *An Enemy of the People.* In W. Archer (ed.), *Ibsen's Prose Dramas.* New York: Scribner, 1903.

ICF, Inc. *ICF Community Relations at Hazardous Waste Sites: A Report to the U.S.E.P.A.* Washington, D.C.: ICF Inc., 1980.

Ingraham, P., Selden, S., and Moynihan, D. "People and Performance: Challenges for the Future Public Service: The Report from the Wye River Conference." *Public Administration Review,* 2000, *60*(1), 54–60.

Jamieson, K. H., and Campbell, K. K. *The Interplay of Influence: News, Advertising, Politics, and the Mass Media.* Belmont, Calif.: Wadsworth, 1992.

Jehl, D. "Whitman Calls for Patience on Environmental Policies." *New York Times,* Apr. 7, 2001, p. B1.

Johnston, J., and Romzek, B. S. "Contracting and Accountability in State Medicaid Reform: Rhetoric, Theories, and Reality." *Public Administration Review*, 1999, 59(5), 383–399.

Kammerman, S. B. "The New Mixed Economy of Welfare: Public and Private." *Social Work*, 1983, 28(1), 5–10.

Katzenbach, J., and Smith, D. *The Wisdom of Teams*. Boston: Harvard Business School Press, 1993.

Kaufman, H. *The Forest Ranger: A Study in Administrative Behavior*. Baltimore, Md.: Johns Hopkins University Press, 1960.

Kaufman, H. *Administrative Behavior of Federal Bureau Chiefs*. Washington, D.C.: The Brookings Institution, 1981.

Kaye, B., and Jordan-Evans, S. "Retaining Key Employees." *Public Management*, 2001, 83(1), 1–11.

Kelman, S. *Making Public Policy: A Hopeful View of American Government*. New York: Basic Books, 1987.

Kettl, D. F. *Government by Proxy: (Mis?)Managing Federal Programs*. Washington D.C.: Congressional Quarterly Inc., 1988.

Kettl, D. F. *Sharing Power: Public Governance and Private Markets*. Washington, D.C.: The Brookings Institution, 1993.

Kettl, D. *Reinventing Government: A Fifth Year Report Card*. Washington, D.C.: Brookings Institution, 1998.

Kingdon, J. W. *Agendas, Alternatives, and Public Policies*. New York: Little, Brown, 1984.

Kleeman, R. "How to Deal with the Nonproductive Federal Employee." *Civil Service Journal*, 1979, 19(4), 46–48.

Lambright, W. H. *Transforming Government: Dan Goldin and the Remaking of NASA*. PricewaterhouseCoopers Endowment, 2001.

Lane, F. S. *Current Issues in Public Administration*. New York: St. Martin's Press, 1999.

Lane, L. M., and Wolf, J. F. *The Human Resource Crisis in the Public Sector*. Westport, Conn.: Quorum/Greenwood, 1990.

Lee, M. "Reporters and Bureaucrats: Public Relations Counter-Strategies by Public Administrators in an Era of Media Disinterest in Government." *Public Relations Review*, 1999, 25, 451–463.

Lee, M. "Public Relations Is Public Administration." *Public Manager*, Winter 1998–1999, 27, 49–52.

Lee, M. "Public Information in Government Organizations: A Review and Curriculum Outline of External Relations in Public Administration." *Public Administration and Management: An Interactive Journal*, 2000, 5, 183–214. [http://www.pamij.com].

Lenkowsky, L., and Perry, J. L. "Reinventing Government: The Case of National Service." *Public Administration Review*, 2000, 60, 298–307.

Levin, M. A., and Sanger, M. B. *How Entrepreneurial Executives Turn Bright Ideas into Real Results*. San Francisco: Jossey-Bass, 1994.

Lewis, C. W. *The Ethics Challen ge in Public Service: A Problem-Solving Guide*. San Francisco: Jossey-Bass, 1991.

Light, P. *The True Size of Government*, Washington D.C., Brookings Institution, 1999.

Light, P. "Government Grows Under Either Plan." *The Times Union*, Albany, N.Y., Oct. 25, 2000, p. A11.

Lindblom, C. E. "The Science of 'Muddling Through.'" *Public Administration Review*, 1959, *19*, 79–88.

Linden, R. "A Guide to Reengineering Government." *Governing Magazine*, May 1995, pp. 63–74.

Linsky, M. *Impact: How the Press Affects Federal Policymaking*. New York: Norton, 1986a.

Linksy, M. *How the Press Affects Federal Policymaking: Six Case Studies*. New York: Norton, 1986b.

Lippmann, W. *Essays in the Public Philosophy*. New York: Little, Brown, 1955.

Locke, J. *The Second Treatise of Government*. New York: Liberal Arts Press, 1952. (Originally published 1690.)

Mansfield, R. As quoted by B. Williams. *Los Angeles Times*, Oct. 1, 1978, p. 1.

Mansnerus, L. "Ties to Neighborhood at Root of Court Fight." *New York Times*, July 24, 2001.

Martin, L. *How to Compare Costs Between In-House and Contracted Services*. Los Angeles: Reason Foundation, 1993.

McDavid, J. C., and Clemens, E. G. "Contracting Out Local Government Services: The British Columbia Experience." *Canadian Public Administration*, 1995, *38*(2), 177–193.

McGrath, J. *Federal Civil Service Reform: A Report*. Washington, D.C.: Congressional Research Service, Mar. 30, 1978.

Melkers, J., and Willoughby, K. "Budgeters' Views oif State Performance Budgeting systems." *Public Administration Review*, 2001, *61*, 54–64.

Mercer, J. *Strategic Planning for Public Managers*. Westport, Conn.: Quorum/Greenwood, 1991.

Michaels, J. E. *Becoming an Effective Political Executive: Seven Lessons from Experienced Appointees*. New York: PricewaterhouseCoopers Endowment, 2001.

Mikesell, J. L. *Fiscal Administration: Analysis and Applications for the Public Sector*. (2nd ed.) Florence, Ky.: Dorsey Press, 1986.

Milbrath, L. W. *Political Participation: How and Why Do People Get Involved in Politics?* Skokie, Ill.: Rand McNally, 1965.

Milward, B. "Nonprofit Contracting and the Hollow State." *Public Administration Review*, 1994, *54*, 73–77.

Milward, B. "Symposium on the Hollow State: Capacity, Control, and Performance in Interorganizational Settings: Introduction." *Journal of Public Administration Research and Theory*, 1996, *6*, 193–195.

Milward, B., and Provan, K. G. "Governing the Hollow State." *Journal of Public Administration Research and Theory*, 2000, *10*(2), 359–379.

Milz, M. "Managing Family and Work: How One Iowa State Agency Plays the Balancing Act." *Philadelphia Times*, Aug. 2001, p. 4.

Mintzberg, H. "Crafting Strategy." *Harvard Business Review*, 1987, 65(4), 66–75.

Moore, M. H. *Creating Public Values: Strategic Management in Government.* Cambridge, Mass.: Harvard University Press, 1995.

Mosher, F. C. *Democracy and the Public Service.* New York: Oxford University Press, 1968.

The National Commission on the Public Service. *Leadership for America: Rebuilding the Public Service.* Lexington, Mass.: Lexington Books, 1990.

National Performance Review. *From Red Tape to Results: Creating a Government That Works Better and Costs Less.* A report of the National Performance Review. Washington, D.C.: U.S. Government Printing Office, 1993.

National Science Foundation. *Science and Technology Indicators 2000.* Arlington, Va.: National Science Foundation, 2000.

O'Looney, J. A. *Outsourcing State and Local Government Services: Decision-Making Strategies and Management Methods.* Westport, Conn.: Quorum/ Greenwood, 1998.

O'Neill, T. P., and Novak, W. *Man of the House: The Life and Political Memoirs of Speaker Tip O'Neill.* New York: Random House, 1987.

Osborne, D., and Gaebler, T. *Reinventing Government: How the Entrepreneurial Spirit Is Transforming the Public Sector.* Reading, Mass.: Addison-Wesley, 1992.

Osborne, D., and Plastrik, P. *Banishing Bureaucracy.* Reading, Mass.: Addison-Wesley, 1997.

Palumbo, D., and Maynard-Moody, S. *Contemporary Public Administration.* White Plains, N.Y.: Longman, 1991.

Panet, P., and Trebilock, M. J. "Contracting Out Social Services." *Canadian Public Administration*, 1998, 41, 21–50.

Parker, J. F. *If Elected, I Promise: 1001 Jokes, Toasts, Stories, and Gems of Wisdom by and About Politicians.* New York: Doubleday, 1960.

Peters, T. J., and Austin, N. *A Passion for Excellence.* New York: Random House, 1985.

Peters, T. J., and Waterman, R. H. *In Search of Excellence: Lessons from America's Best-Run Companies.* New York: HarperCollins, 1982.

Rainey, H. G. *Understanding and Managing Public Organizations.* San Francisco: Jossey-Bass, 1991.

Rice, R., and Atkin, C. *Public Communication Campaigns.* Thousand Oaks, Calif.: Sage, 1989.

Riordon, W. *Plunkitt of Tammany Hall.* New York: NAL/Dutton, 1963.

Romzek, B. S., and Johnston, J. "Reforming Medicaid Through Contracting: The Nexus of Implementation and Organizational Culture." *Journal of Public Administration Theory and Research*, 1999, 9(1), 107–139.

Rosenbloom, D. "Have an Administration Rx? Don't Forget the Politics." *Public Administration Review*, 1993, 53, 503–507.

Rubin, B., and Rubin, R. *Labor Management Partnerships: A New Approach to Collaborative Management.* New York: PricewaterhouseCoopers Endowment, 2001.

Rubin, I. *The Politics of Budgeting: Getting and Spending, Borrowing and Balancing.* New York: Catham House, 2000.

Salamon, L. *Partners in Public Service: Government-Nonprofit Relations in the Modern Welfare State.* Baltimore, Md.: Johns Hopkins University Press, 1995.

Savas, E. S. *Privatizing the Public Sector: How to Shrink Government.* Chatham, N.J.: Chatham House, 1982.

Savas, E. S. *Privatization and Public-Private Partnerships.* New York: Chatham House/Seven Bridges, 2000.

Schattschneider, E. E. *The Semisovereign People: A Realist's View of Democracy in America.* Orlando, Fla.: Dryden Press, 1975.

Scholtes, P. R. *The Team Handbook.* Madison, Wis.: Joiner, 1996.

Sclar, E. "Public Service Privatization: Ideology or Economics." *Dissent,* 1994, *41*, 329–336.

Sclar, E. *You Don't Always Get What You Pay For: The Economics of Privatization.* Ithaca: Cornell University Press, 2000.

Seelye, K. "Bush Endorses Rule on Lead Emissions Proposed by Clinton." *New York Times,* Apr. 18, 2001, p. A1.

Seidman, H. *Politics, Position, and Power.* New York: Oxford University Press, 1980.

Selznick, P. *Leadership in Administration: A Sociological Interpretation.* New York: HarperCollins, 1984. (Originally published 1957.)

Shalala, D. "Are Large Public Organizations Manageable?" *Public Administration Review,* 1998, *58,* 284–289.

Simon, H. *Administrative Behavior.* (2nd ed.) Old Tappan, N.J.: Macmillan, 1957.

Skjei, S. *Information for Collective Action.* Lexington, Mass.: Lexington Books, 1973.

Steers, R. M. *Organizational Effectiveness.* Santa Monica, Calif.: Goodyear, 1977.

Steinbruner, J. D. *The Cybernetic Theory of Decision: New Dimensions of Political Analysis.* Princeton, N.J.: Princeton University Press, 1974.

Sutherland, J. W. (ed.). *Management Handbook for Public Administrators.* New York: Van Nostrand Reinhold, 1978.

Sylvia, R. "Public Personnel Administration." In J. M. Shafritz (ed.), *Defining Public Administration: Selections from the International Encyclopedia of Public Policy and Administration.* Boulder, Colo.: Westview, 2000.

Thompson, F. "Matching Responsibilities with Tactics: Administrative Controls and Modern Government." *Public Administration Review,* 1993, *53*(4), 303–316.

"The 2000 Campaign: Second Presidential Debate Between Gov. Bush and Vice President Gore" (Transcript). *New York Times,* Oct. 12, 2000, p. A1.

U.S. Bureau of the Census. *Census of Governments, 1987.* (Vol. 3, Public Employment No. 2, Compendium of Public Employment). Washington, D.C.: U.S. Government Printing Office, 1990a.

U.S. Bureau of the Census. *Statistical Abstract of the United States, 1990.* (113th ed.). Washington, D.C.: U.S. Government Printing Office, 1990b.

U.S. Bureau of the Census. *2000 Census Report.* Washington, D.C.: U.S. Government Printing Office, 2000.

U.S. Department of Housing and Urban Development Office of Inspector General. *Semiannual Report to Congress,* 1993, No. 29, 13–14.

U.S. General Accounting Office. *Management Reform: Completion Status of Agency Actions Under the National Performance Review.* Washington, D.C.: U.S. Government Printing Office, 1996.

Ury, W. *Getting Past No: Negotiating Your Way from Confrontation to Cooperation.* New York: Bantam Books, 1991.

Verba, S., and Nie, N. *Participation in America.* New York: HarperCollins, 1972.

Walters, J. "Who Needs Civil Service?" *Governing Magazine,* Aug. 1997, pp. 17–21.

Walters, J. "Pocket Change." *Governing Magazine,* July 1999, pp. 40–44.

Walters, J. "I Have to Talk to You About Your Job . . ." *Governing Magazine,* Mar. 2001, pp. 44–48.

Wayne, L. "E-Mail Part of the Effort to Turn Out the Voters." *New York Times,* Nov. 6, 2000.

Weber, M. "Characteristics of a Bureaucracy." In H. H. Gerth and C. W. Mills (eds.), *From Max Weber: Essays in Sociology.* New York: Oxford University Press, 1946.

Weintraub, A. "Dead Letter." *Business Week,* Oct. 23, 2000. [Businesswek.com/magazine.

Weisbrod, B. "The Future of the Nonprofit Sector: Its Entwining with Private Enterprise and Government." *Journal of Analysis and Management,* 1997, *16*(4), 541–555.

Weiss, J. A., and Tschirhart, M. "Public Information Campaigns as Policy Instruments," *Journal of Policy Analysis and Management,* 1994, *13,* 82–119.

Wildavsky, A. *The Politics of the Budgetary Process.* (2nd ed.) New York: Little, Brown, 1974.

Wilson, J. Q. *The Moral Sense.* New York: Free Press, 1993.

Wulczyn, F., Orlebeke, B., and Melamid, E. "Measuring Contract Agency Performance with Administrative Data." *Child Welfare,* 2000, *79*(5), 457–474.

Additional Resources

Bower, J. L., and Christenson, C. J. *Public Management: Text and Cases*. Burr Ridge, Ill.: Irwin, 1978.

Cobb, R. W., and Elder, C. D. "The Politics of Agenda Building: An Alternative Perspective for Modern Democratic Theory." *Journal of Politics*, 1971, *33*, 892–915.

Cohen, S. "A Strategic Framework for Devolving Responsibility and Functions from Government to the Private Sector." *Public Administration Review*, 2001, *61*, 432–440.

Globerman, S., and Vining, A. "A Framework for Evaluating the Government Contracting-Out Decision with an Application to Information Technology." *Public Administration Review*, 1996, *56*, 577–586.

Golden, O. "Innovation in Public Sector Human Services Programs: The Implications of Innovation by Groping Along." *Journal of Policy Analysis and Management*, 1900, *9*, 1990, 219–248.

Kettl, D. "Building Lasting Reform: Enduring Questions, Missing Answers." In D. Kettl; and J. Dilulio, Jr. (eds.), *Inside the Reinvention Machine: Appraising Governmental Reform*. Washington, D.C.: Brookings Institution, 1995.

Lavery, K. *Smart Contracting for Local Government Services: Processes and Experience*. Westport, Conn.: Praeger, 1999.

Lyden, F. J., and Miller, E. G. (eds.). *Planning, Programming, Budgeting: A Systems Approach to Management*. (2nd ed.) Chicago: Markham, 1972.

Lynn, L. E. *Managing the Public's Business: The Job of the Government Executive*. New York: Basic Books, 1981.

Prager, J. "Contracting Out Government Services: Lessons from the Private Sector." *Public Administration Review*, 1994, *54*, 176–184.

Schick, A. *Budget Innovations in the United States*. Washington, D.C.: Brookings Institution, 1971.

Schiff, M., and Lewin, A. Y. "The Impact of People on Budgets." In W. E. Thomas Jr. (ed.), *Readings in Cost Accounting, Budgeting and Control*. Cincinnati: South-Western, 1983.

Sharpe, M. "Outsourcing, Organizational Competitiveness, and Work." *Journal of Labor Research*, 1997, *18*, 534–549.

Walton, M. *The Deming Management Method*. New York: Dodd, Mead, 1986.

Whitfield, V. P., and Apsan, H. N. "The Hardest Part: Implementation." *The Bureaucrat*, 1985, *14*(3), 43–46.

Whitman, L. "Television and the 1981–84 Review of the Disability Rolls." In M. Linsky and others, *How the Press Affects Federal Policymaking*. New York: Norton, 1986.

Wildavsky, A. *Budgeting: A Comparative Theory of Budgetary Processes*. New York: Little, Brown, 1975.

Index